*Blue Triangle*

© Venture Publications Ltd April 1994.

ISBN 1 898432 04 X

Typeset and produced electronically for the Publishers by
Mopok Graphics, 128, Pikes Lane, Glossop, Derbyshire
Printed and bound in Great Britain

# *Blue Triangle*

*Alan Townsin
takes a nostalgic look at*
**AEC buses**

**Venture** *publications*

# INTRODUCTION

This book is intended to be a eulogy for AEC and the buses it produced, as seen by someone who was, and remains, a sometimes critical admirer. I have tried to give as accurate and balanced a picture as possible, but this is to some degree a personal history. It tells the story from the viewpoint of someone who was involved, albeit in a modest capacity and only for a few years, over forty ago.

I was a draughtsman, and latterly a section leader, in the main drawing office at Southall in 1951-55. My interest in the make goes back considerably further, however, for it was Newcastle Corporation's fleet of AEC Regents mainly dating from 1930-31 that first aroused my admiration when travelling to and from school in them in the 1937-39 period. Peter Ustinov has said that when he was twelve, he was a Bugatti. When I was about the same age I was a petrol-engined Regent, and continued to be able to make a passable imitation of one until my voice broke – it was essential to have a soprano range to reproduce that exhilarating gearbox scream at high engine revs !

My interest did not lessen as further investigation brought greater knowledge, for the 'blue triangle' era from 1929 was a fascinating kaleidoscope of rapid development and fresh ideas. From its formation, AEC had played a key role in the evolution of the motor bus, and one is bound to respect the pioneer work in such aspects as volume production methods, the development of the forward-control half-cab layout and lower floor levels. But it was when AEC buses began to take on that livelier character first associated with G. J. Rackman and the 6-type engine that they began to evoke enthusiasm. Subsequent models, for all the changes in design that took place over the succeeding half-century, retained this to varying degrees but always sufficiently to maintain a sense of continuity.

On 25th May 1979 the story came to an end, and AEC buses and coaches, already dwindling in numbers in most of their former strongholds when this book was first published in 1980, will soon be found only in museum collections. Whether this could or should have been avoided will doubtless be debated for may a day, but some of the importance of their contribution to the story of the bus is, I hope, conveyed in this book. I would like to dedicate it to all those who served this memorable concern.

Steventon, 1994                                                    Alan Townsin

# CONTENTS

# ACKNOWLEDGEMENTS

Although this book is largely an expression of my own interest in and views on AEC, it could not have been written without knowledge and comment gained over the years from people far too numerous to mention. I can only apologise for any omissions in this regard.

However, more specifically, I would like to acknowledge help obtained, whether in the past, or more recently, from the work of John Hibbs whose *History of British Bus Services* and Charles E. Lee whose booklet *The Early Motor Bus* helped to put the events in Edwardian times in perspective; from the late John Rackham, for explaining some of the reasoning behind his designs; from former colleagues at AEC, notably Gavin Martin and the late E. J. (John) Smith; several members of London Transport's staff, from Kenneth Shave to Robin Allen-Smith and his colleagues; the Motor Bus Society of America and its journal *Motor Coach Age* for information on AECs in South Africa; many people in Leyland Vehicles, notably Lord Black, Marcus Smith, Doug Jack, Bob Smith, Stewart Brown, Ray Carpenter and Ron Hall; among individuals, John Gillham and Bob Scanlan for information on LGOC activities. Material from *Bus & Coach* and *Commercial Motor* is reproduced by kind permission of the Editors, with assistance from Charles Hall, Eric Ogden and Stephen Shencoe.

Doug Jack and Robin Hannay read the proofs and made many helpful suggestions, while John Senior took far more than the conventional publisher's interest in the project, triggering off many fresh trains of thought which have helped to broaden the picture I have attempted to give. The opportunity has been taken to extend and update the colour section and I record my thanks to the Board of Venture Publications Ltd for making the reissue of this book possible.


Alan Townsin

# PHOTOGRAPHIC CREDITS

The photographs used in this publication have come from the Author's collection, from the Senior Transport Archive, or from the photographers named below whose assistance we gratefully acknowledge.

| | |
|---|---|
| John Aldridge | 223, 228(bottom) |
| Stewart J. Brown | 233, 234, 235(both top), 237 |
| R. C. Davis | 54 |
| D. L. G. Hunter | 125(top right) |
| Roy Marshall | 4, 220(bottom), 238(bottom left), 240(top right), 245 (top centre) |
| Gavin Martin | 95(bottom), 112(bottom left), 113 |
| R. A. Mills | 143 |
| T. W. Moore | 220(top) |
| Eric Ogden | 247 |
| H. Piltz | 243(bottom right), 244(bottom left) |
| Eric Surfleet | 182, 187 |

## Colour Section

| | |
|---|---|
| SJ Brown | 239 (upper left) |
| R Marshall | 238, 244 (lower), 251 (upper right) |
| H Piltz | 248 (upper), 250 (lower) |
| DF Roberts | 246 (lower), 252 (lower) |
| Senior Transport Archive | 237, 239 (upper right & lower), 240 (both),241 (upper), 242 (all), 243, 244 (upper both), 245, 246 (upper),247 (upper right, lower both), 248 (lower), 249 (upper), 250 (upper both), 251 (upper left & lower), 252 (upper) |
| AA Townsin | 241 (lower), 247 (upper left), 249 (lower) |

The Regent helped to widen the popularity of the double-decker in fleets large and small throughout the country. This early example was supplied to Colchester Corporation in 1930 and had Short Bros. bodywork of a style popular on this model at the time. Appropriately for an AEC, it is seen passing the Regal cinema a year or so later. Note the preponderance of shiny new cars – all British – in evidence, with examples of Humber, Austin and Morris prominent.

(Right) The London General Omnibus Company Limited had over half-a-century of horse bus operation behind it before it became involved in motor bus manufacture. This was a typical example of the standard London horse bus as built at the end of the nineteenth century, seating 26 passengers (14 on top) and hauled by two horses. The LGOC fleet reached a peak of just over 1,400 such vehicles around 1905.

(Lower right) The LGOC's first venture in motor bus operation was a failure, despite the confident expression on most of the passengers' faces in this posed photograph. The vehicle was a Fischer petrol-electric and ran into legal problems as soon as it arrived from the United States in 1903 because of slightly excessive width, but it was heavy and even when allowed to run was found so unsatisfactory that it was rejected before entering service.

# 1 HOW IT ALL BEGAN

The AEC story officially began on 13th June 1912, with the registration of the Associated Equipment Company Limited. However, its origins go back considerably further and the creation of a separate company, with so mundane a title, to take over the vehicle manufacturing activities of the London General Omnibus Co. Ltd. attracted little interest at the time. Indeed there was little evidence of the change at first, since the Walthamstow factory had been producing the famous B-type bus chassis since 1910 and simply carried on doing so. Output, hitherto solely for the LGOC, began to include a few vehicles for other operators but the firm was still very largely the LGOC's "equipment" supplier.

The word equipment even had faint echoes of horse terminology, hardly surprising as the LGOC's origins went back as far as 4th December 1855, when it was incorporated in Paris as the Compagnie Générale des Omnibus de Londres, to amalgamate existing bus operating businesses in the English capital. That was, of course, in horse-bus days and the LGOC did not get involved in operating—or attempting to operate—motor buses until 1902. The first vehicle, a Fischer petrol-electric imported from the

The De Dion of 1905 had, by the standards of the period, a clean and practical appearance and the LGOC was sufficiently impressed with the robustness of its flitched wooden frame to copy this feature on its own subsequent designs. Some 54 chassis formed part of LGOC's first bulk order for motor buses.

By comparison, the Straker-Squire, nee Büssing, had a self-effacing look given by its low-mounted radiator. Even so, the examples bought by LGOC had features which were reproduced on its own chassis. This one evidently dated from 1906, judging by the registration number.

United States, arrived the following year but never ran in service and a steam bus only ran for a few months in 1904-5. But other operators' early successes prompted a bolder course of action and in 1905, some 54 De Dion chassis were imported from France and 50 Büssing chassis from Germany—the latter sold under the Straker Squire name, who subsequently built buses in England using engines of Büssing design. A mixed fleet was rapidly built up, but there was little experience of how to keep vehicles in service, quite apart from the many shortcomings of these early designs.

Frank Searle, trained as a railway locomotive engineer, had become interested in motor buses in 1905. After serving with smaller companies he was invited to join LGOC as garage superintendent at Mortlake garage in February 1907, being promoted rapidly to take charge of the chief motor bus garage at Cricklewood three months later and in June 1907 to become Chief Motor Engineer at LGOC. Just over a year later, on 1st July 1908, the LGOC merged with its two largest competitors among London motor bus operators, the London Motor Omnibus Co. Ltd. (which had adopted the fleetname "Vanguard" in 1905) and the London Road Car Co. Ltd. (which used the "Union Jack" fleetname).

Vanguard was in fact then the largest motor bus operator in London, with some 386 vehicles, mostly of Milnes-Daimler make. Milnes-Daimler Ltd. had been formed in 1902 by G. F. Milnes & Co. Ltd., one of the leading British tramcar builders and the Daimler Motoren Gesellschaft, of Cannstatt, Germany, which owned the Continental patent rights of Gottlieb Daimler, and had by then no connection with the Daimler Motor Co. Ltd. of Coventry, formed to exploit Daimler's patents in Britain.

The combine, which retained the London General Omnibus Co. Ltd.'s title and "General" fleetname, re-appointed Searle as Chief Motor Engineer. New vehicles for the combined fleet of 885 motor buses were required and Searle heard, quite by chance, that the directors were contemplating buying about 200 Wolseley buses, then regarded as one of the most advanced designs available. He put forward a scheme for the LGOC to manufacture its own vehicles, using the two-year-old premises at Blackhorse Road, Walthamstow which had been taken over with the Vanguard business and which were superior to anything the new combine had elsewhere in London for this purpose. The directors, with their horse-bus background, knew little of the implications of motor bus production but an initial fleet of twenty vehicles was sanctioned.

Although the Vanguard name disappeared from London's streets following the merger, the telegraphic address used by AEC right up to the end in 1979 was "Vangastow", which was an abbreviation of "Vanguard, Walthamstow". Vanguard is said to have intended to build buses itself before the merger, but it does not seem that much progress had been made.

The LGOC had decided to use a classified system of fleet numbering in the summer of 1909 and many of the letters of the alphabet were already in use, so the new model was given the letter X. Searle confessed later that its design was an amalgam of the features of many of the types in the combine's fleet, and some writers described it, somewhat cheekily, as the "Daimler-Wolseley-Straker". It was of orthodox design for the period with the so-called normal-control layout, with driving position behind the engine, a straight frame and bodywork very similar to that of the final types of London horse-bus. The distance between the lower parts of the side panels was narrow enough for the rear wheels to pass outside them, which meant that the seats within had to be arranged longitudinally down each side.

The prototype, as completed in August, 1909, had a conventional sliding mesh gearbox with straight-cut gears, but the Metropolitan Police Public Carriage Office, which was responsible for approving the design of buses for operation in London until 1931, objected that it was noisier when the indirect gears were in use than when

The Vanguard fleetname of the London Motor Omnibus Co. Ltd. disappeared soon after that company was merged with LGOC in 1908. However, it was to be commemorated for over 70 years by AEC's telegraphic address "Vangastow", which was an abbreviation of Vanguard, Walthamstow. Most of the Vanguard vehicles, then the largest motor bus fleet in London, were Milnes-Daimlers as shown here. This make was perhaps the most successful motor bus of the 1904-08 period.

The LGOC had also been favourably impressed with some Wolseley buses, but its proposal to buy about 200 more, following the merger with Vanguard and Union Jack, led to the scheme for it to build its own at the ex-Vanguard works. Note the "cab-over-engine" layout, favoured on several French and American vehicles of the pre-1920 era, but uncommon on a British bus chassis.

The first product of the Walthamstow factory was the LGOC X-type, introduced late in 1909. Although not differing much in general appearance from other contemporary buses, the design attempted to combine the best features of the mixed fleet of buses already in use. X54 was one of the last built.

in top gear. Helical gears were tried, with a distinct improvement, but it was not until Searle obtained the so-called silent chain gearbox from the Coventry Chain Co. that the meticulous Chief Inspector Bassom was satisfied. In this unit the pairs of gears for the various ratios were replaced by sets of sprockets and chains, giving quiet operation and having the more robust dog-clutch form of gear engagement later combined with gear drive in constant-mesh gearboxes.

The chain gearbox was to remain a feature of most buses built for the LGOC until the 'twenties. Curiously enough, the use of helical gears in gearboxes was never subsequently favoured by AEC throughout its existence, apart from about 300 of the first NS-

type buses in 1923 and the bought-out ZF gearboxes used in the later types of Reliance coach chassis from the early 'sixties.

A total of 60 X-type buses and one lorry were built, the first vehicle finally entering service on 16th December 1909.

# The famous B-type

In effect they acted as prototypes for the much more famous B-type, on which design began in March 1910, the first bus being completed at Walthamstow on 7th October 1910. Early B-types

The B-type in its original form was almost identical-looking to the X-type, but incorporated numerous improvements. It set new standards for reliability and was soon in volume production, enabling the 1,100 or so horse buses surviving at the time of its introduction in October 1910 to be replaced within the following year. B293 is seen in the rather sombre dark red livery favoured at that date.

looked almost identical to the X-type, but numerous detail changes made it a much more successful model. It soon acquired a similar degree of respect among operators as the Milnes-Daimler designs of about six years earlier. Moreover the manufacturing methods at Walthamstow formed one of the earliest British examples of volume production, and the first applied to a commercial vehicle of this size. In the next three years, no less than 2,678 B-types were produced, transforming the London bus scene. At the time of the introduction of the B-type, there were as many horse-buses as motor buses licensed for operation in London, 1,142 of each type on 31st October 1910. Just under a year later, the LGOC ran

its last horse-bus, on 25th October 1911, though there were still independently-owned examples up to 1914.

The credit for this achievement was largely due to Searle's vision, but he was ably assisted by a talented team of engineers. Notable among several later famous names was George Alan Green who had left Vanguard before the merger, was taken on by Searle and soon became Chief Assistant Engineer at LGOC. He subsequently became General Manager of Fifth Avenue Coach Company in New York in 1912 and Vice-President of the Yellow Coach Manufacturing Company, being better known latterly as Colonel Green. Another even more notable name in the subsequent story

The manufacture of some 2,678 B-type buses within the short spell of three years transformed the London street scene, making this type of vehicle as familiar as the Routemaster of 50 years later. With later additions, the B was to dominate the London bus population from 1911 until outnumbered by more modern types in the mid 'twenties. This photograph conveys what must have been the usual relationship, with only a minority of other models — in this case one of the white-painted National fleet of Clarkson steam buses near the centre of the picture, preceded by a Rolls-Royce Ghost which brings a touch of glamour to this scene photographed around 1914.

of AEC who was later (in 1922) to follow Green to the United States was George John Rackham, who had joined Vanguard as a draughtsman in 1906 and then joined LGOC as Chief Draughtsman at the age of 22, in 1907, first at Cricklewood and then left briefly in 1910-11 to join David Brown Ltd. at Huddersfield but returned to Walthamstow in the same post until 1916. Charles Bullock is credited with much of the design work on the X-type and Walter James Iden was appointed Works Manager in December 1909—he was later to be Chief Engineer of LGOC.

The design of the B-type was again generally orthodox, with a typical four-cylinder petrol engine of the period, having the T-head layout, with side valves, inlet and exhaust being on opposite sides of the engine. The cylinders were cast in pairs and mounted on an aluminium crankcase. The cylinder bore was at first 110mm and the stroke 140mm, giving a swept volume of 5.3 litres. The Royal Automobile Club formula for horse power, based on number and bore of cylinders only, gave a figure of 30 and, as was often the case with early engines, the measured ''brake'' horse power was, indeed, the same figure, developed at a mere 1,000 rpm, although a 'Modern Transport' article in 1942 quoted 30 bhp at 750 rpm. The X-type had a 28 hp engine.

A cone clutch took the drive to the chain gearbox, which had only three speeds with very widely-spaced ratios, making for slow progress on gradients, but a worm-drive rear axle helped to eliminate noise from this quarter. Brakes operated only on the rear wheels, as virtually universal on buses until the mid 'twenties, similar remarks applying to the solid rubber tyres.

It may seem surprising that a wooden frame was used, though this was flitched with steel reinforcement plates. Mr. Rackham told me this was copied from De Dion practice of the time, as early steel channel-section frames as used by Milnes-Daimler and others were prone to cracking. The normal-control layout of those days produced a high stress concentration at the front of the bodywork, and oddly enough I recall being involved in hastily designing flitches for steel frames for normal-control AEC goods chassis supplied to Egypt when similar trouble occurred in the early 'fifties.

Early B-types, like the X-type, had a very plain-looking radiator of a shape rather like that used by Leyland (with whom there was of course no connection) and small initials 'LGOC' cast near the centre of the top tank. Subsequently there were several variations of design, and an early AEC design, used for some vehicles supplied to other operators, had the full title ASSOCIATED EQUIPMENT CO.LTD. cast in a much larger and more elaborate design; another version had an inter-twined monogram of the AEC initials. Another version had LGOC in larger letters

The B-type engine was a typical four-cylinder design from the Edwardian era, with T-head layout, inlet valves being on the nearside of the engine and exhaust on the offside. The pairs of cylinders were cast integrally with the cylinder heads and were mounted on an aluminium crankcase. Contemporary observers report that it was a quieter-running unit than most of that period. Note the massive flywheel. Although of 5.3-litre swept volume, the engine gave an output of 30 bhp, considerably less than that given by a modern Mini car engine, though the unit was designed to pull well at slow speeds.

but it was not until 1919 that the style of radiator that was to remain standard until 1926 first appeared, bearing the Underground group's bulls-eye motif on a central ''hump'' in the top tank and bearing the name General when on vehicles for LGOC and, at last, the familiar initials AEC for other customers.

The reputed manufacturing cost of the B-type chassis was £300 and the Metropolitan Police's insistence on a gross weight with passengers of no more than six tons kept operating costs down, though passenger capacity was also held down to 34 (eighteen 'outside' and sixteen 'inside'). Unladen weight of this very simple design of vehicle was 3 tons 10 cwt., or a few cwt. more on later examples. Its success tended to frustrate other manufacturers and, in particular, the Coventry-based Daimler concern, whose directors had approached Searle to see whether he would join them in a new venture to operate buses in London. The LGOC Board got wind of this and offered Searle double his salary to stay with them, a five year agreement and five minutes to make up his mind. Understandably he did not like the condition and left the company the same day, 4th May 1911. He thus had gone before AEC was formed, though he could undoubtedly be regarded as the father of the company.

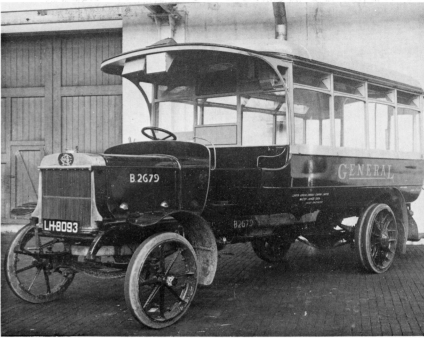

Variations on a theme. In early AEC days, there were several varieties of radiator badge applied to the original shape of B-type radiator.

(Top left) Early chassis supplied to ''outside'' operators sometimes carried this style of radiator with the full Associated Equipment Co. title cast into the top tank. B2623 was delivered to United Automobile Services Ltd., then based in East Anglia, though this vehicle was equipped for operation in Durham. United was to remain a regular AEC customer until the late 'twenties and an occasional one until 1938.

(Above) B2679, one of several types of B-type single-deckers built in small numbers for LGOC, was the first chassis built early in 1914 after a brief pause in production. It carried the intertwined version of the AEC monogram on its radiator, and was the first of a batch of 30 handed over to the War Department as ambulances when war broke out later that year.

(Left) This enlarged version of the LGOC radiator lettering also appeared on B-type buses around 1914.

# Competition from Coventry

The London venture did not succeed but Searle joined Daimler and set to work to design a bus that could compete effectively with his own B-type. The new Daimler CC not unnaturally bore some resemblance to the B but had Daimler's sleeve-valve engine with 110mm by 150mm bore and stroke and 5.7 litre swept volume, which was notably quieter than the decidedly "tappety" conventional poppet-valve engines of that era. It again incorporated the Coventry chain gearbox and so was highly regarded as a refined vehicle, soon destined to play a key part in the AEC story.

Meanwhile the LGOC had, on 1st January 1912, been taken over by the Underground group of companies, with its extensive electric rail and tram operations in London. This was already under the general managership of Albert Stanley, later Lord Ashfield, who had been born in England of Eastern European parents who were on their way to Canada. He had started as an office boy with the Detroit City Railway and had become General Manager of the Public Service Corporation of New Jersey before returning to London to take the equivalent position with the Underground group in 1910.

The Daimler CC was the result of Searle's move from AEC and was a direct and effective competitor to the B-type. These views show D186, one of the fleet supplied to the Metropolitan Electric Tramways Co.'s bus-operating subsidiary. It was this deal that led to the first of several links between AEC and Daimler.

13

A curious episode in the winter of 1913-14 was the staging of a demonstration intended to show how motor buses could manoeuvre between tramcars. This evidently occurred after the amalgamation between MET and the Underground group as one of the new MET Daimler buses, D161, was used, together with B1353. Here the two are seen face to face, together with two of the London United Tramways fleet of W-type cars, Nos. 192 and 196. The demonstration took place somewhere between Twickenham and Hampton Court.

The formation of AEC as a separate concern had been part of the reorganisation of LGOC that followed the takeover and one senses the business flair of Stanley in realising the possibilities of engaging in manufacturing vehicles for sale.

However, only limited progress had been made in this direction when repercussions of Frank Searle's departure to Daimler had an unexpected effect. The Metropolitan Electric Tramways Co. (part of the already sizeable British Electric Traction group), with extensive tram routes in north west London, was worried about bus competition, especially as the LGOC had been able to extend the area of its operating powers in the 1912 reconstruction. It formed the awkwardly-titled Tramways (MET) Omnibus Co. Ltd.

and Searle obtained an order for 100 of his new Daimler CC-type buses, together with a contract for their maintenance, including labour, fuel and materials, of 3½d. per mile. He then approached Albert Stanley to see whether the LGOC would wish to purchase Daimler buses, to which the reply was the suggestion that an order could be placed if none were supplied to any other London concern for five years. He went back to MET, which increased its order to 350, and Searle reduced the maintenance contract to 3d. per mile. He then went abroad.

On his return, Searle found that an amalgamation had been agreed in November 1913 between the Underground group and MET, under which LGOC took over the operation of the Daimler buses. The maintenance contract was not required, and as part of the compensation, the Daimler concern was appointed selling agent for any vehicles built at Walthamstow that were surplus to LGOC requirements.

AEC and Daimler then became linked in the first of several associations of various kinds between the two concerns that were to punctuate the AEC story over the next thirty years. Daimler engines were fitted into some AEC chassis built at Walthamstow, an arrangement which continued into the 1914-18 war period.

The B-type was not affected by this arrangement and production resumed, after a brief pause, in the early months of 1914 at B2679 and continued until war conditions caused production to stop again at B2826. The B-type fleet numbers were also the chassis numbers and a final post-war batch built for LGOC in 1919 were B4879-5132. Most of the intervening numbers were used for other models, without the B prefix, though B3474-3503 were single-deckers (as were a small proportion of the others) and AEC records refer to a quantity of 263 2-ton Russian B-types built in 1916-17, presumably supplied as military vehicles to Russia. The later buses mostly had 115mm-bore engines, putting the RAC rating up to 32.7 hp, and ten chassis were rebuilt with Daimler engines in 1922, mainly for charabanc use. The single-deckers had a slightly longer wheelbase of 14ft. 6in., instead of the 12ft.10 5/8in. of the double-deckers.

# Y-types by the thousand

The Walthamstow factory's ability to build vehicles in large quantity had not escaped the attention of the Government and as the demand for army lorries increased as the 1914-18 war dragged on, orders for vehicles to War Department specification were put in hand. These mainly called for a heavier-duty vehicle than the B-type, having a conventional channel-section frame, by then available in adequately robust form, and an orthodox four-speed gearbox. A larger engine than that in the B-type was called for and apart from some Daimler units, a proprietary engine, made by the Tylor concern, was fitted to almost all the wartime production. This was of slightly more modern design than the B-type unit, with L-head layout having inlet and exhaust valves on the same side. Bore and stroke were 5in. by 6in. giving an RAC rating of 40 hp and an actual claimed output of 45 hp at 1,000 rpm.

The Walthamstow factory was enlarged and reorganised and from 1916, large-scale production of the Y-type 3-ton lorry was put in hand. In a surprisingly frank article in 'The Commercial Motor'

Pioneer assembly-line production of Y-type 3-ton chassis at Walthamstow, 1918

The Y-type chassis. The vast numbers of this model built in wartime—about 8,000 in three years—were not finished to the high standard shown in this photograph, evidently of an example intended for exhibition. But the Tylor JB4 engine fitted to most of them is evident, as is the rugged construction necessary for wartime military operation, and which made the model attractive as a reliable basis for early post-war buses, often used on unmetalled roads. Note the large quantities of worm-wheels, road springs and other parts in the background, evidently part of the component stores.

in March 1918, it was stated that up to twenty War Department lorries a day were produced—a statement that might have been expected to invite a German airship or bomber raid! A moving assembly line running at 1ft. per minute, believed to have been the first in Britain for commercial vehicle production, was used and the factory was reorganised to keep its workers fed with the right parts at the right time.

Some vehicles were designated YA, YB, YC, YD and YE to indicate design variations and some were rated as of 4- or 5-ton capacity as well as the decidedly conservative military figure of 3 tons. Total production quoted for the 1916 to 1921 period was the remarkable figure of 12,002, of which about 8,000 were built in wartime, easily beating the output of any comparable British vehicle. Approximate figures for Dennis, Albion, Leyland and Thornycroft were respectively 7,000, 6,000, 6,000 and 5,000, all of these being vastly greater than respective pre-war outputs. Chassis numbers of the AEC Y-type vehicles were at first interspersed between those of the B-types and then continued, reaching 16145 in 1920.

Inevitably the end of the war brought a drastic cut in production, but AEC had a well-equipped factory with which to meet the demands of not only LGOC but other customers. 'Outside' orders were to be pursued much more energetically in future. Moreover, the AEC name was already familiar to thousands of ex-army drivers. Many of the AEC Y-types built for military service were converted for civilian use, quite a sizeable number becoming buses or charabancs. Even in London, ex-War Department AEC lorries were pressed into service as buses during the latter part of 1919 by simply fitting seats into the goods bodywork. In an least one case, examples of these were passed on to other operators—the Rhondda Tramways Co. began its bus operations with nine such YC models with Tylor engines and 'lorry-bus' bodywork, ex-LGOC. This was only a temporary measure, but outside London, ex-WD AEC chassis with new bus bodywork formed the basis of several immediate post-war fleets. In one sense, these prevented or delayed new vehicles from being sold, but their sturdy construction helped to give the firm a good reputation for building solid, if unexciting, vehicles.

Among numerous operators who adopted the Y-type model in one or more of its variations was the Great Western Railway, whose road motor department was then growing rapidly. This charabanc was typical of the immediate post-war concept of a vehicle suitable for touring, whether a private car or intended for public use. The frontal appearance, with hood straps each side of the radiator, had distinct echoes of military vehicles of World War I. The muddy state of the ground highlights the still great extent of un-made roads for which the military vehicles' ruggedness was an asset.

Lorry-buses, converted from War Department AEC Y-type chassis, were used in several places immediately after the 1914-18 war. This example joined the fleet of United Automobile Services Ltd. Note the use of a registration number beginning with figure zero— Norfolk County Council was still following this unorthodox practice, having issued only 556 numbers since the AH series began in 1904.

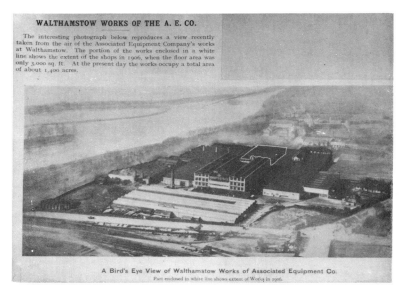

A Bird's Eye View of Walthamstow Works of Associated Equipment Co.
Part enclosed in white line shows extent of Works in 1906.

The war had greatly expanded the production capacity of the Walthamstow works, seen here as it had developed by 1920. The multi-storey buildings in the centre of the picture had been erected in 1916 as part of the programme to increase output of military vehicles. Note the growth from the original Vanguard premises of 1906 immediately behind them, as indicated in the paragraph from ''Motor Transport'' of 29th August 1920.

# 2  BRAVE NEW WORLD

The 1914-18 war had materially altered AEC's position. It was still a subsidiary of LGOC and hence part of the giant Underground group that dominated London's public passenger transport. But it had shown the ability to build commercial vehicles in very large numbers for other markets. Admittedly this was not in competitive circumstances, but AEC was now one of the leading manuacturers.

However there had also been staff changes. Many of the early team had gone. G. J. Rackham had gone to Heenan and Froude as Works Manager in 1916 but soon after became involved with tank design for the War Office, which brought him into renewed contact with George Green, who had returned to Britain to join the Army, and Frank Searle. He also met Walter Gordon Wilson, whose work on epicyclic gears for tanks was to lead to the design of the pre-selective gearbox, later also to play an important part in the AEC story.

Meanwhile Charles Kearns Edwards, who had joined the AEC drawing office staff as a checker in 1912, had soon risen through the positions of Chief Draughtsman and Designer. He was probably engaged in all three capacities on what was to be AEC's first new post-war design, the K-type bus built for LGOC, for the original design work had been carried out in 1914, though it was not until August 1919 that the first example, K1, was completed.

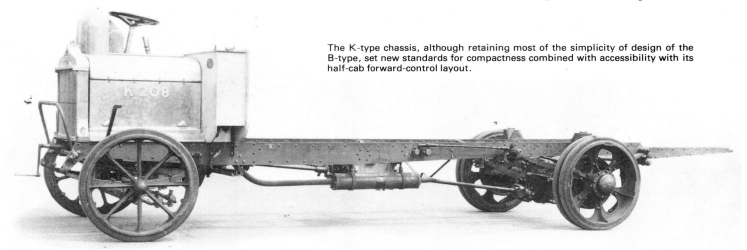

The K-type chassis, although retaining most of the simplicity of design of the B-type, set new standards for compactness combined with accessibility with its half-cab forward-control layout.

An indication of the effect on the proportion of chassis length available for passenger accommodation of the forward-control layout is conveyed by these broadside views of B5015, one of the final batch of this by then venerable 34-seat design built in 1919, and K319, one of the main production batch of this model built in 1920-21, seating 46 passengers. Both were in the immediate post-war LGOC livery, using the familiar bright red associated with London's buses ever since, together with white window frames and darker red lower side panels.

The first three K-type buses were built towards the end of 1919, K2 being seen here in a publicity photograph. Volume production began in the following spring, and this model began the AEC type numbering system with the series beginning at 301.

The basic aim was to materially increase passenger capacity with only slight increase of size and weight. The main difference in layout was the adoption of forward-control. The idea of saving space by moving the driver forward was by no means new. Many early bus designs had the driver above the engine, including the LGOC's original imported Fischer of 1903. The Wolseley was perhaps the best-known British example of the cab-over-engine layout which became quite popular on early American and French commercial vehicles. The concept of putting the driver **alongside** the engine does seem to have been peculiarly a British one, but even here the Scottish Motor Traction Co.'s Lothian design of 1913 was in production before the K-type had even got on the drawing board. However, the K-type was, despite this, a pioneer, establishing the half-cab layout that was to remain usual on full-sized British buses for 30 years and remain common on double-deckers for nearly 50. Lopsided it certainly was, but the principle had important practical merits of good engine accessibility and driver vision which accounted for its popularity for so long. And the K-type had that characteristic emphasis on economy of length devoted to other than passenger space which made for neatness of front-

end layout. "Cab" was perhaps too strong a word for the K, as the driver had only a characteristically rounded dash panel in front of him and even though extending well over 1ft. higher than the radiator this gave only scant protection in wet weather as the driver sat higher than on the B-type.

The wheelbase was 14ft. 2¼in. and the length about 3ft. 6in. longer than the B, at approximately 22ft. 9in. Visually it seemed much wider than the B-type, but at 7ft. 1½in. was only 2½in. more, but the body was almost completely straight-sided, with internal wheel arches over the rear wheels, a concept which made it possible to fit pairs of forward-facing seats on both sides of the interior gangway. All these changes enabled the seating capacity to go up to 46, with 22 inside and 24 on the open-topped upper-deck.

The unladen weight was about 4 tons 4 cwt., the vehicle being designed to comply with a laden weight limit of 7 tons. No attempt was made to materially increase power, and indeed this larger bus had a smaller engine than even the earlier B-types; with cylinder dimensions of 100mm by 140mm, the swept volume was only 4.4 litres. It had the L-head layout used on all AEC engines until the late 'twenties and was sometimes described as of 28 hp and sometimes of 30 hp, the latter figure being quoted as its output at 1,050 rpm, marginally faster than the B. A multiplate clutch helped to give smoother starts from rest, but the three-speed chain gearbox was as before, and the flitched frame and worm-drive rear axle were little altered.

There was a pause after the first three prototypes were produced and volume production did not begin until May 1920, but over 1,000 were built during the following twelve months, and a few more were built in 1924, by which time the LGOC's fleet numbers for this type had reached K1077. A few were also built for use outside London. By then it had been superseded in general production by later types, but smaller numbers of later production took the total to 1132. In 1925 a single-deck version was introduced, the original examples being the first pneumatic-tyred buses in London service. The last new K-types were built in 1926.

# Systematic numbering

A new numbering system had been begun by AEC in 1920, and this applied to types of vehicle and individual chassis, major units and individual parts. Much of it was to survive for the remaining life of the Company and I have always felt that its logic was unsurpassed by any other system I know, though as with all schemes subsequently administered by others, the application now and again did not quite live up to the original concept.

Basically models were denoted by three-figure numbers. The original scheme was that there were to be three series, beginning 301, 401 and 501. The 301 was the original K-type, the 401 was a new model then on the drawing board and the 501 was to be the wartime Y-type in its post-war form with AEC-built engine. The original principle was that these were nominally 3-ton, 4-ton and 5-ton ranges of vehicle but as will be seen later this implied relationship with weight was later superseded by other ideas. Improved models or variations took successive numbers; thus succeeding minor variations of the K-type were 302, 303, 304 and 305 and normally each of those would have had its own series of individual chassis numbers beginning 301001, 302001 etc., but the LGOC chassis were numbered from 20001 for K1 onwards. This series was continued for chassis of the subsequent S and NS tyes supplied to LGOC, reaching 23759 by 1925, but all other production AEC chassis had classified chassis numbers beginning 001 for each model number series. Where production exceeded 999 chassis for one model, the chassis numbers simply followed on, so that, for example, Regal chassis number 662999 was followed by 6621000.

Three-figure numbers prefixed by a letter were used for units, the series for engines beginning at A101, which was the 100 x 140mm engine as used on K-type chassis from No.20005 upwards. Most of the other letters of the alphabet were used for other items in a seemingly almost random fashion, and in this respect the system was less easy to follow than, for example, Leyland's E for engine, GB for gearbox, etc. The principal other AEC series of interest from a historian's point of view was probably D for gearboxes, but by the 'thirties the series in use were A, engine; C, pedal gear; D, gearbox; E, change speed; F, rear axle; G, brake gear; J, clutch (or fluid flywheel); K, cardan (i.e. propeller shaft); L, front axle; M, steering; N, radiator; P, bonnet; Q, structure (i.e. dash panels, cab floor, etc.); R, controls (i.e. accelerator linkage, etc.); S, fuel tank; T, silencer; V, electrical equipment and Y, frame. At first B had been used for some petrol tank items and H for starting gear (i.e. handle) but these had been dropped by about 1930.

The same series were used for parts, with four-figure numbers for sub-assemblies and five-figure numbers for individual components. These were again classified so that, for example, L10113 was in the L101 series of front axle beams. When 99 numbers had been used up, the '101' identity was maintained by using L1/10100 up. This system had the immense advantage of listing all items of similar nature together. There were also series with no prefix for items such as bolts and studs and Z, officially 'chassis miscellaneous', was used for special bolts, etc., though the complete chassis arrangement drawing also had a Z prefix. The main exception to the system was the U series, used for experimental and prototype items, which was in one vast numerical sequence which even included occasional chassis numbers for prototype vehicles, particularly after 1945. In practice, most items began

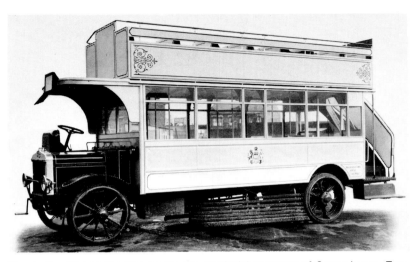

Manchester Corporation was among the provincial operators of S-type buses. Two were delivered in January 1922, the bodywork, to almost identical specification to the LGOC buses, being sub-contracted by AEC to Fry Bus Ltd. of Greenwich. Ten more S-type chassis were supplied early in 1925, but this time the bodywork, with enclosed cabs, was supplied by Davidson of Trafford Park.

with U numbers before being given classified numbers for production. An XU series was used for special versions of chassis or units up to about 1939.

# 4-types . . . .

The success of the K-type was quickly followed up by further development along the same lines and the 401 series of models began with an enlarged version of very similar design. This was the S-type, which took advantage of an increase in the maximum permitted gross laden weight from 7 tons to 8½ tons that had been requested by the LGOC. This enabled the seating capacity to go up to 54 (28 on top, 26 inside), almost as high a figure as was reached for vehicles in volume production until the 'thirties. Indeed 56 seats was then to remain the standard maximum for most double-deckers until the 'fifties.

The S-type was longer, at 24ft. 8¼in., with a 14ft. 11in. wheelbase, and its unladen weight complete with standard body went up to 4 tons 10 cwt., a very modest figure by later standards and

reflecting its simple design. Engine size went up again slightly (though the 108mm bore was still less than that of the B-type and the stroke remained at the 140mm figure of earlier LGOC types) to 5.1 litres and the quoted output was 35 bhp at 1050 rpm. The first units to have these dimensions were designated A107. This time a single-plate clutch was used, but the remainder of the chassis was much the same as the K, complete with its flitched wooden frame.

The first example appeared in December 1920, about half-way through the main production run of the K-type, and 895 had been delivered by September 1923, including a few single-deckers. A few more were built up to 1927 and total figures for the type have been quoted as 1066, of which 928 were operated by LGOC or its agents, with S-series fleet numbers.

Some chassis with the chassis numbers in the 401 and 403 series were supplied to provincial operators such as Manchester Corporation—it should perhaps be explained that the adjective "provincial", which tends to recur in the AEC story, was used to refer to versions of buses built for operators outside London and differing from London specification to a greater or lesser extent. Even the East Surrey Traction Company, already part of the LGOC empire, was "provincial" in this sense.

# and 5-types . . . .

As well as having some 403-type buses, East Surrey had some examples of the very similar-looking 502 model. This was basically an S-type chassis with the more powerful 5-type 6.8-litre engine. This had originally been produced to succeed the Tylor unit used in the Y-type. It had slightly smaller dimensions of 120mm bore and 150mm stroke, but the quoted output of 45 bhp at 1,000 rpm was the same, as was the L-head layout. Thus the 4-type and the 5-type series of chassis were being offered at the same time and quite often the passenger versions had many common features, apart from the engine. Hence the East Surrey 502 models (and their examples of the later but similar 507) were given fleet numbers in a special PS or "Provincial S" series. A total of 50 of the 502-type were made, but the almost identical 503 was more popular, with 148 built between 1922 and 1925, including fifteen for Birmingham Corporation. The 501 model, with normal-control layout and appearance much the same as the Y, was primarily a goods vehicle, although still also offered for passenger bodywork. With far more experience of building double-deck buses than

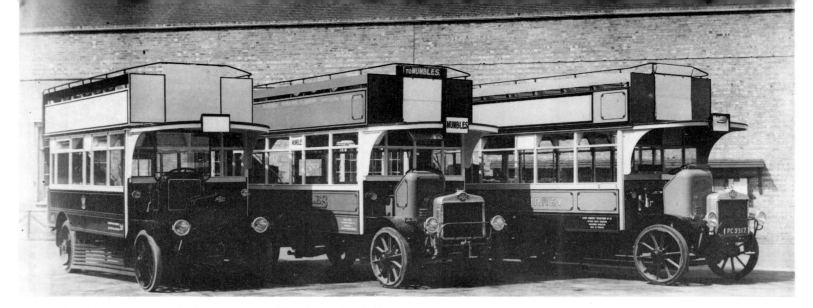

An indication of the growing breadth of the market for AEC double-deckers is given by this picture of vehicles for Birmingham Corporation, South Wales Transport Co. Ltd. and East Surrey Traction Co. Ltd. The Birmingham bus, No. 59, a 503 with Fry bodywork, was the first of many hundreds of AECs for service in that city. The South Wales bus was one of four 403 models which were also the first of many AEC double-deckers for this fleet, and the East Surrey vehicle was the first of six 403 models. All were built in 1922.

The 5-type 6.8-litre engine was the largest of AEC's range of standard production power units of the early and mid 'twenties. Like almost all commercial vehicle engines of that period it was a four-cylinder side-valve petrol unit. Maintenance advice included resetting tappets weekly, and lifting the cylinders to decarbonise the engine every 10,000 miles.

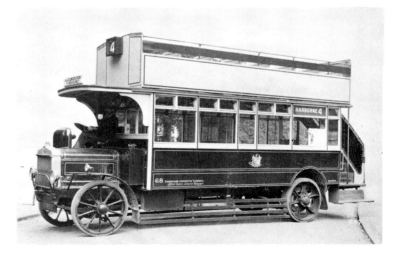

The first production batch of buses for Birmingham consisted of 14 more of the 503 model, this time with Brush 54-seat bodywork in 1923, No. 68 being seen here. The external resemblance to the S-type can be judged by comparing this view with that of the Manchester bus on the opposite page. Advances in design were such that in both fleets all had been withdrawn from service by 1930.

An early export venture was the supply of a 404 model, a North American equivalent to the S-type, to the Toronto Transportation Commission in 1921-22. The vehicle, as well as having left-hand steering, was of normal-control layout. The front-entrance position was unusual on a double-decker of that period—note the forward-ascending staircase. It did not attract volume orders, but Canada was later to become a significant AEC export market.

Contemporary press reports described this vehicle, with two others of the same type, as the first AEC S-type chassis to have charabanc bodywork. In fact they were 503 models with Strachan & Brown 31-seat bodywork and were supplied to the South Wales Transport Co. Ltd. in 1924. The description ''S-type'' was apt to be very loosely applied at the time, being given not only to chassis such as this, which could be described as largely of S-type design apart from the engine and gearbox, but even to bonneted 5-type chassis. Passengers could not have seen much of the countryside on a wet day.

The forward-control 5-type chassis was also used as a basis for single-deck bus chassis. This example was supplied in 1923-24 to Alexanders' Motor Service, Falkirk, later to grow into the largest bus fleet in Scotland. The totally-enclosed cab was by then becoming accepted practice outside London.

any other manufacturer, because of its position as supplier to the LGOC, AEC was tending to be regarded as the obvious choice when provincial operators wanted to buy double-deckers. In those days, the market for such vehicles outside London was still small, since all the major city transport systems outside London relied mainly on trams, but AEC was clearly in a strong position for future orders.

The next major step was the development of the top-covered double-decker. The open-topper was attractive on a summer's day but effectively became a single-decker in wet weather. The LGOC was well aware of this and its buses were unable to compete in this respect with the tramcar, which by then generally had a top cover. However, in London, the Metropolitan Police view was one of nervousness about stability—unlike a tram, a bus might have to swerve, and would not an upper-saloon roof and windows make it top-heavy? Charles Edwards, by then Chief Engineer of AEC, had been to America and was impressed by efforts to reduce bus floor levels. Here was a means of improving stability while allowing adequate headroom on both decks when a top cover was fitted—simply make the whole bus lower.

# Nulli Secundus

The result was the LGOC NS-type, which was derived from the S-type, with which it shared its basically similar 108mm x 140mm engine, front-end layout and general proportions, though it was slightly longer at 25ft. overall (compared to 24ft. 8¼in.) and had a wheelbase of 15ft. 6in. instead of 14ft. 11in. However, the differences behind the front bulkhead were profound. Instead of the straight frame, a new design with lowered centre section and even lower rear end was adopted. The flitched timber frame had to go to achieve this result and the pressed steel sidemembers were of a shape that was, with variations, to remain characteristic of most subsequent British double-deckers—and many single-

The major step forward—or downward—in design made by the NS is conveyed in these two photographs, which contrast the frame profile of S747, with that of NS3, seen in the lower picture, both built during the winter of 1922-23. The low-level-cranked frame was soon to be accepted as the normal form of chassis for British double-deckers. The inclined transmission line, already standard practice on AEC double-deckers, allowed the amidships-mounted gearbox to be mounted almost flush with the frame sidemembers. NS3 was evidently used as a test chassis by AEC as it was not delivered to LGOC until August 1923.

deckers—for the next forty years or so.

Even more interesting was the rear axle design. Instead of the "plain" underslung worm-drive axle of previous models, a double-reduction axle was used. The centre part had an underslung worm-drive unit, generally similar to those on the K, S and related

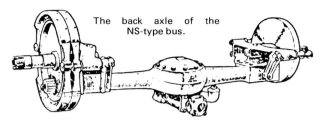

The back axle of the NS-type bus.

chassis, which in itself put this end of the propeller shaft below axle level instead of above. But the whole of this part of the unit was further lowered by the drive to the wheels which was via an internally-toothed ring gear attached to the brake-drum assembly. In principle, the idea was not new, since a similar idea had been used on the Milnes-Daimler buses of nearly twenty years previously, but that design had made no attempt to exploit the possibilities of reducing floor height and had suffered from noise problems from the exposed ring gear drive.

The NS rear axle incorporated a means of adjusting the meshing of these gears and with better lubrication and means of excluding dirt, the noise level ceased to be a problem. With this design of rear axle, the propeller shaft was considerably lower at the rear than the front. The designers therefore mounted both the engine and gearbox at the right level and angle to produce a straight but quite markedly inclined transmission line from starting handle to the rear axle worm shaft. The inclined engine tended to be an AEC characteristic and indeed on some later models it was common practice to mount it out of square in all three planes.

This ingenuity enabled the lower saloon floor level and hence the whole build of the passenger-carrying part of the body to be almost a foot lower than the S-type. Yet when the first example, NS1, was submitted to the Metropolitan Police complete with covered top early in 1923, permission to operate it was refused.

(Below) A line-up showing LGOC and hence AEC progress in double-deck bus design up to 1923. From left to right can be seen B256, of 1911; K95, of 1920; S546, of 1922, and NS29, of 1923.

(Above) An experimental design of top-covered bodywork as introduced by the LGOC for the NS chassis and submitted to tilt tests during 1924. The Police had rejected the original version, with detachable top cover, as built on NS1 in 1923 and most of the NS class entered service in 1923-26 with open tops. The extended front mudguards, reaching down to axle level in front of the wheels, do not seem to have been adopted in London, though they were used on a few AEC chassis supplied to provincial operators at that time—they give a falsely "modern" look. The single-step platform and rear end design of the NS set the basic standard for most of the open-staircase top-covered double-deckers built until about 1931—the spiral shape of the advertisement panel on the staircase decency screen always reminded the author of the Sam Browne type of leather shoulder strap formerly worn by Army officers.

An earlier top-covered double-decker design had been produced by Liverpool Corporation in 1920. This was on an AEC Y-type chassis dating from 1918. The body, obviously intended to closely resemble that of a tram, was built in the Liverpool undertaking's workshop. Note the cow-catcher in the front view on the opposite page.

As the LGOC's efforts to introduce top-covered double-deckers were delayed by the initial refusal of the Metropolitan Police to sanction their use, it fell to Birmingham Corporation to put the first example of the classic forward-control top-covered double-decker into service in 1924. This was No. 101 (OL 8100), a 504-model chassis with Brush bodywork, seen here when new. As also applied on the NS, a peak was subsequently added as the front of the upper-deck, giving a better-balanced appearance on a vehicle with projecting driver's canopy.

Ironically, Birmingham Corporation produced a covered-top bus which met the less conservative requirements for operation outside London (it did undergo a tilt test, incidentally). This was on an AEC 504 model chassis, basically very similar in build to the S-type but having a slightly lowered front axle and frame, wider track as well as the 120mm x 150mm 5-type engine. Although

(Above) Production NS-type buses for LGOC continued to be of open-topped type until 1926. NS898 was typical, with the characteristic step down from the level of the driver's canopy to that of the upper saloon floor. Bodies were built by outside contractors as well as the LGOC's Chiswick works, the largest number being produced by Short Bros.

even it was not the first British covered-top double-deck motor bus (there had been an earlier Liverpool Corporation vehicle based on an AEC Y-type chassis, quite apart from a Widnes Corporation Commer dating from as early as 1909), Birmingham's No. 101 (OL 8100) was the first example of the recognisable classic forward-control top-covered vehicle.

But morally, the LGOC/AEC design deserved the credit, for it was this concept, with some simplification of the rear axle, that became accepted for most British double-deckers for the next twenty years—indeed, even then, the NS idea of the drop-centre double-reduction rear axle was revived by the Bristol Lodekka first introduced in 1950 and put into production in 1953.

LGOC, and more to the point, its passengers, had to put up with open-toppers until 1925, when the Police were convinced

Ironically, a top-covered NS was exported to Buenos Aires before London passengers were given the opportunity to ride in such a vehicle. It was based on the ''provincial'' 409-model version of the chassis, but was officially an ACLO rather than an AEC, possibly the first example of the use of this trade name for the South American market. The Short Bros. body seated 52. It was shipped to Agar Cross & Co. Ltd., the AEC agents in Buenos Aires, on 24th January 1925.

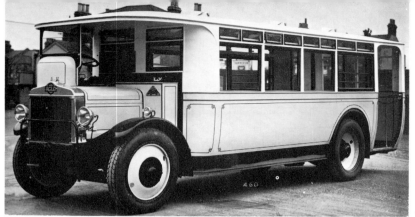

In the event, the demonstrator NS sent to Buenos Aires produced an order, but not for double-deckers. Anglo-Argentina Tramways Co., a company which had been formed in London in 1876 and operated an extensive network, ordered 40 of the 409-type chassis plus one fitted with 28-seat single-deck bodywork by Strachan & Brown; these vehicles being supplied later in 1925. An odd appearance resulted from the high driving position and low-floor bodywork. A repeat order for 70 chassis followed in 1927.

The chassis numbers allocated to the NS chassis supplied to LGOC were in the same continuous series as the K and S models and ranged from 22150 to 23759. At first it was stated that the model would not be supplied to other operators and the model was simply known by the NS-type letters, variously supposed to indicate "New S" "No Step" or, perhaps the most appealing title, "Nulli Secundus" (second to none). Pressure was such on the AEC works that it was decided to transfer assembly of the NS-type chassis from Walthamstow to LGOC's Chiswick Works and in some cases LGOC garages. This took place in September 1924, the last Walthamstow-built example being NS 1605. In 1925, it was decided to apply the model numbers 405, 406, 407 and 408 to the variations already built, which had alternative gearboxes. The first 300 or so chassis had the helical gearboxes previously mentioned but most had the by now traditional LGOC chain gearbox, in many cases transferred from withdrawn B-type buses. (Model 404 had been a left-hand drive version of the S-type intended for export but not built in any great quantity.) When it was agreed to offer the NS design on the open market, the model number 409 was allocated to such chassis. Model 410 was reputed to have been a further LGOC NS series, though few, if any, appear to have been built.

by a further experiment with four vehicles that the closed-top NS design was quite safe. Meanwhile, some 1733 NS buses had been built with open-tops and it was not until March 1926 that production covered-top bodies began to come through, though most of the earlier buses were later fitted with top covers. Inevitably, there was a significant increase in weight, from the 4 tons 10 cwt. of the S-type to 6 tons 6 cwt. for the covered-top NS.

The ACLO 409 chassis for Anglo-Argentina Tramways had pneumatic tyres. One is seen in the works yard at Walthamstow, with one of the ten home-market 409-type NS models supplied to Waterloo & Crosby Motor Services Ltd. just visible behind the radiator. Note the B-type bus also in the background.

After experimental running of four NS buses (NS 1734-37) with covered tops in LGOC service in the Autumn of 1925, the Metropolitan Police approved their general adoption. An order for 200 covered-top bodies was placed, 150 being built by LGOC and the rest by Short Bros. They were all intended for new chassis, but production delays caused the first few to be fitted on existing chassis. One of these was NS 1647, seen here at Trafalgar Square shortly after re-entering service in this form on route 11E in March 1926. The majority of existing NS buses were fitted with top covers in 1926-27.

(Above) The Equitable Auto Company Limited, of Pittsburgh, Pennsylvania, took delivery of two 409-type chassis early in 1926. One was open-topped and the other closed and in both cases the design and finish were of LGOC style, with the important exception that the staircase and entrance suited the right-hand rule of the road in the United States. Similar vehicles were also built for Berlin.

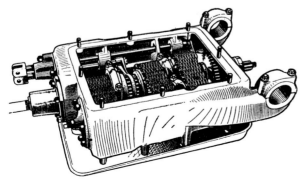

(Left) The chain gearbox in the form introduced for the NS chassis. This differed from earlier versions in having centre bearings, though some existing gearboxes were transferred to NS chassis.

# Early trolleybuses

At about the same time as the development work on the original NS design was nearing completion in 1922, AEC launched into a new market with the introduction of its first trolleybus chassis. This started a new series of model numbers from 601 upwards, but these must not be confused with the later and much better-known 6-type series of motor buses of 1929 onwards.

The 601 design itself does not appear to have gone into production but the 602, based on the S-type chassis, was available in 1922 to 1923 though only six were built. It was a single-decker, like almost all the early AEC trolleybuses.

The 603, announced in 1924, was very much more successful. It adopted the now familiar layout first seen on trolleybuses in the 'twenties of having the entrance ahead of the front axle and consequently had a short wheelbase, 12ft. 6in. at first. Some

chassis at least from the Autumn of 1925 were built as short as 10ft. 8¼in. in wheelbase length for an overall length of just under 23ft. and soon a lively export trade was built up, mainly to the Far East, for the manoeuverable vehicle that resulted. The chassis looked remarkably like underfloor-engined bus chassis of 30 years later in proportions and layout, their date of origin only being given away by such details as the solid tyres and cast spoked wheels. The model was progressively modernised, including pneumatic tyres, and was easily the longest-lived of its generation in terms of production, the last not being built until 1939—Shanghai being a regular customer. Latterly the model was designated 603T, in line with more modern AEC trolleybuses. A total of 282 were built.

What was then thought to be the largest order for trolleybus chassis ever placed was put in hand in 1924. It called for 100 chassis for the Shanghai Electric Construction Co. Ltd., each being designed to haul a trailer. The chassis were built to the Shanghai concern's requirements, including the set-back front axle, which gave the chassis much the same proportions as underfloor-engined diesel chassis of a much later period. They must have been among the world's first of this layout. Ten of them are lined up in the works yard at Walthamstow before the Bull motors and EMB controllers were fitted.

A home-market 603 demonstrator on pneumatic tyres was publicised in the technical press in September 1925. It had a Strachan and Brown 30-seat body and was designed for one-man-operation —by no means the relatively recent concept it is sometimes claimed to be. The wheelbase was ultra-short at 10ft. 8¾in.

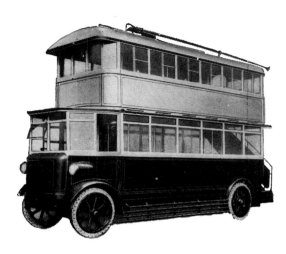

The 2-ton chassis was an attempt to extend AEC's market into wider spheres. Its appearance was very similar to that of larger AEC models of the period.

The 607 trolleybus was, in effect, a 507 bus chassis with electric motor and, understandably, the single demonstrator built went to Birmingham Corporation, the largest customer for the 507 bus chassis, ultimately becoming No. 17 in that fleet, though no further orders resulted. It had bodywork by Vickers of Crayford, then beginning to become prominent as bus bodybuilders.

Models 604, 605 and 607 were less successful, with totals of six, three and five examples built respectively. Three of the 604 models and one of the 607 models were double-deckers supplied to Birmingham in 1926, the former having a set-back front axle while the latter could be described as a trolleybus version of the 507 petrol-engined chassis—there appears to have been no 606.

# Lightweight models

Meanwhile, in 1923, a new range of lighter chassis had been introduced, nominally of 2-ton capacity and hence known as the 2-type, with model numbers beginning 201. Of normal-control layout, they were of similar appearance to larger AEC models of the time suitably scaled down and had a new engine of the 100 mm x 140 mm dimensions and 4.4-litre capacity, the original version being A110. Most were goods—a total of 917 were built, mostly

The neat-looking engine of the 2-ton model. This was AEC's first monobloc engine, with combined cylinder block and crankcase, and had only two main bearings. It had the same dimensions as the K-type unit but differed greatly in design.

in 1924-26 but in a few cases up to 1928, but the 202 was a passenger model on pneumatic tyres designed to seat up to 26 and helping to build up a market for AEC among the numerous independent operators then becoming established in all parts of the British Isles.

However, the first AEC motor bus model to be clearly intended to capture a share of the municipal and company bus market outside London was the 411, introduced in 1925. As the number implied, it belonged to the 4-type family and had the 108mm x 140mm 5.1-litre size of engine that was to remain AEC's standard choice for the majority of passenger models until 1928. The version introduced for the 411 was the A118, described in the handbook for the model as of 35-40 hp. Its RAC rating remained at 29 hp, but this version, also used in the NS, was quoted as having a maximum output of 45 bhp at 1500 rpm, partly reflecting more efficient design and partly a greater willingness to quote the output at maximum speed.

The 411 also had the distinction of being the first AEC model to have a name as well as a number, starting the long line of names beginning with R. This first name to be chosen, Renown, was applied to three completely different series of models over the

The first named models to be introduced by AEC were announced in March 1925. The Renown, model 411 (and 413, which differed only in braking arrangement) was the first of three generations of AEC model with this type name. The chassis was AEC's first full-sized model to be designed for pneumatic tyres, being intended to meet anticipated legislation limiting the weight of such vehicles to 3¾ tons unladen if they were to run at 20 rather than 12 mph. In the event this was not pursued. Many examples had the curious flat-topped front mudguard shown here, giving an appearance reminiscent of Edwardian designs. This example for the AMC Motor Service operating to the west of Leeds had Strachan and Brown bodywork, this firm being particularly active as suppliers of bodywork on AEC chassis around this time.

years. The 411 was described as a light passenger chassis with 14ft. 6in. wheelbase (slightly shorter than the S-type) and was intended to seat about 30 passengers. It was of very simple and straightforward design though it broke new ground among forward-control AEC models in having pneumatic tyres as standard. It had a straight pressed-steel frame and reverted to the cone clutch (the NS had a multi-plate unit) and its four-speed sliding-mesh gearbox and overhead worm rear axle gave a relatively high horizontal transmission line. Like almost all commercial vehicles at that time, its brakes operated on the rear wheels only, though the system of operation, with foot-brake acting on the rear of the gearbox and handbrake acting on the rear wheels, was the reverse of the more usual arrangement.

Mr. George N. Walsh, of Tullamore, Co. Offaly, stands proudly beside his 414 model, which was delivered in November 1926, after the formation of ADC. It had bodywork by United Automobile Services Ltd., then beginning to become one of the regular suppliers of bodywork for AEC or ADC passenger models. The vehicle was used on a daily service to Dublin. The fleetname was typical of the era — AEC was building up useful business with Irish operators.

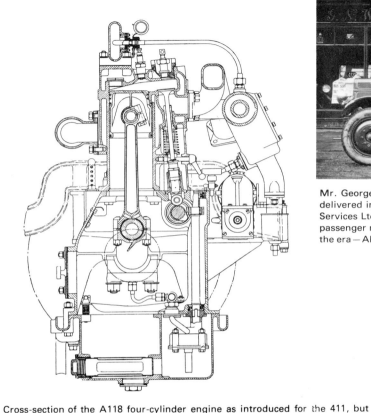

Cross-section of the A118 four-cylinder engine as introduced for the 411, but representative of the whole family of 108 mm x 140 mm engines that powered most of the 4-type models throughout the 'twenties. Originally designed when buses were not supposed to run at more than 12 mph, its limitations were beginning to become apparent when operation at up to 30 mph was becoming accepted, even though still illegal at the time. This drawing shows the somewhat spindly conn-rod and small diameter big-end bearing, together with the trough (marked B) into which the scoop under the big-end dipped.

Early in 1926, the enterprising Greyhound Motors Ltd. of Bristol put four AEC 411 models with fully-fronted Strachan & Brown saloon coach bodywork on the Bristol-London service they had started the previous year — one of the pioneer long-distance services. Note the roof rack for luggage.

A basically similar model with normal-control layout, the 412, was also built and given the type name Blenheim.

Within a few months a revised version of the 411, with both hand and foot brake acting directly on the rear wheels, was introduced. This was the 413, and the 414 was listed as a bonneted (normal-control) version, though this had a transmission handbrake and rear-wheel footbrake. The 411 and 413 were quite successful, with 191 and 214 respectively built for a wide variety of operators in 1925-26, but the bonneted versions were only built in small numbers.

Operators who wanted to continue with what amounted to the Y-type concept could still buy the 505 model in 1925. This example with 31-seat Strachan & Brown body and pneumatic tyres was supplied to Richards' Busy Bee service of Caernarvon, being taken over with that business by Crosville, in which fleet it ran as No. 249 until 1931. The 506 was of similar appearance.

This Ramillies of late 1925, probably a demonstrator, was of interest in being a single-decker and in having the model name displayed on the radiator in the manner to become familiar four years later. In fact, the mid 'twenties model names were not used as universally by AEC or others in referring to types of vehicles as applied later. They were dropped under the ADC regime and rarely used in subsequent reference to these types.

Among the exhibits at the 1925 Commercial Motor Show was this example of the then new 507 Ramillies double-decker, with pressed-steel frame, but retaining the high floor level of previous 5-type models and still on solid tyres. It appears to have been a in Birmingham Corporation livery and the body was clearly to that operators' specification, though the first examples of the 507 model were not taken into the Birmingham fleet until 1927. The chassis price was quoted as £935 and the complete vehicle £1,704.

# More 5-types

Meanwhile the 5-type chassis had also been modernised. This range was built in both passenger and goods versions, with little basic difference in design. The 504 model had been adopted as Birmingham Corporation's standard top-covered motor bus, 107 being added to that fleet in 1924-26, thus accounting for most of the 120 built. The 505 single-decker was less common, but some 530 examples of the 506 bonneted model which replaced the original Y-style 501 model in 1925 were produced, though only a limited number were passenger, in which version some examples were given the type name Grenville.

The 507, introduced in 1925, was to some extent a repeat story of the 504, for Birmingham Corporation accounted for 118, delivered between 1927 and 1929, of the 240 built. This forward-control model was again intended mainly as a double-decker, but with a pressed steel frame instead of the 504's flitched version, and was given another name chosen from ships of the Royal Navy—Ramillies. However, it was also offered as a 6-ton goods model and remained in production in this form until 1932. Models 508 and 509 were basically goods chassis, the former intended as a tipper but the latter, sharing the same 15ft. 9½in. wheelbase as the 507 and differing from it mainly in having an overhead-worm rear axle, was also the basis of some single-deck buses. A model 510 double-decker was also listed in 'Commercial Motor' in November 1926 but evidently never went into production.

# 3 ASSOCIATED DAIMLER
# — MARRIAGE AND DIVORCE

The working relationship with Daimler that had begun in 1913 and had resulted in so marked a similarity between AEC and Daimler vehicles as to almost amount to one of the earliest examples of badge engineering, had withered away at the end of the 1914-18 war. Daimler continued to build buses through the early 'twenties, sales largely depending on the reputation for quietness of the sleeve-valve engine. The basic chassis design was altered but little. and the range of normal-control single deckers had diminishing appeal as operators' interest in higher-capacity buses increased.

Then, on 25th June 1926, a formal marriage of interests was created by the formation of the Associated Daimler Co. Ltd. Its object, as stated in company publications, was to "market all standard types of AEC and Daimler omnibus, motor coach and commercial chassis previously manufactured and sold by Associated Equipment Co. Ltd. and the Daimler Co. Ltd."

Lord Ashfield, as the former Albert Stanley had become, was appointed Chairman, reflecting the position of AEC as a subsidiary of the LGOC and hence the Underground group. Both AEC and Daimler continued as the manufacturing companies, and Daimler continued to sell its private cars under its own name—its best-known customers for these being the Royal family. The key word in the above quotation was "market", for ADC was basically a sales company and trading name, though the original policy was of unified chassis design, and indeed chassis manufacture.

## The move to Southall

Earlier in the year plans had been revealed for removal of the AEC works to a new site at Southall and before the end of 1926 construction of the new factory was well in hand. The address was Windmill Lane, described at the time as "that hitherto and still, in great part, pretty wooded lane running between Uxbridge Road and Sion Corner on the Bath Road". The design of the new factory was significant, for prominent within the site were the single-storey detached offices of the Associated Daimler Co. Ltd. and at the corner of the main factory block those of the Associated Equipment Co. Ltd., in almost identical style.

The formation of Associated Daimler led to the introduction of a new radiator design, though this did not appear until 1927. This example is on a 416 in the fleet of Western Valleys Transport Co., one of the constituents of what later became Red & White Motor Services Ltd. Note the ADC symbol on the filler cap.

In practical terms, the plan was for AEC to build chassis, in many of which would be offered a choice of AEC or Daimler engines. Not for the last time, there tended to be a certain amount of confusion over names. What had hitherto been AEC engines were for a time renamed ADC and indeed carried these initials on the tappet side covers, but no attempt was made to rename the Daimler engines.

The first ADC model number was the 415, though it first appeared under AEC name-plates. In effect the basic design was a longer version of the 413. It was introduced to meet the requirements of United Automobile Services Ltd., which took all but a small minority of the chassis produced This is an example of the version with ADC radiator.

Incidentally, the AEC name itself had run into trouble a year or two earlier, when the German electrical concern AEG objected to the registration of AEC as a trade name in South America as well as Germany itself. As a result AEC vehicles sold in South America were given ACLO nameplates—this standing for ''Associated Company's Lorries and Omnibuses''—an arrangement that continued into recent years. (This trade mark is still in existence at the time of writing).

At the beginning of the ADC regime much of the model range continued unaltered apart from the adoption of a new style of radiator, of somewhat similar style to the previous AEC pattern, but with the ''Associated Daimler'' title spelled out in full across the top tank, and a small ADC monogram on the filler cap. The current 5-type models, 506, 507, 508 and 509 and the NS, in its provincial 409 form, continued unchanged apart from the radiator, etc., and in those cases no Daimler-engined version was offered.

# A choice of engines

It was the 4-type single-deckers that spelled out the implications of the new regime. A new model, the 415, basically a lengthened version of the 413, was introduced shortly before the formation of ADC. It was created to meet the requirements of United Automobile Services Ltd., which was beginning to expand rapidly from its original East Anglian territory, as well as engaging in bodybuilding on a rapidly growing scale at Lowestoft, and acting as AEC agents in parts of County Durham. United took 100 AEC 415 models, forming that company's E class and then a further 140 ADC 415 models, with a new radiator,

which became the F class in the United fleet. The first 115 of the latter had AEC engines and were officially designated 415A, and the last 25 had Daimler engines and were thus 415D. Between them, these United orders accounted for all but twenty of the 415 models built and the model was not publicised to any extent by AEC or ADC.

However, the 416 and 417 were a different story, for the former in particular was to become the best-selling model yet, so far as provincial customers were concerned. These were forward-control and normal-control respectively and the successors to the 413 and 414. They had no model names; these were dropped during the ADC regime.

Apart from adopting the same 16ft. wheelbase as the 415, the 416 and 417 had a new frame with sidemembers cranked over the front and rear axles to give a lower loading line. An underslung worm rear axle was adopted, the amidships-mounted four-speed gearbox was of a new type with shafts side by side rather than one above the other and an inclined transmission line was adopted. Although not so low-built as the NS, the 416 and 417 broke new ground as far as the first lower-framed single-deck models from AEC or ADC.

Mechanically they each had a choice of AEC engine, in which case they were designated 416A or 417A, or Daimler (416D or 417D). The AEC unit was the familiar 4-type 108mm x 140mm 5.1-litre engine in its latest A119 form, still developing a mere 45 bhp, and happier to jog along at say 20-25 mph than if pressed harder, but now including such advanced features for a 1926 design as an air cleaner and an oil filter with throw-away element. However the lubrication system relied almost entirely on splash and the cylinder heads were still fixed—at least until the 1928 season, when detachable heads over each pair of cylinders were introduced on the A127 engine—the first chassis so equipped being 416519. Within AEC, this revised model was known as 416A/2, a method of indicating variations much used later.

The alternative engine was a Daimler six-cylinder sleeve-valve engine (the four-cylinder units used on earlier Daimler buses being dropped). Daimler's designation for it was the CV25, which indicated that it was the commercial vehicle version of the 25 hp (RAC rating) car unit. It was of 81.5mm bore and 114mm stroke, giving a swept volume of 3.568 litres. Though smaller, it was much faster revving, developing its maximum output of 70 bhp at 3,000 rpm, exactly twice the speed of the AEC unit. The 416D and 417D were accordingly lower-geared than the AEC-engined versions.

Operators thus had a choice of the simpler and almost certainly more economical AEC unit or the refined but more complex

The front end of a 416A chassis, showing the AEC A119 engine, officially described as an ADC engine, these initials on the tappet cover just being visible. This was basically the same unit as was being used in the NS and other 4-type models. The photograph also shows the drop in frame level behind the bonnet.

The Daimler CV25 was the first six-cylinder engine to be offered in an AEC-built chassis. Visible in this view are the six separate cylinder heads and the ribbed exhaust manifold.

Daimler. The latter's sleeve valves, allied to the six-cylinder layout, certainly gave quieter and smoother running, but were prone to heavy lubricating oil consumption, of which the characteristic blue exhaust smoke was clear evidence. The remainder of the chassis was a mixture of old and new ideas. The braking system could be either, operators being offered a choice of brakes on the rear wheels only, on both front and rear or even the latter with a Dewandre vacuum servo.

Overall, the 416 was a good average middle 'twenties bus design. Despite being faced with tough competition from such models as the Leyland Lion, the Tilling-Stevens B9 and B10, the Dennis E and the Bristol B and the Albion 30/60 hp, it sold well, some 987 being built in the 2½ years it was marketed, mainly for company and municipal operators. The bonneted 417 tended

to be favoured only by small operators or as a coach, but also did well in its more limited market, with 124 examples.

Model 418 was a straight-framed 3½-ton goods model which had a front-end like the 417 and remained in production until 1931, but the 419 was quite different. The LGOC had built eight special ''all-weather'' coaches using the Daimler sleeve-valve

Representative of completed 416 models are the two examples on the opposite page. The bus for White's Motors of Cardiff and Barry had United bodywork and was among the first vehicles to be photographed outside the experimental department at the new Southall works.
The all-weather coach for Pilcher's of Chatham had Hall, Lewis bodywork of a transitional type between the traditional charabanc and the enclosed coach, having a centre gangway, wind-up glass windows but a canvas hood.

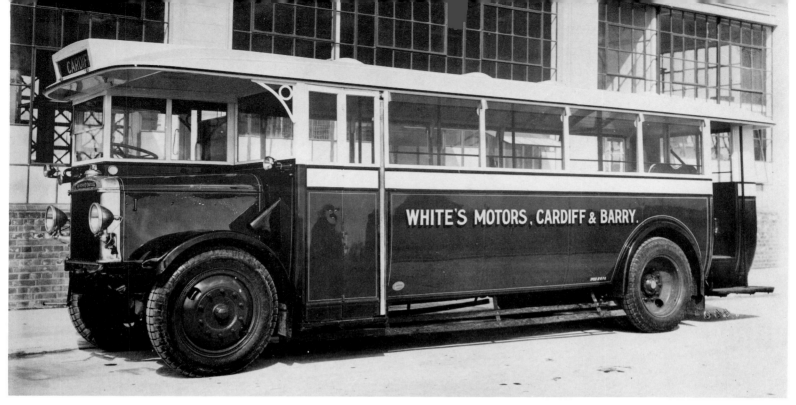

The atmosphere of an excursion to the seaside in 1927 is nicely conveyed by this photograph taken at Timpson's coach station in Catford, south-east London with an ADC 417 about to depart for Eastbourne.

six-cylinder engine at Chiswick Works in 1926. In 1927, 39 more vehicles were assembled, reputedly at Chiswick, to a similar specification and the ADC model number 419 was allocated to the latter. Their transmission was similar to that of the NS, with three-speed chain gearbox and double-reduction rear axle. The LGOC took 33, which together with the original eight ''Daimler experimental'' as they were described, were allocated the fleet numbers AW1-41. The remaining six 419 models were supplied to East Surrey. They had a front-end design unlike any other model with a radiator of well-rounded outline and relatively long bonnet. There had also been one vehicle of similar frontal appearance actually numbered NS1738; this had a saloon coach body, but the reason for its inclusion in the NS class is not clear.

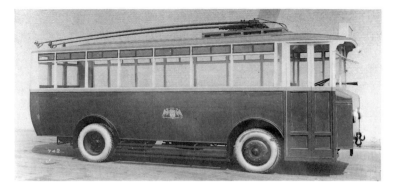

Trolleybus manufacture continued on a small scale under the ADC regime and two 604 models with 31-seat Vickers bodywork were the first trolleybuses to operate in Holland, being supplied to Groningen.

The unusual appearance of the 419, generally unlike that of any other ADC or AEC model, is conveyed by this picture of a chassis, complete with part of the cab. The model was an LGOC creation but echoes of some of its features were to be found in the LS-type six-wheelers.

(Above and left) South America was an increasingly important export market and these photographs of ACLO buses built in the ADC era convey the styles of bodywork favoured—similar designs were fitted to later types of chassis up to 20 years later.

LS1, the first of the London Sixes, photographed before entering service. It had seats for 68 passengers, an enclosed staircase and was provided with a cab door, though as still required in London, no windscreen was fitted. It was shown to MPs in May 1927 and entered service on 4th June of that year on service 16 from Victoria to Cricklewood, causing considerable public interest. Subsequently the conservatism of the Police caused the staircase to revert to the open type and removal of the cab door.

# LS — The London Six

These ADC single-deckers all had pneumatic tyres as standard, but the NS double-deckers were still being put into service on solids. The initial introduction of pneumatic tyres on London double-deckers took a more dramatic course. There was much interest in six-wheelers at this time and word reached LGOC that one of the leading independent operators planned to be the first to operate such a vehicle in London.

The design of a six-wheeler for LGOC was put in hand in the AEC drawing office, then still at Walthamstow, as a matter or urgency. A. W. Hallpike, then a draughtsman there but later to be Director and General Manager of Bristol Commercial Vehicles Ltd., told me of working through the night on the first chassis arrangement

drawing so that Charles Edwards could take it to LGOC headquarters the following day. Mr. Hallpike had begun work on a new engine, AEC's first six-cylinder unit, the A121, which was based on the familiar 108 x 140 four-cylinder 4-type unit, but with two more cylinders and thus a 7.6-litre swept volume.

It was intended that this would be offered in a four-wheel double-decker and indeed such a model, with 16ft. 1¾in. wheelbase, was listed as being offered by ADC in 'The Commercial Motor' for 9th November 1926. It was quoted as model 810, but it seems clear that this was an error for 801. However, none were built and the only ''8-type'' vehicles were the six-wheelers, given the type number 802 and, intriguingly, listed in the same table

One of the model-802 chassis, seen at Southall. The varied paintwork suggests that it had been returned after removal of bodywork, so was probably one of the demonstrators, a theory supported by the type of bonnet, evidently intended to suit a fully-fronted cab. Evident in this view are the deeply arched sidemembers over the rear bogie, which was of the type with third differential which AEC/ADC helped to pioneer. Visible in the background are some of the 24 B-type buses that were used to transport workers from the Walthamstow area. They had been fitted with canvas-tilt top covers and were modified to seat 40 passengers each. Also visible are a couple of 416 chassis.

in 'The Commercial Motor' over five months before any general announcement. (Incidentally, there had been only one 7-type, a heavy haulage tractor with model number 701 built in 1923, which was remarkable in having a four-cylinder engine of some 9.7-litres swept volume, with 135mm x 170mm bore and stroke).

The LGOC code for the new six-wheeler was LS, standing for London Six, and LS1, with chassis number 802001, entered service on 4th June 1927, beating the appearance of the London Public Omnibus Co.'s first Guy six-wheeler on 9th September by three months. Guy adherents claim that the LS ran at first without lights, but in fact LS2 was also in service by then, and it seems hard to believe that it took so long to complete any deficiences in its equipment.

As well as being the largest bus yet seen in Britain, LS1 looked much bigger than the standard NS, partly because of its enclosed staircase (though in fact this feature was found on some special

NS buses designed to operate through Blackwall Tunnel which first appeared a few weeks earlier). No doubt because of the urgency, a Daimler engine was fitted, this being the CV35 Mark I, a commercial version of the 35 hp car engine with 97mm x 130mm cylinder dimensions and 5.7-litres swept volume first introduced in 1923, and given a full-pressure lubrication system in 1925, when it was called the 35/120. No less a person than HM The King had purchased a 35/120 car in 1926 and so passengers in the LS buses similarly powered were in good company.

The transmission system was conventional for the period, with single-plate clutch and amidships-mounted four-speed crash gearbox. Both rear axles were driven through underslung worm units mounted centrally; the rod brakes operated only on the rear axles.

The frontal design was the subject of a competition among the draughtsmen and Mr. Hallpike was successful with his remarkably rounded style, with a bow-fronted radiator and an almost symmetrical bonnet and cab, which owed some of its features to the 419. The steering column was more raked than on other front-control AEC or ADC models and with the front axle well forward, the general front end proportions were to be faintly echoed by the Bristol Lodekka of about 25 years later—Hallpike influence in common perhaps.

The second chassis, 802002, used as a works bus to carry staff from the Walthamstow area to Southall and the third, which was

WORLD'S LARGEST CAPACITY BUS
ASSOCIATED DAIMLER 104 SEATER
THE ASSOCIATED DAIMLER COMPANY LTD. SOUTHALL. MIDDX.

Useful publicity, as well as a major contribution to its staff transport problem was obtained by ADC from the 104-seat works bus built on the second of the 802-type chassis. LGOC built the bodywork on both the works buses as well as all its own LS type buses. To modern eyes, the 104-seater was better balanced in appearance than LS1 because the upper-deck was built further forward over the cab. Surprisingly, the overall length was quoted as only 29ft. ½in. — the high seating capacity was obtained by extensive use of tip-up seats. Contemporary reports refer to the use of Westinghouse air brakes on this vehicle, found on a few buses at that time but not generally found on motor buses in Britain until the era of the RT. It was this vehicle that was also used as a test bed for AEC's first experimental oil engine.

LS2, had the AEC A121 engine. A second works bus was 802007 and these two vehicles, not subject to the general regulations applicable to buses, still less the stringencies of the Metropolitan Police, seated the remarkable totals of 104 and 102 passengers respectively, largely by use of tip-up gangway seats, which have never been permitted on a British PSV. One, believed to have been the 104-seater, was used as a mobile test bed for AEC's first experimental diesel engine from December 1928, and was therefore probably the world's first diesel double-decker. This aspect of the story is covered in a later chapter.

The remainder of the first ten chassis (except 802009) were demonstrators to Westcliff-on-Sea Motor Services, Maidstone & District, Southdown, Birmingham and Sheffield Corporations respectively. Then followed a further ten vehicles, 802011-20, for LGOC, built between January and September 1928, and numbered LS3-12, though not in order. Most were 70 or 72-seat double-deckers with open staircases, the Police being dissatisfied with closed staircases. However, LS6 was a complete exception, as it was a 34-seat single-decker, and had electric transmission, similar to that used on many Tilling-Stevens buses up to that time and then much favoured in the United States—it was the only 802 with either of these features. LS3 and LS12 had A121 engines but the rest had Daimler CV35 units, as built. (All were converted with the later 6-type AEC petrol engines in 1929-30).

After that ...... nothing. No more 802 models were built and most of the demonstrators ended up in the works transport fleet. What had no doubt seemed a promising line of development was abandoned and although the LGOC did subsequently adopt six-wheelers in a big way they were based on a quite different design. On paper, the 802 should have been an effective competitor to the Guy and Karrier six-wheelers of that period, but perhaps ADC's salesmanship was being affected by the strains in the

One of the 802-type demonstrators—almost certainly that supplied to Westcliff on Sea Motor Services Ltd., and subsequently purchased by that operator (802004). All the demonstrators had Daimler 5.7-litre engines and Short Bros. bodywork, of varying styles. Two of them ended up in the AEC works transport fleet, one went to the East Surrey concern and one, that to Sheffield Corporation, was burnt out, leaving this one as the only example operating outside London after about 1929.

(Below) The only 802 single-decker was the LGOC's LS6, with petrol-electric transmission, which spent most of its life on the 104E service between Golders Green and Edgware. It was converted to conventional gearbox in 1929 and withdrawn in 1935.

(Below, right) The appearance of the LS buses during most of their lives in LGOC service is conveyed by this view of LS8 alongside NS975 at Hyde Park Corner in June 1929. This bus had been built with an enclosed staircase but had by then been converted to open staircase. At about this time, its Daimler engine had been replaced by an AEC unit of the type then being fitted to new vehicles.

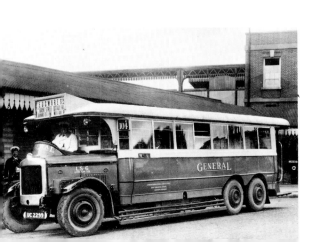

relationship between AEC and Daimler that were beginning to arise.

So for a brief while the NS returned to favour. Pneumatic tyres were eventually accepted by the Metropolitan Police, who had at first objected to the slight increase of width needed to adapt them to the large rear wheels of the model. ADC introduced a new version of the chassis so equipped, with model number 422 and this incorporated other improvements, such as a slightly more powerful, detachable-head engine, the A128, of the same size as before but developing 57 bhp. The LGOC took delivery of its first AEC-built NS chassis since 1924, these being products of the Southall factory and having a variation of the ADC radiator, but with 'General' lettering, 50 being supplied in July/August 1928 as NS2297-2346 and a final six were added in May 1929 (NS2372-77).

ADC 422 buses, mostly with LGOC bodywork, were supplied to several operators in 1927-29, and the writer occasionally travelled to school in one of Newcastle Corporation's six examples for a few months in 1937. By then they seemed very old-fashioned and it came as no surprise when they, like the LGOC's fleet, ceased operation later that year. It was not until many years later that their significance in bus history was realised.

The NS received a further lease of life and 50 examples of the improved 422 model were placed in service by LGOC in the summer of 1928, including NS 2300, seen here. The pneumatic tyres were the most obvious difference although there were several body and chassis improvements, while the radiator could be described as a General version of the Associated Daimler unit.

City of Oxford Motor Services Ltd. took delivery of ten of the 422 version of the NS in 1928-29, including six with LGOC bodywork, one of which is seen outside the experimental department at Southall. Pneumatic tyres had, in fact, been fitted to a 409 model NS supplied to the Greyhound company in Bristol early in 1927 — this must have been one of the earliest two-axle double-deckers on pneumatics.

# Coventry-built ADCs

The first signs of the break-up of ADC came at the November 1927 Commercial Motor Show when models 423 and 424 were announced. Another pair of forward- and normal-control chassis, they broke new ground by being built at the Daimler works in Coventry. Mechanically they were quite similar to the 416D and 417D in having the Daimler CV25 six-cylinder sleeve-valve engine, four-speed sliding-mesh gear box and worm drive axle.They had four-wheel brakes as standard, and a choice of wheelbase lengths, 16ft. 3¼in. and 17ft. 3 7/8in. (the odd fractions were to remain a typical Daimler feature for about twenty years).

The appearance of the 423 and 424 broke new ground in having a marked resemblance to contemporary Daimler cars, though the top of the radiator lacked the characteristic Daimler fluting and, remarkably, bore no name at all. The appearance was greatly

The Associated Daimler stand at the November 1927 Show at Olympia. Prominent in this view are the 423 (right, with Short Bros. body) and 424 (left, in chassis form) which were ADC's newest offerings. They resulted from the appointment in the autumn of 1926 of Laurence H. Pomeroy as Chief Engineer of ADC and, at first, consultant to AEC, Daimler and the LGOC. However, his interests were soon to be concentrated on Daimler's works at Coventry, where these two models were to be built, a decision not advertised at the time. Charles Edwards continued as Chief Engineer of AEC and had been responsible for the Southall-built but Walthamstow-designed 802 (LS) model, of which the demonstration example with Short Bros. metal-framed body built for Birmingham Corporation is visible in the background. Note the rear-hinged bonnet on the 424 chassis, a feature to remain characteristic of Pomeroy-designed Daimler cars and buses during the following decade.

improved and it was hardly surprising that in both forms these chassis were particularly favoured as the basis of coaches. The 424, in particular, had very much the air of a somewhat overgrown Daimler car with the implication of luxury this conveyed.

Production of neither model was large, consisting of 73 of the 423 model and 56 of the 424, probably because of the impending break-up of ADC, but United took 26 of the 423 model, and other prominent customers included Manchester Corporation (12), Wrexham and District (10) and Edinburgh Corporation (8). The largest customer for the 424 was Elliott Bros. of Bournemouth, which concern was then expanding its Royal Blue coach service network, and took 26 examples.

(Opposite page) It would be hard to beat the sheer elegance of this ADC 424 model, one of 26 supplied in 1928 to Elliott Bros. of Bournemouth, who in those days were the proprietors of the Royal Blue express coach network which already covered much of the south of England. This one had bodywork by Duple and is photographed at that concern's premises at Hendon. The one-upmanship of the obvious resemblance to a Daimler limousine was heightened by the then almost exclusive use of such cars by the Royal family for official occasions. RU 6728 would no doubt have been a most pleasant vehicle in which to travel, with smooth running ensured by the six-cylinder sleeve-valve engine. The low gearing required to give adequate performance with the relatively small 3½-litre engine was no doubt acceptable at the modest speeds at which vehicles were supposed to travel — there was still an overall 20 mph limit, though this was widely ignored. Note the advertised price of No. 1 petrol — the contemporary equivalent of four-star — of 1s. 1d. (5½p) per gallon.

## . . . and Southall-built with a Coventry look

United Automobile Services Ltd. was the sole customer for the next model to appear. This was the 425, which had the general appearance of the 423, but the AEC A127 four-cylinder engine and a mechanical specification generally similar to the 416A. The wheelbase length of 17ft. 0 5/8in. almost suggested a Daimler-designed vehicle, but all 125 built were reputedly Southall products, becoming United's J1 to 125. When United's fleet was split in 1931, the newly-formed Eastern Counties Omnibus Co. Ltd. received 28 of these and all were rebodied in 1934-35, surviving into post-war days. Ten of the vehicles kept by United were rebodied by Plaxton with special fully-fronted centre-entrance

Although manufacture of the 423 and 424 models was at Coventry, testing of completed vehicles was carried out at Southall. This view of a 423 was taken on the test hill that had been excavated in a similar manner to that at the LGOC Chiswick works. It was a coach with fully-fronted Short Bros. 20-seat coach bodywork supplied to Mr. J. Glenton Friars of Blaydon, Co. Durham, for his newly-established North Road Coach Service between Newcastle and London. It had been a 1927 Olympia Show exhibit and was used as a restaurant car, being equipped with facilities to keep food collected from hotels en route hot.

(Above) United Automobile Services Ltd. was the only operator of the ADC 425 model, which had the four-cylinder poppet-valve engine in a chassis with the 423 style of radiator. Ten of the 125 built were rebodied in 1935 with fully-fronted centre-entrance bodies for Scarborough sea-front service as an answer to Blackpool's trams of similar layout and thus survived until 1950. By the time this early post-war photograph was taken the radiator of VF 2814 had been given a modified grille—the centre strip topped by a triangle belonged to a later era.

(Right) The next step was to modernise the standard Southall-built 416 and 417 models, using the new-style radiator. This picture shows how closely the radiator resembled contemporary Daimler car outlines—in fact early development of the shape had been done by applying plasticine to a Daimler radiator to eliminate the fluting; curiously, no lettering was applied. Fortunately for the historian, the modernised 416, designated 426, had a different style of dumb iron cover, consisting of a complete aluminium casting, as shown here, rather than the cover strip of the 423 model.

bodies for the Scarborough sea-front service in 1936 and survived until 1950—they could well have been the last ADC buses and the last vehicles with 4-type engines to survive in public service.

AEC itself followed suit with the 426 and 427 models which were respectively face-lifts of the 416A and 417A using the 423/424 style radiator and bonnet, plus curved cast-aluminium dumb-iron cover castings added to the front of the frame, obviously intended to resemble those of the 423/424, though the latter's were more in the nature of aluminium strips over a rounded frame end. Here again the A127 engine was used, but the mechanical design so closely resembled that of the A416A and 417A that the latter's instruction book was used, with a note in the flyleaf stating that it applied to the 426 and 427 except for the radiator and bonnet.

Quite a number of chassis were converted and the first three 426 models, chassis numbers 426001 to 003, supplied to East Surrey in March 1928, were rebuilt from 416-type chassis with the numbers 416930 to 932. Official production figures were 226 of the 426 and 52 of the 427, but 426 chassis numbers were issued at least to 426239, the difference being due to rebuilds or cancelled orders. Customers were a mixed selection of municipalities, company and independent operators, including some coach operators, such as Elliott Bros., although this concern's vehicles were soon to be the subject of a further step in rebuilding.

## The break-up of ADC

By this date, the ADC set-up was beginning to break up. Indeed the design and manufacture of the 423 and 424 at Daimler had been a significant step. Advertisements in The Electric Railway and Tramway Journal convey the change of atmosphere. Those in the February and March 1928 issues refer to Associated Daimler models and quote the ADC address at Windmill Lane, Southall.

The 427 was the corresponding equivalent to the 417. Its overall appearance was almost identical to the 424, though the dumb iron again provided means of identification. This vehicle was evidently a demonstrator, looking much more modern than the solid-tyred lorry with open-sided cab alongside.

A 427 chassis, showing not only the strongly-raked steering column but also the characteristic shape of this generation of chassis frame, with relatively low side-members and comparatively abrupt kick-up over the rear axle and under the rear of the bonnet.

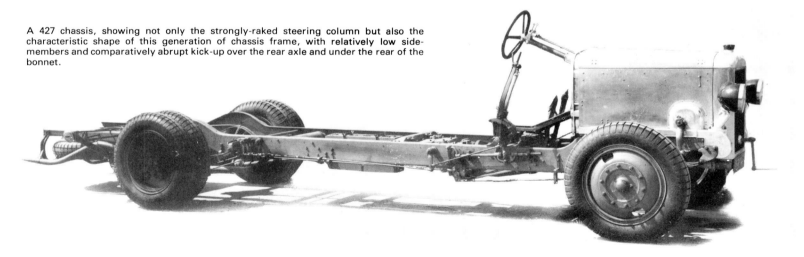

**Associated Daimler....**
This series of advertisments in ''The Electric Railway and Tramway Journal'' during 1928 give a clear indication of how the Associated Daimler Co. broke up. All seems quite normal in this one dated 9th March.

**....going....**
By July 13th, the split was clear, with separate enquiry addresses, even though the Associated Daimler lettering was still the boldest.

**....going....**
By August 10th, the Associated Equipment and Daimler titles had become predominant, though significantly the former was bolder and occupied more space than the latter.

But the July 1928 advertisement, though boldly headed 'Associated Daimler Co. Ltd.', quotes that concern's address as 55 Broadway, London SW1, the Underground Group's headquarters (nowadays those of London Transport) and refers inquiries to either the Associated Equipment Co.Ltd. at Southall or the Daimler Co. Ltd. at Coventry. The August 1928 advert carries matters a stage further with larger billing for Associated Equipment and Daimler than Associated Daimler, though some papering over the crack was conveyed by the association that ADC was "the largest combination of manufacturing and technical resources in the commercial vehicle industry''. But by December the rift was complete, since the AEC advertisment carried the revived bulls-eye and made no mention of ADC or Daimler. It quoted a range of 21 to 68 seaters (thus including by implication the 802, though the illustrations were of an NS-type double-decker which, even with pneumatic tyres, was by then beginning to look distinctly dated, particularly as it had an open cab, and a 426, described as a 35/50 hp model).

For a brief period, what had been the ADC passenger models continued under the AEC name. This Mumford-bodied demonstrator was thus an **AEC** 426, though had there not been an advertising board on the bodywork to say so, it would not have been possible to distinguish it from the ADC version, in view of the "anonymous" radiator. Though up-to-date in appearance, the 426 lacked the smoothness of running at speed required for an effectively competitive long-distance coach in 1928.

**....gone**
By December 14th, all trace of Associated Daimler and Daimler had gone, the AEC bull's eye motif was back and only the slogan "Builders of London's Buses" provided a link with that in the March ADC advertisment.

In fact by that late date, there were far more than mere changes of name afoot, as will be seen in the next chapter. It was not before time, for the models being made by AEC on its re-emergence as a separate make name were ceasing to be competetive.

All were four-cylinder, which in itself was a handicap when operators were turning to such models as the Leyland Titan and Tiger, quite apart from the Guy and Karrier six-wheel six-cylinder ranges. Even Daimler was in an advantageous position in this respect, for the immediate post-split model, the CF6, used the 5.7-litre sleeve-valve engine that had powered most of the 802 model ADC six-wheelers.

However, even among four-cylinder models, the AEC 426, as it had now become, was up against severe competition. The Leyland Lion PLSC model, though of the generation previous to the Tiger, certainly had an engine which offered more refined running at speed and between 1926 and 1929 over twice as many were built as the combined total of ADC/AEC 416 and 426 models. The Tilling-Stevens Express was largely sold to Tilling-associated companies but the latest B10 version was building up a good reputation in the industry as a whole, as were the Bristol B, the Dennis E and the Albion 30/60 hp models. The AEC was particularly handicapped by its engine design, and in particular its absence of a pressure lubrication system was becoming more of a problem as operators' requirements for speed increased.

## Some key men in the story of AEC buses

At this turning point in the history of AEC, it seems appropriate to bring together some of the major personalities who made the decisions that lay behind the design of the vehicles.

**Frank Searle** (left)
Searle had actually left the LGOC before AEC was formed as a separate concern in 1912, but his development of the B-type and the advanced manufacturing methods used for its production made him effectively the father of the company.

**Lord Ashfield** (right)
Although seemingly a relatively remote figure as the Chairman of the Underground group, Lord Ashfield was sufficiently interested in bus manufacture to even influence policy and even detail design. This photograph was taken just before he became the first Chairman of London Transport in 1933.

**Charles Edwards** (below left)
Photographed at the presentation made to mark his departure from AEC in 1929. Perhaps the most impressive of his innovations during his term of office as Chief Engineer was the NS double-decker with its low-level frame.

**Bob Fryars** (above right)
This photograph was taken in 1950, when he was Assistant Chief Engineer and about to concentrate on the design of the Reliance and Mercury ranges introduced in 1953. He became Chief Engineer in 1961, and subsequently held a number of senior posts in the Leyland organisation.

**John Rackham and George Robinson**
This photograph was taken at Rackham's retirement presentation at the completion of 21 years as Chief Engineer. Robinson was his successor and notable among those visible was C. B. Dicksee, standing behind Robinson and looking at Rackham, responsible for much of AEC's early oil-engine design policy. The date was June 1950.

It was significant that Lord Ashfield chose a Yellow Coach Y-type chassis as the basis of his personal 9-seat "parlour coach" delivered in 1927, as it had been designed by G. J. Rackham during the period when he was Chief Engineer of that concern, later to become GMC. Some of this model's features were also to be found on Rackham-designed AEC buses later built in greater numbers for the LGOC. Earlier comparative trials between the previous Yellow model Z and the NS in 1925 had not led the LGOC to doubt the wisdom of its then standard.

# 4 THE BLUE TRIANGLE ERA

The break-up of ADC, officially announced in July 1928, even if partially covered up by continued reference to its combined resources, was only the outward sign of major changes in vehicle design policy at AEC. Lord Ashfield, who had greater interest in the Underground group's vehicle manufacturing activities than is generally realised, had his eye on an engineer who, like himself, had begun to build up a reputation during a period in the United States.

G. J. Rackham (known as John only to his closer friends), who as mentioned earlier had been with AEC until 1916, had joined the famous Colonel Green (whom he had first met when involved in tank design around 1917) as Chief Engineer of the Yellow Coach Manufacturing Co. Ltd. in Chicago in 1922, spending four years there before returning to Britain as Chief Engineer of Leyland Motors Ltd. in 1926.

Yellow had largely built up its reputation with six-cylinder bus chassis for single- or double-deck bodywork of which the final form during the Rackham era was model Y, introduced in 1925. It was of bonneted layout—forward-control in the form generally standardised in the UK had never caught-on in America—and used a six-cylinder sleeve-valve engine similar in principle to that built in Britain by Daimler, together with an offset transmission line. Lord Ashfield was evidently sufficiently impressed to order a model Y from Yellow as his personal "parlour coach". This was delivered in 1927 and came under the care of LGOC's Chiswick Works, where its features were no doubt scrutinised with interest.

Meanwhile, Rackham, back in Britain, had not been idle. Within about a year of his arrival at Leyland, he had supervised the design and construction of the prototypes of the original Leyland Titan double-decker and Tiger single-decker which were to make an immense impact on the British bus scene when exhibited at the Commercial Motor Show at Olympia in November 1927.

Rackham was a controversial figure, and stories of his methods have buzzed around British bus engineering circles for over half a century. There is clear evidence of continuity of thought and deed in such details as the characteristic curve of the dumb irons of the Yellow Z and Y, Leyland Titan TD1 and early Rackham-designed AEC chassis. However, the Titan certainly differed in many respects from the Z. Its six-cylinder engine was of a design new to the British bus industry, with single overhead camshaft operating the valves through rockers. I have heard it said that it was inspired by the American Hall-Scott design which was perpetuated right through to the early 'sixties in the unit used, latterly in propane-fuelled form, in Flxible buses. Though I have been unable to confirm this directly, I was struck by the similarity in general appearance to Rackham-designed Leyland and AEC units of the engines from such buses I saw in the workshop of the Chicago City Transit Authority on a visit in 1973.

Rackham may not have been an innovator and his tendency to continue with ideas developed when with one firm after moving to another sometimes caused difficulties. But I confess that I remain an admirer of a man who had a quite uncanny flair for selecting features which, if only occasionally original, combined to produce outstandingly successful chassis. To have been responsible for both the original epoch-making Titan and the succession of outstanding AEC models from 1929 up to 1950 puts him firmly among the all-time leaders of bus design.

However, to return to the story, Lord Ashfield persuaded Rackham to return to AEC as Chief Engineer, the announcement of the new appointment coinciding with that explaining that AEC and Daimler were henceforth to go their separate ways, in July 1928, though it seems probable that it may have already been in effect.

# The 6-type engine

His first job was to design a new engine and incredible as it may seem by the standard of half a century later, by 29th September, only two months after his appointment was announced, the first unit was on test. Not surprisingly, most of the design features followed much the same pattern as those of the Leyland T-type unit. It was again a six-cylinder engine with single overhead camshaft and the two designs were similar in many respects.

It would be wrong to suggest that the AEC unit was a direct copy of the Leyland. In the first place, it had metric dimensions, as was to remain standard practice at Southall until the late 'forties. The bore, at 100mm, was probably intended to be similar to the 4in. of the Leyland—the latter dimension being equivalent to 101.6mm. However, the stroke of 130mm was appreciably shorter than the 5½in. (139.7mm) of the Leyland unit and the swept volume therefore worked out at 6.12-litres compared to the latter's 6.89-litres.

However, the shorter stroke made the AEC a slightly faster revving unit and minor changes in valve timing etc. no doubt contributed to the claimed power output being much the same. The AEC engine, which was given the type number A130 in original form to suit the Reliance chassis, was generally advertised as a 95 bhp engine, this power being developed at 2,500 rpm; 102 bhp at this speed was quoted for the prototype on test, but this may have been without auxiliaries. Early Leyland publications quote 98 bhp for the early T-type engine without quoting speed, but slightly later units were quoted as developing their maximum power at 2,200 rpm.

Despite these differences, the resemblances between the two units were striking. Both were handsome engines, with domed aluminium valve covers and prominent ribbed exhaust manifolds mounted high on the left hand or kerb side—the driver's side was devoid of auxiliaries. Internally, both had seven-bearing crankshafts and it is interesting to note that both were advertised as having 2¾in. main bearings, the same size as on the six-cylinder engine offered in the Yellow model Z and Y chassis.

The visual similarity between the AEC 6-type petrol engine as introduced for the Reliance in 1928-29 (above, left) and the Leyland T-type engine as introduced for the Titan and Tiger just over a year previously (left) can be judged by comparing these two views. The AEC engine, one of the earliest A130 units, has magneto ignition and an exposed flywheel to suit the 426-based Reliance chassis whereas the Leyland engine has coil ignition and a clutch housing to suit a unit construction gearbox. Even so, the general similarity of appearance and layout is striking.

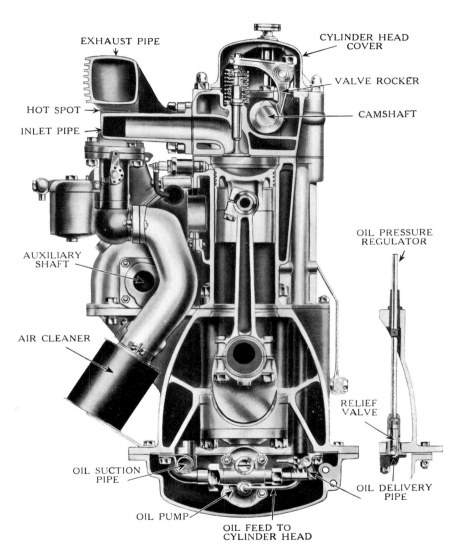

EXHAUST PIPE

CYLINDER HEAD COVER

HOT SPOT

INLET PIPE

VALVE ROCKER

CAMSHAFT

AUXILIARY SHAFT

OIL PRESSURE REGULATOR

AIR CLEANER

RELIEF VALVE

OIL SUCTION PIPE

OIL DELIVERY PIPE

OIL PUMP

OIL FEED TO CYLINDER HEAD

More revealing is an internal comparison. Though these two sectional views of the AEC engine (this time in early Regent form, as built in 1929-30), above, and the early Titan unit, above right, are cross sections facing in opposite directions, the similarities of proportion and such details as combustion chamber shape and valve gear layout are striking. This view faces forward, and shows the inlet port.

This view of the Leyland engine faces towards the rear, with the exhaust port included in the section taken. Note the similar outline of the crankcase and cylinder block on the two units. The sparking plugs on the Leyland unit are on the driver's side, which was inconvenient from a servicing viewpoint, and they were moved to the kerb side on the AEC engine.

The 6-type engine looked impressive as well as giving a much livelier and more refined performance as compared to the 4-type unit. Compare this under-bonnet view of an early Reliance with that of a 416A on page 41. The amount of polished aluminium was reduced somewhat on later versions, but this engine would not have looked out of place in a high-quality contemporary car — indeed, its behaviour would not have been far out of line.

Another characteristic feature was accelerator-pedal control of engine oil pressure.

There was clear evidence of second thoughts on some detail features on the AEC unit. The sparking plugs were on the left instead of the right, for greater ease of access. Aids were given to simplify timing when replacing the cylinder head, minimising this complication of the overhead camshaft layout.

But overall, Rackham clearly felt that the basic design was the best all-round proposition for bus and coach operation and the introduction of the AEC unit accelerated the major influence on bus engine design set in train by the Leyland T-type. Engines with 'fancy' valve gear were to appear from Dennis, Morris-Commercial and Sunbeam within the following year or two. Yet Rackham later told me that his reason for adopting the overhead camshaft was the somewhat mundane one of simplifying the cylinder block casting—complex castings of that size were apt to give problems with the foundry techniques available at that time.

Certainly, the power output, though far greater than that of previous AEC bus engines, could have been achieved by a simpler engine. Midland Red, with the aid of the cylinder head design wizard Harry Ricardo, had achieved a lively performance from a simple side-valve design, but units of this type required attention to valves to be carried out in situ, whereas Rackham advocated fleet use of an overhauled spare cylinder head complete with valves

etc. to minimise time out of service. In fact, both engines set new standards of reliability as well as refinement. I have to admit that I think the Leyland engine was marginally even quieter than the AEC, in fleet service, but both were much superior to today's diesels—idling was virtually inaudible. AEC made play of the engine's ability to run at any speed between 300 and 3,000 rpm and, although drivers were recommended to change up early, a very lively performance was available if freer use was made of the gearbox.

## The first Reliances

The decision was made to fit the new engine to what was basically the existing 426 chassis, the resulting vehicle being given the type name Reliance and the model number 660, thus starting a new 6-type series, the second figure denoting the number of cylinders. No doubt this saved time and allowed AEC to get a competitive chassis on to the market without delay, but it was probably also influenced by the need to use up stocks of parts.

Only minor modifications were made to the chassis, notably the introduction of Marles steering, and though worthy enough

Believed to have been the first AEC Reliance to have entered service with an operator, East Surrey No. 78 (PK 4243) had the third chassis, 660003, and Hall, Lewis two-doorway bodywork, being delivered in November, 1928. It was a rebuild of a 426 model chassis, number 426067, and retained that model's style of radiator, its true identity only being revealed by the slightly more forward mounting of the radiator needed to accommodate the longer engine.

This early Reliance chassis had a style of radiator not used on production models, with central strip continuing down from the new triangular version of the AEC badge. The casting of the model name in the bottom tank of the radiator was another new feature which was not repeated on later types of AEC chassis.

it was becoming outdated. The rather ponderous right-hand gear change was a case in point, but even more surprising was the retention of the cone clutch, with its propensity to kangeroo starts, even with a skilled driver. The general appearance was only slightly altered, the radiator moving forward about 3in. to accommodate the longer engine.

However, the familiar blue triangle AEC badge appeared on the radiator for the first time. A prototype chassis had a radiator with a central dividing strip rather like that on later models, but

Elliott Bros. (Bournemouth) Ltd. took delivery of 25 of the new Reliance model, all with Duple bodywork, and put them on the road between March and June 1929. This delightful picture of one of them, taken soon after delivery, conveys the atmosphere of coach travel half a century ago. The ice-cream tricycle was obviously proving an attraction in the noonday sun and the combination of a horse-drawn cart and the inevitable Ford Model T, in this case a van, underlines the big transition to motor transport by then well under way despite the lack of traffic.

The biggest single customer for the Reliance was the London and North Eastern Railway, which chose this model for a planned major expansion of its bus services in Durham and Northumberland. These were operated by companies whose shares had been purchased and hence the vehicles bore such fleetnames as Robert Emmerson and Eastern, often in addition to the LNER initials. These photographs show No. 73, with fully-fronted Strachan and Brown bodywork, ready for delivery and a small exhibition featuring a similar vehicle on the left with an Eastern half-cab vehicle with Dodson bodywork, apparently on an earlier chassis, in the background. This appears to have been held at Southall, possibly in the running shed. One of the two chassis is a normal control model similar to that shown on the opposite page, while the bodied vehicle on the right was evidently a demonstrator.

production Reliances simply had the triangle set on the face of the header tank with the downward point projecting over the radiator core—and, incidentally, being prone to becoming removed in later years.

The first three chassis, 660001 to 3 were all rebuilt from 426 models and had engine numbers 1, 3 and 2 respectively. The first two appear to have been used as test vehicles or demonstrators before being delivered to J. Sharp of Manchester and Brown of Sapcote respectively in May and April of 1929. The first to enter service was probably 660003, which was delivered to East Surrey

Competition on the Great North Road route was becoming intense and Orange Bros. of Bedlington, Northumberland, ran a Glasgow-London service via Edinburgh, Newcastle and Doncaster. Two Reliances were supplied in August 1929, and the chassis number of this one, 660419, gives an indication of the model's success despite its basically mid 'twenties chassis design. Strachans built the 26-seat bodywork, producing a smart and comfortable vehicle—this picture was taken just outside the AEC factory gates in Windmill Lane, a favourite spot for publicity pictures. These vehicles were taken over by United Automobile Services Ltd. with part of the Orange Bros. business in 1935 and, with the Reliances acquired from LNER, brought the total of this model in the United fleet to 60, the largest in the country.

No normal-control version of the Reliance was listed, but at least one chassis was produced bearing the Reliance radiator on a model otherwise resembling the 427. This could have been merely a cosmetic variation, but the radiator position suggests that this coach may have had a 6-type engine. It was built for Smith's Tours of Southport.

York street scene circa 1929-30. One of three Reliances supplied to Corcoran Bros. (Ideal) Ltd. of Tadcaster passes one of the very few Reliances to receive goods vehicle bodywork, in this case a removal van, such vehicles often being based on passenger chassis because of their low load line and softer suspension. The Corcoran Reliances, used on local services including that to Leeds, were fitted with bodywork by Cravens, who also built the somewhat similar-looking bodies on those supplied to Stockport Corporation. The Corcoran business was taken over by West Yorkshire Road Car Co. Ltd. in 1933.

as No. 78, PK 4243, in November 1928, the model being announced generally at the beginning of January 1929.

Some 484 Reliances of the 660 type were built, or in a few more cases rebuilt, the last not being delivered until 1932, although volume production appears to have reached about 400 by about the end of 1929. The largest single user was the London and North Eastern Railway, which during its brief spell of direct bus operation, ordered some 74 for service in the North-East of England, though before the order was completed some of these were delivered to United Automobile Services Ltd., which took over most of the LNER routes and vehicles, though seventeen of the LNER Reliances went to the Northern General Transport Co. Ltd. Other company users included the National Omnibus and Transport Co. which had 25.

The Reliance often tended to be regarded primarily as a coach chassis. The LGOC's 39 examples were coaches, and fleets were operated by Elliott Bros.(the original proprietors of the Royal Blue network), Timpsons and Keith & Boyle, for example. The Elliott Bros. vehicles highlighted the limitations of the 426-model coaches delivered in July 1928 and by November 1929 the six vehicles involved had all been redelivered with Reliance engines, reclassified model 426/6 and given new chassis numbers 426601 to 6.

There were some municipal fleets, notably Nottingham's twenty examples, originally hired from AEC and accordingly having Middlesex (MY) registration numbers, and Stockport's eighteen, some of which survived until after the 1939-45 war.

# The first Regents and Regals

However, all this was a stop-gap, while work went ahead on the new chassis for which the 6-type engine was really intended. Rackham was a believer in the future of the two-axle bus chassis and the two new models in which he was primarily interested were to be models 661 and 662, respectively the Regent double-decker and Regent single-decker.

The first prototype to be built was chassis number 661001, the first Regent, for which the service department record card read "built by exptl.", meaning that it was assembled in the experimental department rather than on the production line, always known within the factory as "the track". The moving assembly system had been transplanted from Walthamstow. The date quoted was 13th February 1929, and usually on such cards this was a delivery date, but even if it referred to completion of the chassis, it was a remarkable achievement.

There was hardly a single chassis component of any consequence that was not newly designed for the Regent. Frame, axles, clutch, gearbox, brakes—all were new and, moreover, there were a host of minor parts of fresh design. Many of these were to remain standard for over a quarter of a century and some were to survive until the end of production at Southall. Items such as shackle pins were incorporated without alteration in many later models.

The engine, designated A131, was, of course, the 6-type unit basically as just introduced for the Reliance but modified in regard

Almost certainly the first photograph ever taken of an AEC Regent, seen outside the experimental department at Southall. It shows what was presumably the first chassis, no doubt immediately after completion early in 1929—an epoch-making moment. The flowing curves of the frame were designed to minimise the stresses set up by body and passenger loadings and road shocks. One of the most intriguing features of this picture is the single-decker on Middlesex trade plates parked in the background. The body is of the style built by Leyland on early Tiger chassis as introduced just over a year previously, when Rackham had been at Leyland. If it was a Leyland, what it was doing at Southall, and how it came to be there, can only be surmised!

What the photographer saw from the steps on the left of the above picture. This plan view of the Regent chassis clearly shows the offset transmission line and characteristic outline of the frame, as wide as possible at the rear and tapering inwards to give adequate steering lock at the front, that linked this model with Rackham's designs for both Leyland and Yellow Coach. The left-hand sidemember was slightly longer at the rear than that on the right to suit the shape of open-staircase bodywork.

to mountings, sump shape and to suit the new clutch and gearbox. The clutch was a single-plate unit, of very simple design, but with a generous lining area and it gave a very smooth take-up of drive—there was really no excuse for stalling a Regent.

The original D119 four-speed gearbox, mounted on the back of the engine, was generally similar to that of the Titan, with sliding engagement for all but top gear, and straight-cut gears, as was usual at the time. It was a little quieter than the TD1 unit, and possibly the same applied to the comparison with the Reliance D118 unit. But perhaps the most striking feature was the characteristic sound. The Reliance had a fairly typical 'twenties low-pitched tone, and the TD1 a somewhat higher and more strident note but the Regent unit set the sound standard for almost all later AEC gearboxes, other than epicyclics.

The tone was slightly more "pure" than that of the TD1 unit and seldom deteriorated noticeably with age—perhaps AEC's gear-cutting methods were a little better or the construction slightly more rigid—but coupled to the fast-revving AEC engine, the whine could rise to a high-pitched scream if the driver used the gears freely. He was not supposed to—a notice in the cab recommended changing up early, getting into top gear at 14 mph on the level, for example. The engine would certainly pull smoothly down to low speeds, but maximum power in third gear corresponded to about 25 mph with the original low-geared (6¼ to 1) Regent rear axle. In practice, most drivers used the gears fairly freely, being encouraged to do so by the engine's willingness to rev easily, so the whine of AEC gears was a familiar sound wherever these models operated.

The general layout of the Regent followed that of both the Titan TD1 and Yellow Y in having an offset underslung worm drive rear-axle and the whole transmission line, including that of the engine crankshaft, angled both downwards and towards the left. The frame was actually not quite so low built as the NS, to the extent of 1in., at 1ft. 9in. laden, but the gentle curves over the wheel arches and taper in width over the front section were characteristic Rackham features.

The rear axle itself followed the Yellow and Leyland pattern in being of the semi-floating type, generally regarded as inferior to the fully-floating type as used on the Reliance. Rackham told me that the Timken Axle Co.'s design used by Yellow began to suffer from broken half-shafts after he had left for Leyland. The Leyland axles of similar design also began to develop similar trouble after he had gone to AEC and the same happened at AEC. Both firms were to revert to the fully-floating type around 1932, but the trouble cannot have been too serious as several thousand Leyland and AEC examples survived wartime overloading, often remaining in service until about 1950.

The original Regent brake system was rod-operated, the front brakes being operated by push rod through the hollow king-pins, Leyland style, with a single vacuum servo unit to reduce pedal effort to reasonable limits. A conventional pull-on handbrake was used rather than the push-on type favoured on the Titan. Marles steering was at first standardised.

However, perhaps the greatest advance of the Regent over its Yellow and Leyland predecessors was the tidier and more compact front-end design. In this respect at least, the pattern originally set by the K-type was followed, with the radiator mounted well forward, virtually flush with the front dumb irons. The engine was compact enough to allow the front bulkhead of the body to fit closely behind the front mudguards. Compared to the Titan, this economy of space reduced the effective overall bonnet length by 6in.

The radiator was of a completely new style, intended to suit the front end layout. It had a much slimmer polished aluminium surround than other contemporary commercial vehicle radiators and the triangle badge formed part of the overall design, the mounting for it being neatly merged between the top part of the surround and the centre strip. The basic style was set for AEC radiators until the end of the exposed radiator era in the 'fifties and indeed the grilles used on many later front-engined models until the end of the 'seventies was clearly derived from this classic design. The early version was subjected to minor revision before volume production started later in 1929, but the basic original design was an excellent example of Rackham's flair as an artist-engineer. He told me that the original concept was based on something Lord Ashfield had seen in Germany and it was the latter who had given the initial instruction to devise a similar design for AEC.

However, it is important to record that the introduction of the Regent and Regal models was entirely an AEC venture and "nothing to do with LGOC", as Rackham said to me. The relationship between the two concerns was a curious one at this stage—AEC being the talented child that had somewhat grown away from its parent, with Lord Ashfield in the position of indulgent "grandfather". The LGOC had managed to win its case for independent development of new vehicles types in the uncertain period that had seen the break-up of ADC and, indeed, was busy on its own new designs of vehicle, known as types CB and CC, the staff involved including Messrs. Watson, Ottaway and Wicks. So its attitude to the new Regent was more reserved than might otherwise have been expected.

The prototype Regent, and indeed most of the first dozen pre-production chassis, were sent to Short Bros. for bodying. The body style produced for them was based on a detailed AEC specification which, once again, bore clear evidence of Rackham influence. It was of what was later to become known as piano-fronted style, with almost vertical upper-deck front-end framing having a projection at floor level in which the destination indicator was intended to be accommodated. This style was by then familiar on Leyland bodies for the Titan chassis though its origins could be traced to Fifth Avenue Coach Co. designs introduced in New York in the early 'twenties.

The AEC version did not incorporate the side-gangway "low-bridge" layout of the Leyland, but the shape of its roof was evidently intended to give a similar impression of low build when viewed from nearby, as the necessary height to give headroom over the gangway was confined to the centre. The resulting hump effect inevitably gave rise to the nickname "camel-roof" for this style of body. The staircase was open, again with a general resemblance to Leyland appearance, but the seating was for a total of 50, of which 26 were upstairs and 24 down.

The first Regent, chassis number 661001, complete with AEC-design body built by Short Bros. and registered MT 2114. This photograph was taken towards the end of 1929, when it had been repainted from its original demonstration livery into Glasgow Corporation colours — orange, green and cream. Not only was an order for 25 buses from that undertaking obtained, but the officials of Halifax Corporation, impressed with both the bus and the livery, not only ordered similar vehicles but adopted the same livery and purchased the demonstrator, which remained in the fleet until 1935 and was then run for a further spell by Western SMT before ending its days as a furniture van, after the 1939-45 war.

The first Regent to be delivered to an operator's fleet was 661002, supplied to the National Omnibus and Transport Co.'s branch at Colchester as fleet number 2902 as early as April 1929. This offside view shows how closely the design of the AEC-design body followed the style of the standard Leyland body for the original Leyland Titan TD1. This vehicle was handed over to the newly-formed Eastern National Omnibus Co. Ltd. in 1930 and was rebodied by East Lancashire in 1944, being fitted with an AEC 7.7-litre diesel engine at about the same time. It then continued in service, not being sold until November 1954, having thus operated, albeit rebuilt, for over 25 years—an impressive record for what was a pre-production vehicle. It was scrapped in 1957, having just missed survival into the bus preservation era.

Front view of ''No. 1'' Regent, MT 2114, as originally painted in demonstration livery. This view clearly shows the type of radiator fitted to the pre-production vehicles, different from later production in having less flowing curves for the grille outlines each side of the triangle badge. Even so, the general frontal appearance of the chassis set the standard for most subsequent AEC buses with engines at the front until the mid '50s. Note that the humped outline of the roof was not visible from near the vehicle, thus giving an illusion of low build. This vehicle made a 24-hours endurance run at Brooklands.

Chassis number 661001 was registered MT 2114, and began a period of use as a prototype and demonstrator, though at first such activities were carried out quietly as the model was not announced publicly until shortly before the Commercial Show in November 1929. Ultimately this vehicle was sold to Halifax Corporation early in 1930. However, the second chassis, 661002,

(Left) The front view of the AEC-design body, when seen from a greater distance, gave clear justification for the "camel-roof" description. The ninth Regent chassis, supplied to Wallasey Corporation in July 1929 is seen here when in service a few years later.

(Right) The last of the twelve pre-production Regents was a Hall, Lewis-bodied demonstrator, believed to be the vehicle shown. The vehicle shown was of the side gangway low-height type, hence the pointer indicating that it was under 13ft. high. This view conveys the compact front-end design of the Regent chassis, copied by most other British bus makers within the following few years. The Hall, Lewis body was of a type that had been built on earlier Dennis and Leyland chassis, but its up-to-date lines suited the Regent particularly well and similar-looking designs were popular on production Regents in the 1930-32 period.

was delivered to the National Omnibus and Transport Co.'s Colchester branch on 12th April 1929 as fleet number 2902, being registered VW 9565. The third chassis was sent to the AEC agents in South America in May and the fourth, registered UU 9161, to Thomas Tilling Ltd. in June. The next three were allocated to National and only at chassis number 661008 did the LGOC

empire get a look-in, this vehicle being registered UU 6610, from a batch of numbers booked by LGOC, but allocated to East Surrey. The ninth chassis went to Wallasey Corporation, all the foregoing having Short Bros. bodywork of the AEC design, apart from the exported 661003. The pre-production batch of twelve chassis was completed by two for Birmingham Corporation delivered in July 1929 and fitted with Brush bodywork and, finally, a Hall, Lewis-bodied demonstrator.

The first of the Regal single-deckers were a batch of twelve for Plymouth Corporation, with locally-built Mumford bodywork, chassis number 662001 being No. 83, registered DR 5797.

This mysterious early Regal was evidently used for experimenting with an alternative type of radiator, before standardising on the familiar AEC style. If the triangle badge is ignored, the resemblance to the type of radiator introduced on the Leyland Titan in mid-1929 is striking—would this have been how the 1930 Leyland models might have looked if Rackham had not disliked the Lancashire climate? Note that the badge is a "General" one.

The first twelve Regal chassis were supplied to Plymouth Corporation. This was the first one, chassis number 662001; note that it has the same style of radiator as the first Regents. Bodywork was by the local concern, Mumford. Unusually, these vehicles were retained for only a few years by the original operator, though ten of them were purchased by the Bath Tramways concern, then standardising on Regals, in the early 'thirties.

# The Renown six-wheeler

The first vehicle of the new generation to be supplied to LGOC's own fleet was licensed in August 1929, soon after the majority of the pre-production Regents mentioned. This, however, was a six-wheeler, for although Rackham was not an enthusiast for passenger vehicles of this type he found himself involved in their manufacture, just as had occurred at Leyland. But the AEC Renown, as the 663-type six-wheeler was named, was to go into volume production, unlike the Leyland Titanic. Indeed the Renown was to become by far the most numerous three-axle bus chassis built in Britain, despite arriving on the scene just as the majority of operators who had tried six-wheelers were deciding that the two-axle bus was the better bet for their operations. The choice of name, if happier than Leyland's Titanic (the famous liner disaster of 1912 being still of recent memory), was surprising, as Renown had, of course, been applied to the 411 and 413 models up to 1926, though the AEC model names of the mid 'twenties had been used rather half-heartedly.

The LGOC was somewhat wedded to the six-wheeler, partly because of interest in high-capacity buses and probably because

The first of the new generation models for LGOC was the prototype Renown six-wheeler, chassis number 663001, seen here before it left Southall for bodying at Chiswick. Here again an unfamiliar version of the radiator is evident—this one was rejected before the vehicle was completed and replaced by, or converted to, the early standard design as used on the original Regents. The wheel-nut guard rings were to become a familiar feature, though this first set was non-standard. The chassis appears to have been given something approaching a Show finish and it may well be that this was thought necessary to help "sell" the new Southall-built range to the LGOC management, then seriously thinking of introducing its own design of chassis. Though Rackham was not an advocate of six-wheelers, he had produced what was to prove easily the most successful of the species to emerge from a British factory and, in due course, the Chiswick-designed chassis "faded-away".

The first 663-type chassis became the LGOC's LT1, the first vehicle in a new class and the beginning of a whole new family of London bus types. The vehicle is seen here parked alongside the railway embankment at Southall works after the Chiswick-built body had been fitted. This, too, set new standards and provided the basis of LGOC's standard designs of the 1930-31 period. The vehicle was licensed in August 1929.

of the publicity associated with the LS vehicles on ADC 802 chassis. Indeed, an initial order was placed for 50 Renowns, though the first delivery was of one chassis, 663001, given the fleet number LT1 by LGOC and registered UU 6611.

The chassis design was virtually identical to the Regent at the front end, but the frame widened out to a greater extent towards the rear because of the single tyres fitted to the rear bogie axles. Both of these were driven, as on the LS, though the worm drive units were offset to a greater extent, and unlike some other six-wheelers there was a third differential to distribute the drive evenly between the axles regardless of tyre wear or inflation pressure. This eliminated many of the stresses that had caused problems with other six-wheelers and the bogie design was to serve AEC well for trolleybuses as well as the Renown itself. The brake

LT1, photographed within a few days of entering service on route 16, in August 1929. The contrast with the NS it is overtaking underlines the immense progress in bus design at that time—what had seemed a considerable advance in 1926 was, within three years, made to appear obsolete. Although the Renown chassis had been a purely AEC venture, LGOC's body designers had produced a style of body which married up particularly well with its shapely front end design. The NS happened to be one of those which carried the Metropolitan fleetname, being operated by LGOC on behalf of the Tramways (MET) Omnibus Co. Ltd., the concern that had played a key role in the AEC story before World War I.

system incorporated two additional frame-mounted slave servo units to operate the front brakes, a feature that was found to give better braking response than the single servo of the two-axle models and was later adopted as standard for them, too.

At first, a surprising variant of the new radiator design was used, with two vertical strips, one each side of the triangle badge, but sanity prevailed by the time the vehicle was bodied and the centre-strip type substituted.

The LGOC built a quite different style of open-staircase body for LT1 as compared to the AEC specification design—more old-fashioned in only having the upper-deck extended forward to a slight degree over the cab, but setting new standards for harmonious outlines and detail treatment.

# 6-types by the thousand

Production of the new models began in earnest in the Autumn of 1929, with several minor modifications. Most noticeable was

"The track" in Southall works in the winter of 1929-30, as production of the new range of models got under way. The chassis receiving finishing touches in the foreground was Regal 662157, one of a batch of twelve for the East Surrey Traction Co. Ltd. and accordingly to LGOC specification — it later became T397 in London Transport days. Its rear wheels are still on the moving platform which moved forward slowly at intervals to bring the chassis opposite the appropriate points for assembly of the various units. The overhead runways with electric hoists used to bring the heavier items such as engines and gearboxes over from the unit assembly lines to the right of the picture can be seen above the second chassis. Note the coats, lifted out of reach during working hours — standard practice in many factories in those days. The board just visible on the left of the picture listed daily production quantities.

There is an air of slightly frenzied activity, no doubt exaggerated by the slow shutter speed needed for an interior photograph at the time, and the bits and pieces lying about in the foreground look a little disorganised. However, there can be no doubt that the works was busy, with about 40 passenger chassis alone being produced every week.

The photograph also conveys the slightly "softer" curves of the production version of the new radiator design — in the author's view this ranks as one of the most attractive commercial vehicle radiator styles of all time.

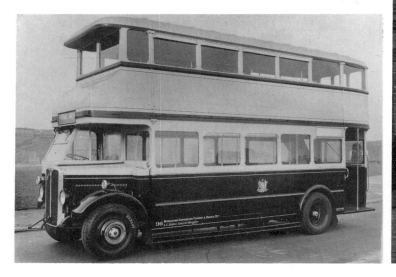

Birmingham Corporation continued to be an important customer for AEC double-deckers. This Regent was at first numbered 96 in the series used by that undertaking for demonstrators, evidently because of its experimental Short Bros. metal-framed bodywork. Although it was an early chassis, 661035, Birmingham had been operating two of the pre-production Regents for about six months by the time this bus arrived in February 1930. It was later renumbered 368 and registered OF 8368, being withdrawn in 1944. Most of Birmingham's Regents with original bodies were withdrawn in 1944-45.

An even earlier production chassis for Birmingham was 661020, one of the first batch of ten chassis which with the two pre-production buses were included in an initial total order for 40, delivered in 1929-30. They had Brush bodywork with the somewhat exaggerated version of the piano-front outline then favoured by Birmingham. Ultimately a total of 167 petrol-engined Regents and one Renown were delivered to this fleet in 1929-32, but AEC was never again to be the principal supplier, Birmingham standardising briefly on locally-made Morris Commercials and then Daimlers. No. 352 (OF 3984) survived until 1950, having been one of 45 rebodied in 1943-44.

In London, delivery began of production Regents early in 1930, and ST 264 is seen in Holborn in August of that year. Although the prototype LT and ST buses had windscreens, the Metropolitan Police withdrew permission for further buses to be so equipped and hence vehicles were entering service without them until officialdom relented a few months later. Even so, these vehicles must have seemed very smart and up-to-date when new, and drivers were no doubt discovering how nimble they could be in traffic.

(Opposite) Regents soon began to be a familiar sight in most parts of the country. The concept of the double-decker as being suitable only for city transport was being abandoned as the Leyland Titan and AEC Regent showed themselves suitable for operation in most places where headroom existed and traffic justified a larger capacity vehicle. These two vehicles with the camel-roof AEC design body were operated between Camborne and Redruth by Cornish Buses Ltd., later taken over by Western National Omnibus Co. Ltd. Evidently someone's brakes had not been quite good enough, judging by the rear panelling!

the radiator, for the use of larger radii for the top inner corners of the grille panels alongside the triangle badge softened the slightly harsh look of the version fitted to early examples. The front wheel nuts had guard rings added (though these had also been a feature of LT1), front hubs were re-shaped with an enamel badge added, though the latter feature was evidently found unsatisfactory and the embossed bullseye AEC motif was reinstated on a less domed casting during 1930. There were also minor changes to the engine, early production units being of type A136, and slightly later provision for an alternative dynamo was the reason for the introduction of type A138. Similarly type A135 was an improved Reliance version.

Orders soon began to come in unprecedented quantities from bus and coach operators of all types. Birmingham Corporation took

40 of the earliest Regents (including the pre-production 661010 and 11, which were in fact returned to AEC after a year's operation and replaced by new 1930 chassis, probably by prior arrangement). LGOC licensed its first Regent in October 1929. This was ST1 (UU 6614), built on chassis 661074, and fitted with a new style of body similar at the front to that of LT1 but with straight enclosed staircase. AEC chassis numbers were generally allocated when the chassis were ordered, and it is significant that the production batch of ST buses which entered service early in 1930 had chassis numbered 661211 upwards, in other words after over 200 had been ordered by other concerns.

The key to LGOC's choice of type letters came in November-December 1929 with the appearance of 50 Regals numbered T1-50, with chassis numbers 662028-77. Illogically, it had been decided that the Regal (26ft. long at that time) would be counted as the "basic" T-type, and the shorter (25ft.) Regent would be ST and the longer Renown six-wheeler would be LT. Incidentally, wheelbase lengths were 15ft.6½in. for the original 661, 17ft. for the 662 and 16ft. 6in. (measured from front axle to the centre of the rear bogie) for the 663.

Third of LGOC's new types was the T, this "basic" letter being allocated to the Regal single-decker despite clearly being bound to be in the minority compared to the LT and ST versions. T31, one of the original 50 supplied at the end of 1929, is seen here in early London Transport days after having been rebuilt from rear to front entrance layout.

The first long-wheelbase Renown six-wheelers were two vehicles supplied to Warrington Corporation in 1930. They had Massey two-doorway bodywork seating 59 passengers but, despite their imposing appearance, did not influence this operator to become a repeat customer.

A longer version of the Renown, given the model number 664, was introduced early in 1930. This had a wheelbase of 18ft. 7in. and was intended for an overall length of 30ft. The first two examples were double-deckers for Warrington Corporation and had two-doorway 59-seat bodywork. The first bulk order was for 50 single-deckers for LGOC, numbered LT1001-50, and mostly placed in service early in 1931, though later the engineering code given to this version by Chiswick was LTL. A further 150 of these were built later in 1931, though one, LT1137, was completed as a double-deck Green Line coach.

By April 1930, AEC was able to boast that 1,180 "new type" passenger vehicles had been "sold", presumably meaning ordered since the November 1929 Show. Yet there was no air of complacency. Despite the refinement of the standard 6-type engine, some experimental eight-cylinder units were built. These were in-line engines, similar in design to the six-cylinder version but with cylinder bore of 87 mm which combined with the standard 130 mm stroke to give a swept volume about the same as the standard 6.1-litre unit. They were, however, longer and those fitted to four of the LGOC's double-deckers (two Renowns, LT35

The first bulk order for long-wheelbase Renowns came from LGOC and a fleet of 199 were built, mostly entering service in 1931, accounting for more than half the total output of this model. Some wag invented the unlikely nickname "Scooters" for these impressive looking vehicles and it stuck. The round-fronted cab with windscreen was by this time standard on new vehicles for LGOC and the appearance was aided by the provision of glass louvres over all the side windows. However, no doors were provided at the relatively wide entrance and these were draughty vehicles in winter. LT 1041 is seen at Chiswick when new.

(Left) The only export order for the Renown six-wheeler in the early 'thirties was for one 664 model chassis for Copenhagen Tramways, supplied in 1931. This had right-hand steering—left-hand forward-control AEC bus chassis were not offered until the late 'forties—but had doorways on the right-hand, kerb, side. The locally-built bodywork had square-cut but modern lines.

(Below) The Regal found municipal as well as company buyers. This one was delivered to Bury Corporation in 1930 and had Brush two-doorway 31-seat bodywork. It remained in service until 1948, by which date it had run nearly a million miles.

and 41, and two Regents, ST4 and 84) had projecting radiators in the style later to be familiar with some oil-engined buses. One of the single-deckers, T43, was also fitted with an eight-cylinder engine, and in this case the limitation on overall length then in force made it necessary to shorten the rear end of the body by 6in. All the eight-cylinder units were removed after a year or so and it seems incredible that what would nowadays be a prohibitively expensive experiment could ever have been sanctioned, particularly since the only motive possible was to gain even more smoothness of running. Truly, those were very different times.

The standard models were soon seen to be effective competitors to other makes. Glasgow Corporation, hitherto a Titan stronghold, took 25 Regents early in 1930. Even in Lancashire, the Regent made its mark. Manchester Corporation's newly appointed General Manager, the famous R. Stuart Pilcher, recommended in the autumn of 1929 that a similar number of Regents and five Reliances should be part of the first tramway replacement fleet, only to be over-ruled in order to help maintain local employment by purchasing only Leyland and Crossleys. However, both municipal and company fleets in almost all parts of the country put examples of the new models in service, though the AEC-design body had only limited success—Halifax Corporation being

almost the only major user to retain it as standard until 1931. The Regal also had strong appeal as a coach chassis, with its modern appearance backed up by lively, quiet and smooth performance, and large numbers were sold to independent as well as company coach operators.

(Below) Publicity mention of particular makes of coaches in operators' posters has never been a common practice, but Blue Belle, then one of London's better-known coach concerns, thought it worth specifically mentioning in this 1930 poster.

(Below right) A. Timpson & Sons Ltd., of Catford, an even better-known firm, employed about sixteen of its Harrington-bodied Regals on a regular contract to take the staff of Kennards Ltd., a Croydon department store, on its annual seaside outing. They didn't seem to have much luck with the weather this time.

The Regal appealed to many independent operators, including some whose allegiance normally lay elsewhere. Pennine Motor Services, of Gargrave, near Skipton had standardised on Leylands since 1926, but in 1931 an AEC Regal with Burlingham 30-seat coach body was purchased. Although new vehicle orders reverted to Leyland it was considered worthy of rebodying as late as 1949 and remained in service until the late 'fifties. This view shows WX 7431, when quite new and conveys the attractive lines of the standard Burlingham body of the time, which particularly suited the early Regal chassis.

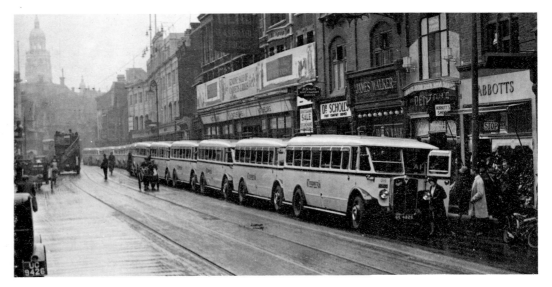

# More power

Even so, those were fiercely competitive days and significant design modifications were made, sometimes to meet operators' varying requirements. Many fleet managers or engineers had decided views about makes of dynamo, magneto or carburettor, for example, and such minor variants were reflected in a succession of new engine type numbers. There was a demand from some quarters for more power and by early 1930 several operators were specifying a newly-introduced alternative 110 mm-bore version of the standard 6-type petrol engine, for which provision had been made in the original design. The first production version was the A137, and others were A141 and A143, though a more widely used variant appears to have been the A145 unit. The swept volume was 7.4-litres and within a year or so this size was to become, and remain, AEC's standard six-cylinder petrol engine. The 100 mm engine continued to be available for a while, however, and itself was built in further variations, including types A140 and A152. LGOC specified 110-bore engines for most of the 800 LT-class Renown double-deckers delivered in 1931, for example, these having 56-seat enclosed-platform staight staircase bodies and being quite heavy vehicles by contemporary standards at 8 tons 1 cwt. unladen. The 100-bore engine continued to be used for the ST Regents; though these were heavier than most Regents at 6 tons 12 cwt., their seating capacity of 49 (later 48) kept the gross weight down and they were nimble vehicles in traffic in the hands of skilled drivers.

# . . . and less power

However, some operators continued to prefer four-cylinder engines and the Regal 4 single-decker (not to be confused with the much later Regal Mark IV) was introduced in 1930 to cater for their needs. This was model number 642, and was the 662 chassis with a new four-cylinder engine of similar type to the 6-type six-cylinder units and having a bore size of 112 mm combined with the standard stroke of 130 mm to give a swept volume of 5.1-litres. The prototype, 642001, was produced by converting a standard Regal. Sales were not as brisk as those of the Leyland Lion LT models with which the model was clearly intended to compete, and only about a dozen were built in the 1930-31 period, though they picked up somewhat subsequently.

# A bonneted version

Another new single-decker was the Ranger, which was a bonneted (or normal-control) version of the six-cylinder Regal, mainly intended for export, though also sold to some of the more traditionally-minded British coach operators who continued to favour the "large private car" image that had been established with such models as the 424. One of these, Timpsons, had already ordered some examples of the AEC Mercury normal-control

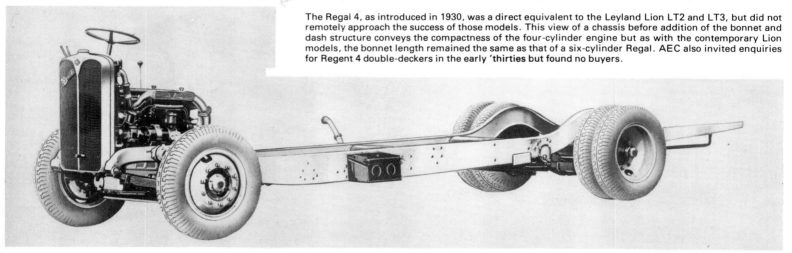

The Regal 4, as introduced in 1930, was a direct equivalent to the Leyland Lion LT2 and LT3, but did not remotely approach the success of those models. This view of a chassis before addition of the bonnet and dash structure conveys the compactness of the four-cylinder engine but as with the contemporary Lion models, the bonnet length remained the same as that of a six-cylinder Regal. AEC also invited enquiries for Regent 4 double-deckers in the early 'thirties but found no buyers.

(Top) Johannesburg Municipal Tramways began a long association with AEC bodies taking eight Ranger 19ft. wheelbase buses with locally-built bodies by R. T. Millhouse in 1931. The bonnet line did not match too well with the low-waisted bodywork.

(Above) This early home-market demonstrator had bodywork which appeared to have been styled to minimise its apparent size. It had a short rear overhang and was thus probably only about 26ft. long but the single-panel windscreen added to the effect.

(Right) The first left-hand drive Rangers were supplied to Athens, where the local transport system was run by a British concern. The frontal styling looked better, as here, without a bumper.

goods chassis (model 640) for passenger bodywork. This had the same design of four-cylinder engine as the Regal 4 and looked very similar to the Ranger apart from having a slightly higher frame.

The first Ranger, 665001, was built for service in South Africa in the summer of 1930 and a left-hand drive version was introduced the following year, mainly intended for the Canadian market, being given the model number 670. Some of these had Delco-Remy coil ignition, no doubt to suit transatlantic preferences, the distributor being mounted on top of the front end of the engine in exactly the same way as on Rackham's early Leyland engines. Most of the export Rangers had a longer frame with 19ft. wheelbase.

By about the end of 1931, with a little over two years' production completed, over 1,700 Regents, about 1,100 Regals and over 1,160 Renowns had been built, of which 836 Regents had been supplied to LGOC to form its ST class. Of the Renowns, 950 double-deckers (type 663) and 199 single-deckers (type 664) had been delivered to form LGOC's LT class, only a handful going to other operators at that stage. The LGOC's own efforts at chassis building were abandoned on Lord Ashfield's orders, in the face of the success of the new generation of AEC buses, though four of the six-wheel CC model double-deckers were numbered LT1000, 1051, 1202 and 1203 and three of the four-wheel single-deck CB became T1000-2. All these originally had Meadows six-cylinder petrol engines of LGOC design, believed to have been of twin overhead-camshaft layout; most, if not all, were later fitted with standard AEC petrol engines.

The British Columbia Electric Railway Co. was an early customer for the Ranger. The interior view gives a good idea of what it must have been like to travel in or even drive such a vehicle. Note the simple but effective method of driver operation of the front door, the impressive-looking heater and the hinged quarter-light beside the steering wheel.

## Trolleybus developments

Trolleybus production had quietly continued through the late 'twenties with the 603. However, the new range of chassis introduced in 1929 had obvious trolleybus potential and were offered in 661T, 662T and 663T versions from the following year. The first to be built were 663T six-wheel double-deckers, 663T001 being a demonstrator originally registered HX 1460. Like many subsequent trolleybuses, it had an English Electric motor and

The 663T trolleybus was the equivalent of the Renown six-wheel bus and London United Tramway's initial fleet of 60 understandably resembled the contemporary LGOC LT-class buses in layout. However, despite the fact that both operator and bodybuilder (the Union Construction Co.) formed part of the same Underground group as LGOC, their appearance was an uneasy mixture of tram and bus styles. This photograph was taken at Kingston Bridge.

The first home-market examples of the 661T two-axle trolleybus chassis were four vehicles built in 1932 for Southend Corporation with both bodywork and electrical equipment by English Electric. They had dummy radiators of a style clearly intended to resemble the contemporary AEC bus design, but bearing the English Electric winged emblem as well as the AEC triangle. The vehicle overtaking appears to be a Westcliff Dennis.

electrical equipment and such vehicles were marketed as AEC-English Electric. This one had English Electric bodywork, a feature associated with some but by no means all of these, and was subsequently sold to Southend Corporation where, unusually, it was re-registered JN 2086.

The first big order came from London United Tramways, which took delivery of 60 of the 663T model in 1930-31 to inaugurate what was later to be expanded into the largest trolleybus system in Britain. These vehicles had bodywork by the Union Construction Co. and had some resemblance to the contemporary "Feltham" design of tram by the same builder, but like many trolleybuses of that period had "half-cab" front-end layout and a motor bus-style bonnet. The motor bus image was fostered on the first four-wheelers to be delivered to British operators, as early 661T models for Southend Corporation had polished "radiator" grilles and the first 662T single-deckers for the Notts & Derby company fleet had half-cabs and these "radiators". Motors on these early vehicles were at the front.

The Nottinghamshire and Derbyshire Traction Co., understandably better-known by its fleetname Notts & Derby, began trolleybus operation with this fleet of ten 662T models in 1932. They also had English Electric bodywork and equipment and with their half-cab styling, resembled contemporary single-deck motor buses to an extent greater than vehicles in any other trolleybus fleet.

# 5 ALL MOD CONS

Despite the success of the Regent, Regal and Renown in their original form, the early and mid 'thirties was a period of continuous development. The LGOC, having abandoned the idea of building its own vehicles, took a more active part in developing the AEC designs. Drivers had found steering early Renowns, in particular, rather heavy when pulling out from behind another vehicle, a manoeuvre frequently used in London traffic. So an improved design was requested and the result was the AEC worm and nut system used on most AEC-designed vehicles thereafter. It began to be used on AEC vehicles for LGOC and associated fleets about the beginning of 1931, becoming standard on all AEC passenger models by the end of the year as well as being fitted to earlier LGOC vehicles on overhaul. It could readily be distinguished by the enlarged bearing housing just under the steering wheel as compared to the plain tubular column of the Marles type.

From a driver's viewpoint, the pleasantly light yet positive steering, even on a high mileage vehicle, was a characteristic feature of most post-1931 AEC models, particularly after lower gearing was introduced a few years later, and I regarded it as possibly the best heavy-duty bus steering in the days before power assistance became common practice. It certainly played a major part in the pleasure I recall in driving various AEC models.

Similarly some work was done on brake systems. LGOC extended the use of triple-servo brakes to models other than the Renown and, as an experiment, converted ten of its first 50 Regals to vacuum-hydraulic brakes in 1931. This principle, with Lockheed hydraulic operation of the brakes from the vacuum servo unit, was then new to buses in Britain. Some new Renowns for LGOC were fitted with similar systems and, again, AEC took it up as standard for all passenger models from about 1932 until 1939.

Another feature originally introduced towards the end of 1930 for LGOC but standardised about a year later was the D124 gearbox. This was based on the D119, as introduced for the original Regent, but had constant-mesh (dog-clutch) engagement for third gear instead of simply sliding one gear into mesh with the other. The method used was simple to the point of crudity. Both of the pair of third-speed gears slid together on their respective splined shafts, giving a shorter lever travel for this gear and reducing the damage to gear teeth that was being experienced, due to rough gear changes. This alteration gave no reduction of gear whine, and claims to the effect that it was a "silent third" gear in AEC literature were no more than wishful thinking.

T207, the first chassis for a further fleet of 100 Green Line coaches delivered early in 1931, seen before delivery to the bodybuilders. These had the 110 mm bore petrol engine and could reach 60 mph. The photograph shows two other changes in design which became standard AEC practice for many years. Two holes were provided in the bonnet side to permit checking and topping up of engine oil levels without opening the bonnet, and the engine oil filler became a screw-on cap inclined at a convenient angle for this purpose. The steering was the then new worm-and-nut type, distinguishable by the enlarged bearing housing under the steering wheel. Note that AEC was still supplying chassis to LGOC and associated fleets with the bonnet number, as it was called, already in place.

However, this gearbox was a reliable, robust unit which remained in large-scale production until the early 'fifties, when it began to prove inadequate for the torque of engines then in production which were considerably more powerful than those for which it was designed.

The unmistakable sound of this standard Regent gearbox, with its high-pitched tone, was to continue and be echoed to varying degrees in later AEC-designed "conventional" gearboxes.

The reports of occasional failures of the semi-floating rear axle had by this time caught up with John Rackham, and a new fully-floating rear axle was introduced during 1933, though the semi-floating type was not completely dropped until some time later. The new unit had a larger hub and, again, was to remain little altered on subsequent AEC passenger chassis for many years.

A new more powerful version of the 110-bore engine was also introduced about the same time. The cylinder head was modified to give better breathing and this "high power head" engine was put into production as type A162. It developed 120 bhp at 2,200 rpm and was thus more than twice as powerful as the unit used in the later NS-type buses of only four years earlier. A corresponding 112 x 130 four-cylinder unit was designated A163 and developed 80 bhp. The A162 engine was to remain the standard petrol engine for the Regent, Regal, Renown and Ranger until petrol models ceased to be available about 1940. However, a military version, A193, continued to be built not only during wartime but even until the early 'fifties. I recall the valve cover casting drawing being redrawn at that time so that the "Associated Equipment Co. Ltd." lettering on the last few orders could be replaced by the revised company title "AEC Ltd." by then in use.

The A162 brought British bus petrol engine design very near its peak of development. Most buses and coaches fitted with it were of modest weight, and performance was decidedly lively,

Rackham gave the development of bus styling another major push forward with the AEC-design double-decker body introduced for the then new 16ft. 3in. wheelbase Regent at the November 1931 Olympia Show. One example, built by Brush, was on the AEC stand and another, seen here outside the experimental department at Southall, was bodied by Park Royal. The overall concept was altogether more sleek and considerably in advance of typical designs of that period, acting as a foretaste of common practice in the mid 'thirties—indeed the frontal profile was still being echoed in some new buses nearly twenty years later. Perhaps the only impractical feature was the curious long rear-hinged cab door. The lightweight body was designed to seat 56 or even 60 passengers.

even by the standards of nearly half a century later—a Regent at the new maximum legal gross weight of 10 tons for a two-axle double-decker introduced in 1931 had a power-weight ratio of 12 bhp/ton, which is equivalent to that of a modern double-decker, running at 15 tons gross, with about 180 bhp. The idea that an old petrol-engined bus chugged slowly along is quite untrue so far as the AEC models of the early 'thirties were concerned. I well recall Newcastle Corporation drivers getting

Not everyone went along with the new ideas on appearance. E. Brickwood Ltd., proprietors of the London independent Redline concern chose this decidedly conservative style, built by Birch Bros. for the first 16ft. 3in. wheelbase Regent to operate in London, built in May 1932. However, its 1920's style frontal appearance belied an up-to-date mechanical specification, for it had a preselective gearbox of the Daimler type described later in this chapter. Ironically, its one ''modern'' body feature, the enclosed staircase, was lost as the result of an accident after it was taken over by London Transport and became numbered STL 558. The rear-end damage was such that an open staircase from an otherwise similar Daimler bus was fitted. It thus became the only open-staircase STL, remaining in service until 1946. The front mudguard design had also been revised for the 1932-standard Regent—the Regal was a little slower in changing, perhaps due to a need to use up existing stocks.

Thomas Tilling Ltd. also beat the LGOC in getting long-wheelbase Regents on the streets of London, its fleet of 80 entering service from November 1932, a couple of months before STL 1. They had Tilling-built 56-seat bodywork of generally up-to-date outline, though the detail treatment was less modern in style. By this date Tilling was in close association with LGOC and fleet numbers in the latter's series were allocated. This photograph shows that the first example originally carried the fleet number ST 837 on the front dumb irons, the next vacancy in the ST series at that date. Howevver, it was subsequently decided to give the longer chassis a new code, STL, and the ex-Tilling examples became STL 51-130. ST 837 was later allocated to the first of the open-staircase short Regents taken over from Tilling's.

wheelspin when moving away from traffic lights in wet weather, and although this was partly due to the slippery wood block road surface, it gives an indication of the responsive performance available.

The altered legal requirements also fostered changes in the wheelbase and overall length of the two-axle models. The Regent, hitherto having a 15ft. 6½in. wheelbase and an overall length of 25ft., was now offered with 16ft. 3in. wheelbase for a length of 26ft., the new maximum permitted. The Regal, and also the home market Ranger, wheelbase length went up from 17ft. 0in. to 17ft. 6in. to suit a length of 27ft. 6in.—hitherto bodywork was built to a length of either 26ft. or 27ft. to suit varying local authority requirements. LGOC was to give the new Regent the type code STL, signifying ''short T long'' when its first examples appeared in 1933, but the basic T class was not affected.

The new dimensions prompted interest in higher-capacity two-axle double-deckers. At the 1931 Olympia Show, examples of a new ''AEC specification'' double-decker based on the 16ft. 3in. Regent chassis were shown, that on the AEC stand being bodied by Brush while another of virtually identical design had bodywork by Park Royal. Both had a then new front-end profile, with continuous unbroken slope from the windscreen pillars to the upper-deck front dome, but with a prominent rounded projecting cab front panel. Brush built only a very few examples, but Park

The fully-floating rear axle became standard on two-axle AEC passenger models early in 1933 and this example for the Mansfield District fleet was one of six Regal 4 models with Weymann 32-seat bodywork to be supplied. The Regal 4, externally virtually indistinguishable from a standard six-cylinder Regal, had by this date found a few more customers, with just over 50 sold. The operator had specified a radiator badge bearing the MDT initials on a green background to match the livery. Note the provision of a sliding roof, quite common practice at that time on company-owned single-deck buses.

Royal was to adopt the basic design as standard and continued producing very similar bodywork until 1940 for certain customers. Seating capacities tended to go up from the 48, 50 or sometimes 52 to 56 or even 60. The writing was on the wall for continued large-scale orders for six-wheelers, but not before LGOC placed some more examples of exceptional technical interest in service, playing a key role in both engine and transmission development.

The foregoing changes in design were introduced gradually and often offered as an option before being standardised. Thus specification tended to vary among vehicles built during the 1931-32 period. In some cases, for example, the fully-floating rear axle appeared on early examples of the long-wheelbase chassis, yet slightly later vehicles were also built with the semi-floating type. Six-wheeled models retained the semi-floating rear axles for several years after they became obsolete on four-wheeled chassis.

# Oil engines

AEC's involvement with oil engines, or as more generally called nowadays, diesels, went back to 1928, but I have held back from introducing them into the story until this point because they had largely been experimental—though well-publicised from late 1930—and because the thread of continuity would

otherwise tend to be lost amid all the other activity at the time.

The first vehicle engine had evidently been built at about the same time as the first Reliance chassis. To what extent Rackham was involved is not clear, but circumstantial evidence rather points towards it being Charles Edwards' swan-song with AEC—it is significant that his entry in "Who's Who in the Motor and Commercial Vehicle Industries" includes the entry, doubtless written by himself, that he was "responsible for the design, development and research work on all London bus chassis and engines including first "one-step" entrance, and covered-top buses **and first diesel-engined bus to run in London**"—my emphasis. His period with AEC and ADC is quoted as 1912-29, despite Rackham's arrival publicly announced in June 1928. So was he working out his notice to good effect on this epoch-making project? Incidentally, he then became Chief Engineer of Morris Commercial to take charge of the design of the Dictator and Imperial models, of which the appearance bore a distinct resemblance to that of the ADC 423 and 426 and hence the Reliance.

British commercial vehicle makers had been well behind the Germans and Swiss in the adoption of compression-ignition engines. The Swiss Saurer concern had connections with Bosch, who had pioneered the development of efficient fuel-injection pumps, and had thus been able to convert petrol engines to diesel in 1923 and was soon building purpose-built diesels.

The first AEC diesel was built under Acro licence and may well have been based on a Saurer design, being intended merely to gain experience of the practical needs of manufacturing such engines. Certainly it resembled no other AEC engine before or since and had a somewhat Teutonic appearance. The cynic might conclude that it was imported, but close examination of one of the photographs that have survived, but never hitherto published, clearly shows a U-series part number as well as flywheel timing marks using the conventional English TDC initials.

Nothing was published about the design details of this six-cylinder unit, but it is clear that it had a one-piece cylinder block but three separate cylinder heads each covering two cylinders. A Bosch pump was used—no other make was available until well into the 'thirties—and both inlet and exhaust manifolds were on the right-hand side (as still found on Gardner engines today). Surprisingly, no provision seems to have been made for an electric starter, there being merely a throw-out dog for a handle at the front. The engine was fitted in the 104-seat ADC 802 works bus, chassis number 802002, which was on the road between Walthamstow and Southall in this form in December 1928, thus fitting the rather careful wording in Charles Edwards' biographical note.

It is also reasonable to claim this as the first British diesel bus, even though not in public service. Significantly, the negative

AEC's first attempt at oil engine manufacture was more of a research project than one intended for volume production. The six-cylinder engine made in 1928 had very little in common with previous or subsequent power units. The view shown above right gives a misleading impression of size, due to the camera angle chosen, but it was a fairly lengthy engine, as indicated by the historic photograph on the right. This shows it installed in the 104-seat works bus on ADC 802 chassis, which can thus be claimed as the first British diesel bus, even though not licensed for public service; it was running in this form by December 1928. Note the simple fuel supply from a tank suspended from the front over-hang of the upper-deck—driver vision to the left must have been somewhat limited. This was before the introduction of legislation requiring fuel tanks to be located separately from drivers and passengers. The vertical ladder in the foreground was a means of an emergency exit from the upper-deck.

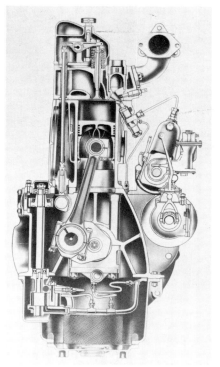

More easily recognisable as an AEC engine, the first production A155 oil engine was in fact a fresh design, though it shared the Acro combustion system with its experimental predecessor — the characteristic upward-pointing injectors can be seen just above the triangle badges on the side of the cylinder block.

number of the photograph of this installation (reproduced herewith) is immediately before the first to be taken of the original Regent chassis — a historic time at Southall. How long the 104-seater ran in this form is not known — the vehicle and the other works bus had been registered MY 2274-5 (not necessarily in order) probably about the beginning of 1930, and with two of the 802 demonstrators, were transferred to the oddly-named Walthamstow Wayfarers' Club probably in 1931 (the date is not confirmed for 802002, but for the others was March of that year), evidently for further workers' transport service, though for some reason no longer operated by AEC itself.

The next step in the AEC oil-engine saga was the development of the first unit for sale to operators. In 1929 Rackham engaged C. B. Dicksee for this work — he was still a familiar figure in the drawing stores himself whenever he wanted a print, despite his drawing stores himself whenever he wanted a print despite his considerable eminence among engine designers by that time.

The result of his first efforts was the A155 engine announced by AEC in October 1930. This was again a six-cylinder unit incorporating the Acro indirect-injection combustion chamber, but the design was otherwise very different from the 1928 unit. It had a superficial resemblance to contemporary AEC petrol engines, with ribbed exhaust manifold mounted at a high level on the left-hand side, but differed considerably from them, too. It was of push-rod overhead-valve form, as was to be the case on all six-cylinder AEC diesels, and the merging of the inlet manifold with the valve cover was also repeated on several later engines. The bore and stroke were 110 mm and 142 mm, the latter dimension familiar on many later AEC engines, being an indication of a chain of continuity of design that was to run through the larger-capacity units for nearly half a century. The swept volume was 8.097-litres and the power output quoted as 95 bhp, exactly the same as the contemporary 100-bore petrol engine. However, it was about $4\frac{1}{2}$ in. longer and vehicles fitted with it had to have the radiator moved forward by a similar amount. This projecting radiator was to be a characteristic of most AEC oil-engined buses until the mid 'thirties and in some cases later.

The first engine appears to have been fitted to an existing Regent demonstrator, chassis number 661131, — an internal AEC document of October 1930 gave the instruction to "fit oil engine to XU 440" to this chassis. The vehicle had been registered MY2102 in December 1929 and had already visited Birkenhead and Bassett of Gorseignon before conversion. The following month a further instruction was issued to "fit oil engines numbers 2, 5 and 6" in accordance with the XU 440 parts list to three more Regents which became LGOC ST 462, 464 and 466. Engine

This vehicle is believed to be the first oil-engined Regent. Although the photograph, taken during the course of the special oil engine Show laid on at Southall in December 1930, does not provide direct evidence of its identity, it was clearly a demonstrator (with AEC-design "camel roof" body) built before mid-1930 and yet having the projecting radiator required to accommodate the AEC-Acro oil engine. These factors fit other known characteristics of MY 2102, thought to be the historic vehicle concerned; it seems odd that it should have an open staircase, then rapidly becoming obsolete. Visible in the background on the right is LGOC ST 466, one of the three buses of this type fitted with others of the first batch of oil engines.

numbers 3 and 7 were at the same time allocated to Mammoth and Majestic goods chassis. Hence it seems likely that engine number 1 or number 4 went into MY 2102. It is possible that it was used purely as a demonstrator or works test vehicle as no news of its movements seem to have been recorded until it came into the Northern General Transport fleet as number 561 about 1932, though whether it was still oil-engined then is not known. I first became aware of this bus in January 1945, when it was fitted with a new wartime-style Northern Coachbuilders body, by which date it had a much later 7.7-litre AEC oil engine.

However, ST 462/4/6 were put into operation from LGOC's Willesden garage in December 1930, with seating capacity reduced

Another photograph taken during the oil engine Show, on the occasion of a visit by the Municipal Tramways and Transport Association. The figure in the foreground is none other than R. Stuart Pilcher, the famous General Manager of the Manchester Corporation undertaking, who was a major advocate of oil-engined vehicles, and even though not an AEC customer, by no means unsympathetic to its products as mentioned in the previous chapter. The vehicles behind him were a petrol-engined demonstrator, with Short Bros. body of a popular style on Regents of the 1930-32 period, and ST 464, another of the experimental oil-engined Regents for LGOC. The comparison clearly shows the difference in radiator position. As the engines in these three vehicles were transferred to LT-class buses in 1932, photographs of them in this form are very rare. Note that they belong to the no-windscreen era of London buses.

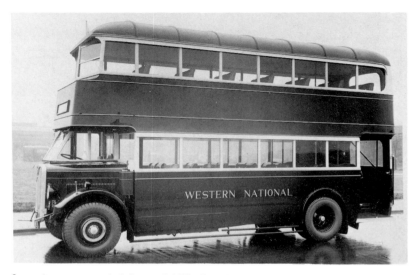

Several operators took delivery of AEC oil-engined buses during 1931. Among them was the Western National fleet, which was one of the minority of English bus companies to take an active interest in oil-engined vehicles at this early stage. The arrival of this Short Bros.-bodied Regent with the AEC-Acro oil engine just about coincided with the taking of a controlling interest in the National companies by the Tilling group. Although the latter were later to take enthusiasm for diesels to the extent of large-scale conversions of existing vehicles, little progress was made until the mid 'thirties.

to 44 because of current weight restrictions, and were probably the first AEC diesel buses in regular public service. AEC was not quite first in the race to get a British-made diesel bus on the road, for Leeds Corporation had a Gardner-engined Crossley in September 1930, but this had a slow-revving light marine engine whereas the AEC could be regarded as a true automotive diesel. However, Crossley also introduced it own-make diesel in December 1930 and the atmosphere of competition was intense.

Several further chassis with the A155 engine were put in hand before the end of 1930, including Regents for Glasgow, Walsall, Halifax and Birmingham municipalities, a Regal for Scottish Motor Traction Co. Ltd. and nine LT-type Renown double-deckers for LGOC. These latter, LT 191-9, entered service from Harrow Weald garage in March 1930. Further orders, mainly for single vehicles, came in during the first half of 1931, but meanwhile a new and improved engine was being developed—not before time, for the A155 units were proving prone to bearing and crankshaft failures. This was partly because they were ungoverned and partly because the need for heavier construction to withstand

the harsher pressure rise in a diesel had not been fully appreciated.

The new engine, though still of the indirect injection type, had a new combustion chamber design known as the Comet, developed by the Ricardo consulting engineering concern at Shoreham, Sussex. Heavier-duty bearings were used, the cylinder bore size was increased to 115 mm, increasing the swept volume to 8.850-litres and on the first A161 and A164 versions of the unit an AEC-designed governor was used. Some 130 bhp was available, at first at 2400 rpm, but later, by increasing the fuelling the same power was made available at 2000 rpm. The 8.8-litre was an altogether more reliable, economical and powerful unit, and in A165 form, with CAV governor integral with the CAV-Bosch fuel pump, was to remain AEC's standard oil engine until 1935.

It was decided that twenty Renowns for LGOC would have this improved unit and the first, LT 643, was completed with A161 engine in September 1931, the remainder entering service from November 1931 to February 1932. The earlier engines in A191-9 were thereupon converted to the new specification and those in the three ST-type buses were soon removed, being now considered too powerful for that model, and transferred to LT chassis. The subsequent history of oil engines in the LT class is complicated and the reader is referred to "Development of the London Bus 1929-33" by Gavin Martin for a fuller account. Suffice it to say at this stage that 60 (LT 1355-1414) of the next orders for the 260 60-seat Renowns delivered in 1932 had 8.8-litre engines. The 60-seat LT was nicknamed "Bluebird" because of the colour of upholstery.

The oil engine was now well-established, and if AEC's unit was not quite as economical as some of its competitors, it was more readily acceptable in fleets where the liveliness and flexibility of the new generation of petrol engines was regarded as essential to maintain schedules in traffic or over hilly terrain. LGOC did, in fact, specify the then recently-introduced Gardner 6LW engine for conversion of a Renown (LT 741) in July 1932 and the ten last Renowns for LGOC (LT1417-26), delivered in November, were fitted with Gardner 6LW engines from new. This had followed an inconclusive test of a five-cylinder 5LW unit in LT 1051, one of the LGOC-built CC-model six-wheelers, which hardly surprisingly had been considered under-powered. The 6LW was longer than the AEC oil engines and the Renown installation involved a forward projection of the radiator of no less than 9in. as compared to the petrol version. However, I suspect that no particular pains were taken to produce a compact installation of this competitive power unit—some operators' subsequent conversions were less obtrusive.

The LGOC's LT class of Renown double-deckers played a key role in the technical development of AEC buses and, indeed, buses in general. Most of the early London bus oil engine development was carried out using such vehicles. Although LT 610, dating from 1931 but seen here in Trafalgar Square in May 1934, had at that time only recently been converted with an 8.8-litre A165 oil engine, the earlier experimental vehicles were of similar appearance. Indeed the success of this work resulted in almost all of the class being converted and thereby having the characteristic 8.8-litre look, with projecting radiator set at a slightly inclined angle, which seemed to the author to give such buses a slightly haughty air.

The last ten buses of the LT class, LT 1417-1426, were fitted with Gardner 6LW engines and thus had an even longer ''snout'' as conveyed by this view of LT 1419, seen when operating from Gray's garage in 1947. These vehicles had been built in 1932 and thus had the ''Bluebird'' style of 60-seat body then standardised in place of the 1931 56-seat style shown above.

Understandably, AEC made use of this attractive picture of two Dundee Corporation Regents in advertisements for some time after it was taken, soon after the vehicles were delivered in 1932. It shows, on the left, No. 58 (TS 9874) one of two 8.8-litre engined examples with bodywork by the local Reid concern and No. 56 (TS 9872), one of three petrol models with Metro-Cammell metal-framed bodywork of that concern's first standard production type.

What was claimed to be the first long-distance operation by oil-engined coaches began on 10 March 1932, when Midland Bus Services Ltd. of Airdrie put two 8.8-litre Regals in service on the overnight run between Glasgow and London. One ran in each direction and the northbound coach is seen after arrival at Glasgow, recording a fuel consumption figure of 8.3 mpg—a rather poor figure by later oil engine standards, but appreciably better than would have been given by a petrol model. The bodywork was by Wycombe Motor Bodies Ltd., a firm more usually associated with Gilford chassis but in this case building to Scottish Motor Traction Co. specification—Midland being an SMT subsidiary.

All the LGOC oil-engined buses were by then operated from what was in those days called Hanwell garage (now Southall) only a few hundred yards along the main Uxbridge Road from the AEC works. There must have been some concern at AEC as the comparative fuel consumption figures came through, for the Gardner engines gave good results. But the Hanwell operating staff did not like the low governed speed of 1700 rpm and neither LGOC nor London Transport bought any more Gardner-engined buses, other than wartime Guy Arabs, until the first Daimler Fleetlines of 1965.

Most of the early A155 oil engines were either updated to later specification, replaced with later units, or in some cases simply replaced with petrol engines. So it was with some surprise that in 1973 I came across AEC engine number A155 58 in the Ford Museum in Detroit. It was coupled to a D123 gearbox with gear lever for a normal-control vehicle so had probably been in a Ranger of which several had been delivered to an operator in Ontario, just a few miles across the Canadian border from Detroit, and other Canadian operators. It is almost certainly the only A155 engine to have survived. Incidentally, it had been planned early in 1931 that a petrol-engined Renown chassis to the then latest specification would be supplied to "Henry Ford Ltd., USA", presumably for the Museum, Henry Ford having considerable respect for other manufacturers' products if of technical interest. Unfortunately the order was cancelled, the stock chassis in question, 664057, being supplied to Imperial Motors of Abercynon, registered TG 4487, and subsequently passing to Red & White.

A particularly significant order was that for three oil-engined Regals placed by Midland Bus Services of Airdrie in the autumn of 1931. They were placed on the Glasgow-London service which was claimed to be the first long-distance service to be operated by oil-engined vehicles. Though it was to be another couple of years or so before the numbers of oil-engined AEC buses on order began to rival those with petrol engines, the pioneer work was laying a sound foundation for the future.

# Fluid transmission

Much the same could be said for another development that was taking place around this time. Even the D124 gearbox required a fair amount of skill if quiet changes were to be obtained and as city traffic increased an easy-change system was becoming more and more desirable. John Rackham had known Walter Gordon Wilson, the inventor of the preselective gearbox that bore his name since they were both involved in tank design in World War I.

The London LT class was also used for early experimental application of the Daimler fluid flywheel and preselective gearbox to AEC buses. Plumstead garage was the base from which the first examples were operated and a total of 54 were allocated there when introduced in 1931-33 and remained throughout their lives. For some curious reason these buses were not converted to diesel and so, right up to 1949, the unmistakable sound of a "Plumstead petrol preselector" could be heard as they worked their way through central London on route 53. LT 1330, one of the 60-seaters built in 1932, is seen looking very smart after overhaul at Chiswick in June 1934, lettered with the then new London Transport fleetname.

However, it was the Daimler concern, under the guidance of its Chief Engineer, L. H. Pomeroy, which had made the near-perfect marriage of the Wilson gearbox and the Vulcan-Sinclair fluid coupling to which they gave the title "fluid flywheel". By the autumn of 1930 a bus version had been put on the market in the CH6 model chassis, which had the 5.7-litre sleeve-valve engine that had originally been fitted to most of the LS six-wheelers. Lord Ashfield was interested in this transmission and, despite the comparatively recent break with Daimler resulting from the collapse of ADC, placed an order for three CH6 models for LGOC which entered service in February 1931 as DST 1-3.

The transmission gave good results. Gear engagement did not involve any clashing of gears, the "clutch" pedal bringing in whatever ratio had been pre-selected with the lever by applying either a brake band or clutch within the gearbox. The fluid flywheel ensured smooth starts from rest under any conditions. Gear changes could be very quick, though they could also be rather

One of the author's all-time favourites. Newcastle Corporation took delivery of three Regents of this type in 1932, numbered 152-154. Though of the short, 15ft. 6½in. wheelbase they were very up-to-date in specification, fitted with 120 bhp high-power-head petrol engine, fluid flywheel transmission and vacuum-hydraulic brakes. The Metro-Cammell built metal-framed bodywork complemented the chassis features, for it too gave a high standard of comfort and finish. Yet the unladen weight was only 6 tons 7 cwt. 1 quarter so performance was distinctly lively. They were involved in a complex body transfer procedure at the end of the war period and thus had shorter lives than their all-round merit might have suggested.

jerky if unduly hurried. However, reliability was, from the start, better than that of conventional systems.

Later in 1931, sets of the same type of transmission were supplied by Daimler and fitted to two new Renowns for LGOC, LT 439 and 448, and one Regent, ST 746. In quick succession twenty more sets were ordered and fitted to LT-class buses. These, like the original two, were allocated to Plumstead garage and subsequently two more were added to this fleet of Renowns of the 1931 standard 56-seat pattern. The vehicles of this type were to remain at Plumstead for the whole of their operating lives of up to eighteen years and the same applied to 30 of the 1932 style with 60-seat bodywork, both types being a familiar sight on route 53 and, incidentally, being noticeably smarter than average even when almost due for withdrawal—distinctive vehicles evidently promoted garage pride. A further 60-seater was converted in 1933.

The AEC petrol engine performed very well in conjunction with the preselective transmission, producing exceptionally smooth running and a fascinating combination of AEC engine and Daimler gearbox sound effects. AEC did not favour the quadrant type of selector attached to the steering column as used by Daimler, and most petrol-engined AECs with Daimler-made transmission (AEC's unit number for the gearbox being D128) had a selector looking rather like an engine-room telegraph to the left of the driver, though later a longer and more conventional-looking lever was used, distinguished from the crash gearbox type by the use of a flatter type of knob. This form of transmission was also offered to other operators and early users included Newcastle Corporation, which took three Regents with A162 ''high power head'' engines, preselective transmission, Lockheed brakes and well-appointed Metro-Cammell bodywork in 1932—if the writer could have the

Although the fluid flywheel and preselective gearbox had obvious appeal in urban traffic, some coach operators were quick to adopt it as an aid to smoother running. A small operator in Bishop Auckland, J. E. Smith, was one of these and placed this Regal with preselective transmission in service in 1932. Duple bodywork was fitted. UP 7310 was later transferred to W. Emmerson of the same town, better known by the fleetname OK Motor Services. It continued to be a regular performer on the route to Newcastle until after the 1939-45 war.

It was not only home market operators who were impressed by the new form of transmission. In July 1932, this Ranger was one of two examples with fluid transmission and Lockheed brakes supplied to Gray Coach Lines Ltd., of Toronto for use on the route to Buffalo. The bodywork was by the Canadian Car and Foundry Co. of Montreal, itself to be a user of AEC engines in CCF-built vehicles in later years. Gray Coach Lines came back for a further Ranger, again with fluid transmission, but this time complete with British-built Duple bodywork.

choice of a bus to preserve (and the means to do so) it would have been one of these, but two had bodies transferred to new Daimler CWA6 chassis in 1945-46 and although other bodywork was fitted, they disappeared long before the preservation movement began. Other early users of AEC "petrol preselectors" included Leeds and Huddersfield (both with Regal single-deckers), City of Oxford Motor Services (with one batch of Regents) and a number of coach operators.

Clearly, however, it was the combination of oil engine and preselective gearbox which held most promise for the future and, here again, LGOC was the pioneer. The first such vehicle is believed to have been a Renown, LT 590, which was one of the twenty petrol-engined preselective Renowns placed in service in August 1931 but which was fitted with one of the updated oil engines removed from the three experimental ST-type buses in February 1932. The preselective transmission on these vehicles

(Left) The next logical step was the combination of oil engine and fluid transmission and once again it was the LGOC which took the lead with twenty of the 60-seat LT-class Renowns built in 1932. These vehicles were thus of remarkably advanced specification for their time. This illustration from the November 1932 issue of ''Bus & Coach'' shows LT 1362, one of the vehicles in question, equipped with Hanwell (HW) garage plate. The smaller views show the 8.8-litre engine installation (note the horizontal oil filler characteristic of this engine) and that of the Gardner 6LW engine used in the last ten LT-type buses.

(Right) The 8.8-litre fluid transmission LT-class buses were the first to have this form of preselector lever, looking very like a conventional gear lever, and with similar movements, but fitted with a flattened knob for ease of identification in mixed fleets. It was much more positive in operation than the quadrant type of lever often used with preselective gearboxes.

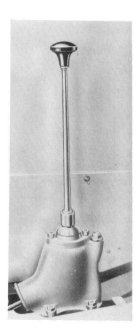

could be, and often was, removed as a set and replaced by standard transmission on overhaul, but it is believed that LT 590 then ran with the oil engine and Daimler transmission for a period, though the latter was removed later.

In any case, twenty of the 1932 batch of 60 oil-engined LT-buses also had fluid transmission, as AEC tended to describe the Daimler system. These buses, LT 1355-74, also had Lockheed hydraulic brakes and hence were of remarkably modern specification for 1932. They could be said to be the forebears of the modern British bus, for the combination of diesel engine, fluid flywheel and epicyclic gearbox is nowadays standard in almost every major fleet in the country. Although Daimler was later to find a highly effective combination of Gardner oil engine and preselective transmission, AEC were first off the mark in this sphere. Thus, in 1932, AEC had the genesis of much of the development that was to follow. The A165 8.8-litre engine, with its output of 130 bhp, was the most powerful British bus engine in volume production, and was to remain so until well into the post-war era, even though by then no longer available. It was, in fact, rather more powerful than most operators wanted and its length meant that body space had to be reduced slightly on maximum length models to keep within the law.

# 6 THE Q-TYPE —
# A MAGNIFICENT FAILURE

However, a completely different approach to bus design was being pursued at Southall, of which more compact engine design was a by-product. Rackham had paid a return visit to the United States to keep in touch with developments there, accompanied by Lt-Col. J. T. Moore-Brabazon, later Lord Brabazon, who had joined the AEC board in 1929 and was to remain a Director until his death in the 'sixties.

Incidentally, AEC seemed to attract personalities from the more glamorous sides of the automobile world. Brabazon had been an early aviator, his proud possession of the first pilot's licence to be issued in Britain being commemorated when he managed to secure the registration number FLY 1 for his car when this was issued in the late 'thirties (this being before the days of buying and selling so-called "private" numbers, though Brabazon did transfer this number to subsequent cars he owned). It was probably he who obtained useful publicity for AEC by arranging for a Regent demonstrator to be used as a timekeepers' or press stand at Brooklands. This association no doubt played its part in the subsequent construction of a record-breaking diesel car, using a specially-tuned AEC 8.8-litre engine in a Chrysler chassis, driven

The inspiration for the Q-type came from the Fageol Twin-Coach introduced in 1925 which had become very popular by the time Rackham made a return visit to the United States about five years later. This was a 1929 example used by the Pacific Electric Railway in the Los Angeles area. It seated 40.

by Capt. G. E. T. Eyston and Mr. A. Denly, which created the first official diesel car endurance record of 24 hours at the Montlhery track near Paris at an average speed of 94.99 mph—also a 50 kilometre spell at 98.75 mph on 15th February 1936. Another motor racing personality who became an AEC director was Earl Howe, who had raced Bugattis at Brooklands and elsewhere.

However, to return to the bus story, Rackham was impressed by the success of the Fageol Twin Coach. He must have been aware of its introduction in 1925 during the period he had been with Yellow Coach, but by 1930-31, the American urban bus operators had adopted it (or competitive designs) in a big way, to the extent that the term "transit bus" tended to imply a vehicle with driving position and entrance ahead of the front axle. On the Twin Coach as the name implied, there were two engines, mounted in the sides of the vehicle between front and rear axles. Once again, he came back to Britain with the intention of adapting an American idea to British bus design.

The result was the AEC Q-type. This differed from the Fageol in having only one engine, thus considerably simplifying the design. It was mounted almost immediately behind the off-side (right-hand) front wheel and to minimise awkward angularities

Although not strictly relevant to the story of AEC buses, this picture of Capt. Eyston's AEC Fuel Oil Safety Special, as it was called, gives an indication of the potential of the 8.8-litre engine. It was taken at Brooklands, where the car was timed at 104.86 and 106.63 mph in opposite directions over a kilometre, in October 1933.

The first Q-type chassis, number 762001, later to become LGOC Q1, at Southall before being sent to Chiswick for bodying. The exact date of the photograph is not known, but the lack of leaves on the trees suggests no later than March 1932. The crash gearbox, mounted on the rear of the engine on this chassis, is just visible beneath the rear end of the engine cover. The building in the background is the works canteen.

(Below) Q1's petrol engine and crash gearbox, ready for installation. This view clearly shows the inclination of the cylinder block used on this model to minimise the intrusion of the engine into the passenger space.

or other complications in the transmission, the rear axle was moved as near to the rear of the vehicle as practicable and single tyres used to allow the differential to be as far to the right as possible, thus giving only a mildly angled transmission line. The frame was splayed out at the rear to permit this.

It was primarily intended as a double-decker, and the engine position was designed to be accommodated behind the stairs. Thus the basic layout, with entrance in the front overhang and stairs behind the driver, was very much akin to that of present-day conventional rear-engined double-deckers. When introduced, the new model was far from conventional, however.

The engine used in the earlier Q models was an adaptation of the standard 110 x 130 petrol engine of the period, with type numbers A167 (standard head) or A169 (high power head). However, it was built in opposite-handed form so as to bring all auxiliaries to the outside of the vehicle, making them easily accessible once a panel had been removed. It was also inclined to the right to minimise the space intrusion into the body, and rubber-mounted

This model, evidently about 3ft. long, was used by AEC to provide styling guidance to bodybuilders. Here again the exact date is unknown, but circumstantial evidence points to the winter of 1931-32. It was clearly used as the basis for the Q1 body design, including the choice of livery, although Chiswick's interpretation was not as well proportioned. It was a remarkably modern concept for that period and undoubtedly influenced not only Duple and Weymann in their Q designs but the whole direction of PSV single-deck styling.

This picture of the first Q, taken at almost the same spot as the chassis illustrated opposite, shows how LGOC had interpreted the body design. The roof curvature was shallower and the waistline higher while the repositioning of the headlamps had a quite disastrous effect on the frontal appearance. The progress of the leaves on the trees indicates perhaps the end of April 1932. Note that the vehicle is unlettered, though in the same livery as the model.

—a feature not adopted on other models until the RT era. Moreover the direction of rotation of the engine was reversed, being anti-clockwise when viewed from the front. The first prototype vehicle, a single-decker, chassis number 762001, had a conventional clutch and crash gearbox. Brakes were of the vacuum hydraulic type.

This initial vehicle was bodied by LGOC at Chiswick as a 35-seat bus with entrance behind the front axle and, following minor body modifications and application of LGOC lettering, entered service on the famous route 11 running across central London as fleet number Q1 in September 1932. This seems to have been largely a publicity stunt as the seating capacity and layout were far from ideally suited to so intensive a route. The crash gearbox also proved unsatisfactory when removed about 8ft. behind the driver, and all subsequent Q-types had preselective gearboxes.

Q1, as modified and lettered, ready to enter service with LGOC in September 1932. Note that a larger destination indicator and modified windscreen design had been incorporated, while glass louvres had been fitted over the windows. This view gives an almost direct comparison with that of the model on the facing page. The LGOC bodybuilding department had produced an eye-catching vehicle, but had not captured the subtleties of outline in the rear dome, for example, where the model was a clear pointer to future orthodox practice.

A model was also produced for the double-deck design and this, as well as being quite faithfully followed by all the bodybuilders who produced Q double-deckers, had an even greater long-term influence on future design trends. Note that it, too, was painted in a special version of the LGOC livery with maroon roof, etc.—it seems likely that the choice may have been influenced by the style used by City of Oxford Motor Services Ltd. However, in this case, no real "General" Q-double-decker ever materialised—by the time the Chiswick management had, after some delay, decided to buy a couple, the London Passenger Transport Board had been formed.

A double-deck chassis, with wheelbase of 15ft. 10in. and a longer front overhang than the 18ft. 6in.-wheelbase single-decker, was also bodied and revealed to the press the following month. This was chassis number 761001 which at first was painted in a light-coloured demonstration livery. The 60-seat bodywork was of a remarkably modern style for 1932, with a curved front profile and generously rounded lines throughout. This followed the style of a wooden model, painted in a similar version of LGOC livery to the single-decker and with "General" fleetname, of which an

This view of one of the early double-deck Q chassis, almost certainly the first, conveys the ingenious layout very effectively. Note how the use of single rear tyres allowed a comparatively simple transmission line to be used. Also visible is the light style of gear engaging pedal used with the vacuum-operated pre-selective gearbox—this particular chassis had the Daimler quadrant type of preselector lever on the steering column—most Q chassis had a conventional-looking vertical lever by the driver's seat.

Translated into reality, the double-deck Q was even more startling to contemporary eyes than the single-decker. This is the first one, 761001, in its original demonstration colours. Today, the long front overhang seems normal, though normally balanced by a rather longer rear overhang on a rear-engined double-decker than is shown here. The unladen weight of 6 tons, admittedly related to 26ft. by 7ft. 6in. dimensions and a petrol-engined vehicle, contrasts very favourably with that of today's double-deckers. Note the vacuum cylinder for the gearbox just visible under the side panels in front of the rear axle.

AEC experimental department photograph is reproduced. It seems clear that this had been constructed as design guidance for body-builders, as all the double-deck Q-types followed its pattern in general appearance, though a few were of centre-entrance layout. Rackham considered appearance important and thought the addition of a false radiator at the front of some contemporary trolleybuses ''crazy'', so he was keen to ensure that the dramatic impact of the new design was not dissipated by unsatisfactory styling. Not only was this effective but it set the pattern for future body designs on conventional chassis.

Contrary to some official records, it appears that this first Q double-deck body was also built by LGOC. It was soon decided to deliver this vehicle, by then registered AHX 63, as a demonstrator to Birmingham Corporation, entering service in the early weeks of 1933. Its livery was altered, again to a non-standard version of the operator's livery and a number of minor body design changes made, presumably to meet Birmingham requirements.

This close-up shows the fluid flywheel, just behind the exhaust pipe on the right, and in the foreground the vacuum-operated preselective gearbox, as used on several early Q double-deckers.

The above two pictures show the first Q double-decker, 761001, as originally delivered in demonstration livery — it was subsequently registered AHX 63 while in this livery — and after a number of minor modifications to opening windows, handrails and the tramcar-style lifeguard (as provided on most early Q buses) had been made for service in Birmingham. Curiously, the livery was not an accurate reproduction of Birmingham's characteristic style.

The interior of AHX 63 seems somewhat austere in relation to the exterior. The resemblance to LGOC practice in ceiling contour and the 1931-style seats is striking. The longitudinal seat on the right is over the engine.

It seems possible this work was done by Park Royal Coachworks, by then regularly involved in building bodywork for AEC demonstrators, and this may account for the reports that Park Royal built this body. In fact, despite its curvaceous exterior, the interior had distinct LGOC characteristics. The seats were similar to those in 1930-31 LGOC buses and the shallow curve of the lower-deck ceiling was reminiscent of contemporary "Bluebird" LGOC LT bodies.

Overall it had distinct resemblances to the LGOC body on London United Tramways trolleybus No. 61 built shortly afterwards. This was built on a special 30ft.-long six-wheel chassis, number 691T001, with amidships underfloor motor, and chassis frame designed to suit the entrance position a few feet behind the front axle. This seated 74 and was for many years the largest capacity trolleybus in the country. It also had a curvaceous exterior and "Bluebird" style interior, though rather better finished than the prototype Q double-decker.

The Q-type transmission was interesting in several respects. A special version of the preselective gearbox to accommodate the opposite-hand torque reaction of the anti-clockwise engine rotation was necessary, and Daimler produced this, apparently without demur — yet another example of the adaptability of bus engineering policy in those days. This was designated D129 by AEC. Several of the early Q vehicles did not have the direct mechanical linkage from the gear-operating pedal, but instead had a vacuum-operated system, reducing the fairly sizeable pedal pressure of the standard system to a gentle dab with the left foot — the pedal was of "mushroom" style like the AEC accelerator pedal of the period.

Although not a member of the Q family, it is logical to include the sole 691T trolleybus in the same group because of its affinity as a pioneer in layout and styling. It was built for London United Tramways in which fleet it was numbered 61 but its registration number AHX 801 indicated its close proximity to the first Q double-decker. It was designed to have a centre entrance and the nearside frame sidemember cranked downwards to give a low step height. The motor was mounted below the floor, rather than at the front as on the early 663T. The body was built by LGOC and, apart from its layout, quite closely resembled the Q design in its smooth outlines. The picture on the right shows it on AEC's test hill—the Southall works was claimed to be unique in its provision of trolleybus overhead over a road circuit within the factory boundary.

However, this was evidently not too reliable as the feature was not repeated, though it pointed the way to the air-operated pre-selective gearbox of the RT era.

Production of Q-type buses proceeded slowly through 1933, about ten double-deck and half that number of single-deckers being built. Most of the double-deckers were bodied by Metro-

Cammell while Duple and Weymann built single-deck coach or dual-purpose bodies, all to styles which would look quite acceptable today. Things picked up a little for the single-deck version in 1934, with another 30-odd produced, but double-deck sales were down, with about another seven sold. Only London Transport, which had by then taken over from the LGOC as described in later pages, and Elliott Bros., the proprietors of Royal Blue, had more than two examples of either version, with five and three respectively. A trolleybus version, the 761T, with side-mounted motor, had done no better, with only five built, three of which went to Australia.

Rescue from complete disaster came in 1935, when London Transport ordered 100 country area buses with 37-seat bodywork by Birmingham Carriage & Wagon Co., although Aberdeen Corporation helped to break the ice with an order for ten following one earlier example and there was also a minor success in South Wales, where the company of that name took five (the only examples for a BET company) and various other companies and

Metro-Cammell double-deck Q bodywork was the most popular, accounting for eleven out of the 23 vehicles built. The Bolton Corporation example, No. 2 (WH 4850), was chassis number 761003, delivered in 1933. This view graphically conveys the impression created by this ultra-modern vehicle on a typical contemporary street scene. Admittedly all the vehicles in sight were a few years old, but noteworthy are the Corporation tram, Ribble Leyland Lion PLSC bus and Albion lorry.

(Left) The entrance layout of most Q-type double-deckers was very like that of modern vehicles of the types not seen until about 25 years later. However, doors were not generally fitted, which must have made them draughty quite apart from questions of danger. This was the second vehicle built, supplied to Crosville Motor Services Ltd.

(Right) A minority of the Q double-deckers were of centre-entrance layout. London Transport took two with Weymann bodywork, painted in Green Line livery and numbered Q4 and Q5 following two front-entrance Q double-deckers for the central fleet. Note that the address quoted for the LPTB was Bell Street, Reigate—the country department being controlled from the old East Surrey headquarters, nowadays the London Country Bus Services headquarters.

The first Q coach was 762002, supplied to Elliott Bros. (Bournemouth) Ltd. in 1933 and registered LJ 8001. It had Duple 35-seat bodywork which combined a front-end design influenced by the AEC styling model with contemporary sloping pillar idiom so far as the side elevation was concerned. It is seen at Lulworth Cove when on a tour of Dorset. Elliott Bros. took two more Q coaches and one wonders whether more might have followed had they continued to operate the Royal Blue services instead of selling out to the Tilling group in 1935.

(Right) Edinburgh Corporation's Weymann-bodied Q also showed influence from the original AEC design. It seated 39, one of the few single-deck examples to show a significant gain in capacity over conventional vehicles.

(Below) Interior of a similar Duple coach. The longitudinal seat over the engine was not popular on a coach chassis. Some later vehicles tried to overcome this by substantially raising the floor level.

The biggest single order for the Q-type was for 100 single-deckers with bodywork by the Birmingham Railway Carriage and Wagon Co. for the country services of London Transport. The second vehicle of the order, Q7B is seen here. This group of vehicles had an unusual appearance due to their sloping roof line, but the overall effect was quite attractive. The "B" suffix indicated "bus" as opposed to "coach".

The oil engine introduced for the Q in 1934 was the original 7.7-litre unit, a size that was to become the most familiar AEC engine in the period from 1935 to 1947. This cross-section also shows the Ricardo Comet indirect-injection system, with the fuel sprayed into a spherical combustion chamber in the cylinder head. As well as the injector, a heater plug was required for each combustion chamber to allow starting from cold.

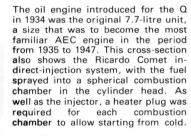

Access to the engine on the Q-type was good, though carrying out any roadside repairs required standing in the roadway alongside the vehicle. This view shows the 7.7-litre oil engine.

municipalities in the area built up a total of sixteen single-deckers in the 1934-35 period. In 1936 London Transport came back for 80 more buses (this time for the central area and the only Q single-deckers with entrance ahead of the front axle) and 50 coaches, all with Park Royal bodywork.

All the production vehicles for London Transport and most of those for major operators from 1934 had diesel engines. These were of a new type, designed for the Q, though a derivative for conventional front-engined chassis was to be built in far greater numbers. In both cases the aim was compactness and this new six-cylinder unit had a bore and stroke of 106 mm and 146 mm respectively, giving a swept volume of 7.731-litres. Indirect injection of Ricardo design was retained and in some ways the engine was a scaled-down version of the 8.8-litre unit, though the camshaft was mounted higher in the cylinder block. The Q version, again with anti-clockwise rotation and inclined cylinders, was the A170.

The A171 version for front-engined chassis had clockwise rotation, but to achieve this from the original design its firing order was 1, 4, 2, 6, 3, 5 instead of the 1, 5, 3, 6, 2, 4 usual for a six-cylinder in-line unit. It fitted the standard Regent/Regal/Renown bonnet length as originally devised for petrol chassis and thus enabled more space to be devoted to passenger accommodation in a given length of bodywork, as well as permitting a standard body to be used for oil or petrol vehicles. The output of the 7.7-litre engine was usually 115 bhp at 2000 rpm, a little less than the 8.8, but still more than almost all competitive chassis, though torque (ie pulling power on hills) was in proportion to its size, and not as good as an 8.4-litre Gardner 6LW, for example.

Despite London Transport's support for the single-deck version, the Q-type was by no means the success Rackham had hoped. His original double-deck concept had not been taken up in production quantities by a single operator. Of the total of 23 examples built, London Transport had taken only four and yet was the largest operator. The first two of these were not taken into stock until April 1934 and Rackham told me that London Transport's opposition to the double-decker model's layout for use in central London was one of the two factors which killed the Q. The other was the AEC management's unwillingness to spread the sizeable development costs over enough chassis to keep the price down. Yet when I visited him in his retirement in 1964, it was clear that he regarded the Q as one of his best designs.

Certainly it was far ahead of its time and nearer to today's practice than any other double-decker built up to the introduction of the production Leyland Atlantean in 1958. It was sometimes inclined to overheat—the radiator behind the offside front wheel

The Q trolleybus, type 761T, was even less successful in terms of sales than the double-deck bus, with only five produced. The first one is seen here in English Electric demonstration livery and with Bradford registration number KY 6210—the EE traction department was in Bradford—though it later ran for that city's transport department as No. 633 before passing to the South Shields municipal fleet as No. 235. The English Electric body was notable for seating 63—the bus versions did not go beyond 60. Note how the styling outlines and prominent mouldings once again faithfully follow the original Q concept.

The chassis of a 761T, showing the motor at about the same position as the gearbox of the motorbus version. This picture also shows the tramway-style lifeguard under the front overhang. There was nervousness about the alleged dangers of vehicles with a long front overhang and most early double-deck Q models were so equipped at first.

did not get a great deal of cool air. There were some reports of inadequate traction on slippery roads due to the lack of enough weight and/or the single tyres on the rear axle and the much greater loading of the offside front wheel—the spring on that side had extra leaves; a double-decker supplied to Newcastle overturned and had a ''jinx'' reputation. The petrol model had a reputation of catching fire easily at the carburettor—if this occurred the correct drill was to rev up the engine until it went out! But none of these were insuperable problems.

Oddly enough, the most remarkable Q of all was the single six-wheeler built after production of four-wheelers had practically stopped. This was O763001 (the prefix O having been adopted for oil-engined AECs from about 1933), which was another double-deck Green Line coach numbered Q188 and, like LT1137 before it, virtually doomed to failure before it was put on the road in 1937. The aim was to give high standards of comfort to 51 passengers in the special Park Royal body, but as the engine was the 7.7-litre, performance was not really up to Green Line standards.

Fleet pictures of Q types were not common as so few operators ordered them in quantity. However, South Wales Transport Co. Ltd. took delivery of these four oil-engined examples with Brush 39-seat bodywork in 1935. The view also shows the office block originally built for AEC when the separate sales and senior management block was an Associated Daimler province. It was, in fact, the headquarters of the production control department.

(Below) Johnston's Bus Service of Germiston, South Africa, was one of the few export users of the Q. One of their vehicles, with locally-built body, is seen alongside two Regals.

(Below left) The only six-wheeled Q, 763001, after it had been sold by London Transport to H. Brown of Garelochhead. Park Royal built the body.

So the Q-type was quietly dropped, though it continued to appear in the catalogue up to the autumn of 1937—yet, forty-odd years later, it is ironical that London Transport is known to have been carrying out investigations into the possibilities of a future side-engined bus design.

# 7 ORTHODOXY AGAIN...
# BUT NOT STAGNATION

In practice, the sales and engineering emphasis went back to conventional chassis from 1934. The LGOC had abandoned the six-wheeler when the high-capacity two-axle double-decker became available. Its first 50 STL-type buses on the 16ft. 3in. wheelbase Regent chassis had 60-seat LGOC bodies, thus equalling the last six-wheel double-deckers in this respect, though this was only possible on the four-wheel chassis within the then gross weight limit by cutting down unladen weight—they weighed only 5 tons 18cwt. Thomas Tilling Ltd., whose London operations were already closely co-ordinated with LGOC, had been slightly earlier with its first 16ft. 3in. buses, which had 56-seat bodies built by Tilling between November 1932 and April 1933, and were numbered in the STL series from 51 upwards. There were to have been 101, but with the formation of the London Passenger Transport Board imminent, the last 22 were cancelled. However, numbers had been allocated to them, so LGOC's second and last batch of 60-seaters was numbered STL 153-202.

Only one of the foregoing, STL 50, had a D128 preselective gearbox, and none had oil engines; the 8.8-litre engine could not readily have been accommodated on either weight or length grounds on the LGOC examples. All had 100 mm bore petrol engines, among the last buses to be so fitted, and, incidentally, twelve Regals ordered by Tillings at the same time had special 95 bore versions of the A136 engine, the smallest variant of that family of engine, with a swept volume of only 5.5-litres. They were numbered T307-318, the first two having D128 gearboxes—suggesting a spark of interest in the fluid flywheel transmission from the former main British protagonist of petrol-electric buses.

LGOC was increasingly sold on the idea and the last buses to be built during its separate existence were 50 STL models with the Daimler fluid transmission and a new sloping-front style of 56-seat body. The first of these, STL 203, was completed a few weeks before the LPTB came into operation on 1st July 1933.

On paper, this was a major event for AEC. The new publicly-owned London Passenger Transport Board took over all road and rail transport operating activities of the former Underground group, including LGOC, together with the London bus services of Thomas Tilling and the various independent operators. However, AEC was not handed over and became a separate company. Thus its financial link with the principal operator of buses in London was broken and in theory each could go its own way.

The first LGOC bus based on the 16ft. 3in. wheelbase version of the Regent entered service in January 1933 and was thus a contemporary of the first Q-types. Numbered STL 1, it was to form a more successful basis for future development, as the STL chassis eventually numbered 2701 vehicles, although the majority differed considerably in design from this version, of which 100 were built in the months before London Transport took over. This photograph was taken in early post-war days.

In practice, the links remained close. Not only had LPTB inherited a combined fleet almost entirely of AEC make, but LGOC's technical policy was continued. In almost all cases, the same senior and junior management and engineers were sitting at the same desks in both organisations. It was agreed that AEC would continue as principal supplier of motor buses and although Leyland began to take a minority share of orders, usually for the more specialised vehicles, this was not new, as the LGOC had sometimes put out some work to other firms, particularly Dennis in the comparatively recent past. AEC maintained close technical liaison with LPTB and, for example, continued to supply copies of all alterations to drawings relating to passenger vehicles to Chiswick, including those relating to models London Transport didn't run—the standard form I used for this purpose when I was in the AEC drawing office in the 'fifties included reference to this.

The definitive concept on which the volume production of the STL was based first appeared with the entry into service of eleven vehicles late in 1933. They had all but one of the first pre-production examples of the 7.7 litre oil engine, type A171, together with preselective gearboxes, a combination which proved very successful. STL 349 of this type is shown here with bonnet open, as if to convey that this "normal"-looking Regent chassis really did have an oil engine. The gearboxes were originally of Daimler manufacture but the demand for such units caused AEC to begin building its own and these vehicles were later converted to the latter. A twelfth 7.7-litre engine was fitted to LT 21, one of the original open-staircase bodied Renown six-wheelers, but no further LT-class double-deckers were fitted with this type of engine. The General fleetname was continued for a brief period in early LPTB days.

In fact, technical design co-operation between AEC and LPTB became of a more positive nature than it had been, particularly in the 1928-30 period, and in due course resulted in the production of two of the world's most outstanding urban bus designs, the RT and Routemaster.

However, in the more immediate future, 100 further STL chassis with sloping-front 56-seat bodies had been ordered by LGOC just before the transfer to LPTB and a further 250 were ordered by the latter, taking the fleet numbers up to STL 608 (STL 553-8 were

used for buses on similar chassis taken over from independent operators). All but eleven of the new buses received existing 110 mm petrol engines taken from LT-type Renown buses supplied in 1931-32, the latter being converted to diesel with new A165-type 8.8-litre oil engines. This rather complex arrangement was used partly because the 8.8-litre engine would have implied a slightly shortened version of the STL body, which was of maximum legal length, upsetting the interchangeability on which was based the system of transferring bodies between chassis after overhaul

AEC began manufacturing its own preselective epicyclic gearboxes in 1934—this is a D133-type unit for a Q-type chassis. The prominent emblem cast into the top cover left no room for doubt about the unit's origin, but the plate alongside it read ''Self Changing Gear Box. This box is manufactured under patents granted to Walter Gordon Wilson and now vested in Improved Gears Ltd.'' A list of nine patent numbers followed, the first having been granted in 1919.

(body repairs taking longer than those of chassis). Also it put the oil engines where their economy was of most benefit. Mr. George J. Shave, LGOC's Chief Engineer, had quoted 5 mpg for a petrol-engined LT and 9.1 mpg for the Ricardo-head 8.8-litre version in an article on the early oil-engine experiments in the November 1932 issue of ''Bus & Coach''. Both strike me as creditable figures but may reflect the modest traffic congestion on the suburban routes run by Hanwell in those days.

The remaining eleven STL buses (STL 342-352) received new 7.7-litre oil engines of the A171 type, derived from that designed for the Q-type. This fitted in the same space as the petrol engines and thus enabled the original bonnet length to be retained. These buses, like all but 100 of the sloping-front STL type, also had preselective gearboxes. The combination of the lively 7.7 engine and this transmission was found most effective, producing a nimble bus that was easy to drive in London's traffic and giving good fuel consumption, even if not quite so good as some of its more efficient competitors.

With a sizeable market for preselective gearboxes assured, early in 1934 AEC began manufacture of its own units of this type, similar in principle to those made by Daimler, but indentifiable to a practised ear by a slightly different tone. They were possibly marginally quieter, though they could develop quite a ''fruity'' note when worn after many years of city operation. The new unit was built in two versions, D132 for front-engined chassis and D133 an anti-clockwise version for the Q, which at that date was still regarded as a production model—indeed the single-deckers for London Transport which formed the majority of production

were yet to be built and incorporated this unit. The last 100 of the ''sloping-front'' STL's also had D132 units.

So the pattern was set, with the A171 7.7-litre engine and D132 AEC-built preselective gearbox as useful units in the battle for sales, particularly in the growing but fiercely fought city bus market. Apart from normal fleet replacement, many cities and towns were embarking on replacement of some or all of their hitherto dominant tramway systems. Accordingly bigger orders for buses were in the offing. AEC was quite well placed to compete and from 1934 until the War intervened in 1939 the Regent with 7.7-litre engine and preselective gearbox was to be the standard not only in London but also Leeds, for example.

Officially the A165 8.8-litre engine remained standard until 1935, and the choice had been further widened by the introduction in 1933 of the A166 and A168 four-cylinder oil engines, available in the Regal 4. For some reason these were of overhead-camshaft type, with a similar valve gear arrangement to that used on the contemporary AEC petrol engines. They had the same 146 mm stroke as the 7.7-litre unit, but bore sizes were 108 mm and 120 mm respectively, giving swept volume figures of 5.35 litres and 6.605 litres.

The latter unit was adopted as the standard Regal 4 oil engine, and a number of operators responded by placing orders, notably Dublin United Tramways (who ultimately took a total of 46), Scottish Motor Traction (for 33) and the Gosport & Fareham Omnibus Co., several of whose eight examples were particularly long-lived, although extensively rebuilt and re-engined before their withdrawal about 30 years later. The year 1934 was the peak for the Regal 4, with about 80 sold, or almost half the total production, which ended in 1937, with the final chassis O642178 being

Demand for the Regal 4 perked up somewhat in 1934, largely as the result of the availability of the A168 four-cylinder oil engine introduced the previous year. Eight examples were supplied to the Gosport and Fareham Omnibus Co., which used the fleetname ''Provincial'', and the first, No. 23 (CG 9606), is seen here. Harrington built the 32-seat bodywork, which was of an attractive style also found on quite a number of six-cylinder Regals, notably a sizeable batch supplied to Timpsons, which for many years formed the main part of their fleet. The Gosport and Fareham examples were themselves converted with 7.7-litre six-cylinder engines in the post-war period and some lasted, albeit much rebuilt, as late as the 'sixties.

(Above) The 7.7-litre became the standard engine in six-cylinder models from 1935 but the 8.8-litre unit was still available if preferred. One of the first instances of the latter being specified was for three Regals for the Schöyens Bilcentraler fleet in Oslo. This strange scene occurred because the body framing was built by Kuaeruer Brug in one part of the city and the skeleton vehicles taken to the bodybuilders—this one obviously could not be driven because its radiator had been removed. Clearly visible is the amidships-mounted preselective gearbox and the distinctive type of gear lever knob. The vehicles had 19ft. wheelbase for a 10-metre length and were said to be the first diesel buses in Norway when placed in service in September 1935.

supplied to Swindon Corporation. The AEC official figure for the total built was 177, but there were several cases of engines being swapped between four- and six-cylinder versions, before sale, with resulting confusion to chassis numbers. There was also one oil-engined Ranger 4 built in 1934, this being chassis number 650001 (for some reason the 'O' prefix by then usual on oil-engined models was omitted) supplied to Burton-on-Trent Corporation with Brush 26-seat body. Burton at that date was still standardising on normal-control buses, and tried one such each from AEC and Leyland, both of whom supplied special four-cylinder models, before reverting to Guy as its regular supplier.

Although the decision to drop the Q did not take effect until 1936-37, the writing was clearly on the wall by 1935, certainly for the double-decker. Rackham did not wish to lose the public relations impact of the streamlined appearance and resolved to

This mock-up of a fully-fronted cab for a Regent was prepared in 1935, no doubt as a basis for the Olympia Show exhibits for that year, seen outside the experimental department. The London Transport radiator badge suggests that it was based on a "borrowed" STL chassis, but as shown on the opposite page, the design was most closely approached in two Weymann-bodied vehicles. In the background can be seen the experimental department's test body that had been built by Strachans to fit on the front end of a Regal or Regent chassis.

(Opposite page) In an attempt to give adequate engine accessibility, a Garner patent for a hinged split front wing was taken up by AEC and built into the fully-fronted vehicles built. This is London Transport's STL 857, put into service in December 1935 and renumbered STF 1 a few months later. It ran in this form until 1938, but no more were built and this vehicle was then rebuilt with a standard radiator and half cab and reverted to the number STL 857. The body remained different to others because of a greater rake to the front of the upper-deck (only just evident in this picture); it was later transferred to STL 1167.

equip the Regent with streamlined bodywork for the 1935 Commercial Vehicle Show. A mock-up of a fully-fronted cab was produced in March 1935 and efforts subsequently made to give satisfactory access to the engine, by arranging for a nearside cab door to carry part of the mudguard with it.

Two bodybuilders, Weymann and Roe, were persuaded to build special streamlined double-deckers in Leeds City Transport livery on Regent chassis for the Show, one retaining the exposed AEC radiator and the other concealing it. Even London Transport went along with the idea, producing one special version of its improved body design that had been introduced the previous year with full-width cab, concealed radiator and a more raked upper-deck, fitting it to STL 857 which was temporarily renumbered STF 1. The idea mis-fired and the fully-fronted cab did not catch on for front-engined double-deckers, though a few operators adopted it much later.

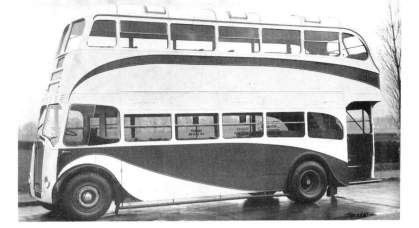

The fully-fronted double-deck bodies built on AEC Regent 7.7-litre engined chassis in 1935 proved to be a passing phase, but between them they had considerable influence on other designs, notably the Manchester "streamline" buses of 1936-40 and post-war Midland Red double-deckers.

(Top right) Weymann not only built a vehicle in Leeds City Transport colours exhibited at the 1935 Show and becoming No. 201 in that city, but built this duplicate in Sheffield colours.

(Centre right) Easily the most startling of the designs was the vehicle with body by Charles H. Roe Ltd. which carried the modernistic cab styling through to the entire body outlines. It was No. 200 in the Leeds fleet. It remained fully-fronted until 1942 when it, too, was converted to half-cab layout.

(Bottom right) Sheffield Corporation decided almost immediately that it did not want the full-width cab, doubtless because of the greater difficulty of carrying out servicing and repairs. Hence the vehicle shown at the top of the page was converted to half-cab, becoming No. 208 (BWE 526) in the Sheffield fleet.

A new face. The Regal Mark II, model O862, was a lighter single-decker model than the standard Regal. This view of a prototype chassis, shows the slightly smaller radiator with chromium-plated shell and slatted grille that identified this model. The front mudguard shape was also new, though it was altered on production vehicles to have a more nearly level bottom edge. The Regal Mark II lettering on the grille was dropped for production examples of this model.

However, the main AEC development at the 1935 Show was the introduction of a new lightweight Regal model. This was the Regal Mark II, model O862 Its chassis weight, at 3 tons 13 cwt., was about 9 cwt. less than the standard O662 model, and a more compact bonnet gave space for up to 39 passengers though only a handful of vehicles had bodywork seating as many — a more usual figure was around 36 for buses and 32 for coaches.

Its main feature was yet another new engine, the A172. This was an oil engine of 105 mm bore and 130 mm stroke, with a swept volume of 6.754 litres, though usually referred to as the 6.6-litre six-cylinder. Its principal novelty was the adoption of "wet" cylinder liners and monobloc construction, in the modern sense — in other words cylinder block and crankcase were combined into one cast-iron unit. Otherwise it was of conventional design, with Ricardo Comet combustion chamber, and pushrod overhead valve gear. Within AEC it was nicknamed the "bootlace" engine, apparently in some reference to low cost. Certainly this simplified construction was both more economical and eliminated a tendency for loosening of the cylinder block to crankcase fixing nuts which sometimes affected AEC diesels. However, in the early days this engine had a reputation for being rather troublesome, I gathered when at AEC in the early 'fifties. I do not recall the details being specified, but the wet cylinder liners (ie liners that were in direct contact with the cooling water as opposed to the dry type used on other AEC engines) were regarded as something of a problem. In fact this engine was the basis from which the engines used in the Reliance and Mercury ranges introduced in 1953 were derived and the wet liners and related gasket failures were undoubtedly their most common source of trouble.

The Regal Mark II chassis was of different appearance to the standard Regal (which continued in production), having a smaller radiator with a chromium-plated shell and vertical-slatted grille, and the nearside mudguard extended to line up with the bottom of the radiator.

The first chassis, O862001, was sent as a demonstrator to Rhondda Transport and BET companies tended to be among the main early customers. Northern General Transport took 25, Rhondda a further eight and South Wales Transport eight, all during 1936. But after that sales slowed down. They were revived to some degree in the 1937-39 period when a petrol-engined version became available. This engine was the A174, with the same

The A172 diesel engine introduced for the Regal Mark II was a very neat, compact and simple-looking unit. Although only about 70 vehicles so powered were built, it provided the basis from which the thousands of engines used in the Reliance and Mercury ranges from 1953 were developed.

(Above) The largest user of the Regal Mark II was the Northern General Transport Co. Ltd., which placed 25 in service in 1936. They had Weymann bodywork to a modified version of the standard British Electrical Federation design. Note how the appearance of the chassis gave a foretaste of that of the post-war Mark III passenger models.

(Right) One example of the Regal Mark II had the unusual distinction of being operated on derv, producer gas and petrol in that order. This photograph shows it when new in 1936, complete with coach bodywork by Northern Coachbuilders Ltd., standing near their premises in Claremont Road, Newcastle, ready for delivery to Bell's Services Ltd., of Westerhope, near that city. This business was taken over by United Automobile Services Ltd. and, by then in the United fleet, JR 5091 was converted in wartime to run on producer gas, probably using a modified petrol engine taken from one of United's 1929 Reliances. After the war this engine was reconverted to run on petrol.

105 x 130 bore and stroke as the diesel, but had a downdraught carburettor, giving it a more modern appearance than the A162 engine, which retained the low-mounted updraught type to the end. Sheffield United Tours took eight such vehicles in 1937 and Standerwick, Ribble's coach subsidiary, became the largest user of this variant with a total of twenty supplied in 1938-39, these being the last to be ordered. A total of 104 Regal Mark II models were built, including about 24 for independent operators.

The 105 mm bore size had also been standardised for the A170 and A171 7.7-litre engines in place of the original 106 mm during 1935. The reason for this is not known—perhaps simply standardisation with the Regal Mark II unit—but it altered the actual swept volume from 7.731 to 7.585 litres. However, they continued to be known as the 7.7-litre engines, an anomaly that was to cause confusion for many years, particularly as it also applied to a new derivative of the A171, the A173 unit, that had never had the 106 mm bore size. The existence of engines with nominal capacities of 6.6, 7.7 and 8.8 litres was tidy from a publicity viewpoint.

The A173, introduced in 1936 but not publicised until July 1938, was AEC's first direct-injection oil engine. Its introduction was due to the success of direct-injection engines of other makes, particularly Gardner, whose fuel economy was now well-known in the bus industry. Daimler's use of the Gardner unit in conjunction with the fluid flywheel transmission was making that concern an effective competitor in the growing market for municpal buses.

The design of the A173 unit, which was to become AEC's most successful oil engine yet, was influenced by the form of piston used in a new Saurer engine that had been introduced in 1934. In a direct-injection engine, the fuel is sprayed into the space above the piston instead of into, or towards, a separate small combustion chamber as in the indirect-injection type. Hence the shape of the piston top face is particularly important. The Saurer "dual-turbulence" piston had a cavity with a central point, which induced the injected fuel to mix with air in a doughnut-shaped swirl or "Torus", but the design was complicated by the provision of four valves per cylinder. C. B. Dicksee still favoured the Ricardo indirect-injection system, but one of his staff named Semmons produced a revised version of the system used by Saurer, using a similar but simpler toroidal-cavity piston and the usual two valves

The existence of the direct-injection version of the "7.7" engine, the A173, was kept very quiet at first, possibly because AEC had hitherto been so strong an advocate of indirect injection. But by the date it was announced in 1938, sizeable numbers had been in service for up to two years, and a year later it had become standard. It was easily identifiable by the use of two separate cylinder heads, each covering three cylinders, and hence a divided rocker cover. The standard front engine mounting designed to clamp over the tubular front cross-member is evident in this view, as is the "chimney" style of air intake, with no air cleaner. It was to remain in large-scale production until the early 'fifties.

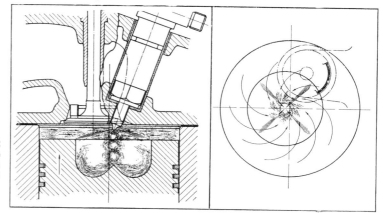

These diagrams of the toroidal combustion chamber were published when the AEC direct injection system was announced. Its success led other makers to introduce similar designs in their immediate post-war engines, notably Leyland, Bristol and, in modified form, Crossley. Dennis also used a toroidal design from 1937 but its version was closer to the original Saurer in concept.

During the 1936-39 period, AEC built bus and coach chassis with both indirect and direct injection. Notable among the former were London Transport's STL-type Regents delivered up to August 1938. In fact, apart from a minority of exceptions the whole of the series from STL 609 to STL 2515 had substantially the same basic specification of A171 7.7-litre engine, D132 AEC-built pre-selective gearbox and well-proportioned bodywork having a gently curved front profile. This example built in 1937 had Park Royal metal-framed bodywork conforming to the contemporary standard appearance. The photograph, taken at Chiswick after the bus was equipped for service from Enfield garage, shows how the advertisements formed an inherent part of the appearance of a London bus of that period — the Black & White upper-deck side display being particularly evocative of the 'thirties. The direct injection system was standardised for 132 more STL buses delivered in 1939 and the earlier vehicles subsequently converted. Vehicles of this general type formed about half of London's double-deck fleet for nearly a decade until the post-war types began to appear in quantity.

per cylinder. This was used in the A173, together with two separate cylinder heads, each covering three cylinders.

The result gave better efficiency than the Ricardo, particularly at low to medium engine speeds, and by using a lower governed speed significantly better fuel consumption figures could be obtained. It also did not require the use of electric heater plugs when starting from cold. However, advocates of indirect-injection claimed that this system was not so demanding in such matters as fuel quality or filtration, and there was some loss of power. Early A173 engines had a maximum output of 90 bhp at 1750 rpm, compared to the A171's 115 bhp at 2000 rpm, but later this difference was narrowed — post-war units gave up to 98 bhp at 1800 rpm, though an economy setting widely used in wartime was 86 bhp at 1800 rpm, only marginally more than the contemp-

orary Gardner 5LW figure of 85 bhp at 1700 rpm, though the AEC engine always seemed more responsive.

The A173 differed only in "top end" design from the A171, and many of the latter were converted, especially during wartime. But at first the two designs were produced side by side, London Transport continuing to favour the A171 for its STL buses until 1938 — some 1,848 vehicles of basically similar design were produced since STL 609 had appeared with an improved curved-front body in August 1934. All, apart from a few experimental vehicles, had the A171 engine and AEC-built D132 preselective gearbox.

A curious one-off vehicle produced in 1937 was Regent chassis number O6615090, built for and briefly operated by Birmingham City Transport as No. 483 (DOB 483) in 1937-38. It had an A168

Among the more surprising of the wide variety of vehicles built by AEC in the late 'thirties was London Transport's LTC class of 24 coaches on the last short-wheelbase 663-type Renown chassis to be built. Their overall length was about the same as by then permissable on a two-axle chassis; the choice of a six-wheeler was purely on the grounds of allegedly improved comfort. For similar reasons they had petrol engines, though these were A145 7.4-litre units from LT-type double-deckers by then converted to oil. Preselective transmission, only 28 luxurious seats, a sliding roof and radio (note the aerial near the rear of the roof) completed a super coach specification. The bodywork was by Weymann, to London Transport design. The fully-floating rear axles were a new feature for Renown chassis, though the 664T six-wheel trolleybus had been so equipped from 1935. These vehicles were refurbished for use during the 1951 Festival of Britain, acquiring 8.8-litre oil engines, again from LT-type double-deckers and an extra row of seats was added, bringing the seating capacity to 32.

four-cylinder diesel engine and D132 preselective gearbox, and carried the Short Bros. body from the original 483 (OV 4483), a petrol Regent of 1931. This was another attempt to produce a vehicle comparable in fuel economy with the Daimler COG5 with Gardner 5LW engine, on which Birmingham, previously a big Regent user, had standardised. It is not known whether the engine was a standard unit, with indirect-injection, but if so was unlikely to have much chance of success. Five complete new Regents with 7.7-litre engines were bought at the same time, these incidentally having Daimler-type quadrant preselector levers on the steering column, but no other Regents were bought by Birmingham until after the War. The chassis of DOB 483 was returned, converted to standard and sold to the Provincial fleet as DAA 848. The original Birmingham 483 resumed service, remaining in the fleet until 1950.

Equally odd was a project to build a Regent 0861 with fluid transmission and self-adjusting brakes, also for Birmingham. A parts list (XU 1449) had been prepared, based on the Regal Mark II 0862 model of which it would presumably have been a double-deck equivalent, but nothing came of the idea apparently.

Despite the variety of models that had been introduced, it was the Regent O661 that dominated the scene. An article in the "AEC Gazette", AEC's magazine for operators, in November 1935 was headed "The acid test—sales" and stated that 3,942 Regents had been sold up to that date. A total of 1,525 AEC vehicles had been fitted with fluid flywheel tranmission and this figure must have been more than doubled by about the end of 1938, when well over 6,000 Regents and about 3,000 Regals had been built. Demand for the Renown six-wheeler had fallen dramatically after the LGOC had abandoned ordering six-wheel buses at the end of 1932, but a further 54 of the long-wheelbase 664 or O664 type versions had been built for various operators up to 1938, and London Transport repeated its engine-transfer procedure in 1938 when 24 petrol-engined private-hire coaches were based on the last of the 663-model chassis to be built, bringing the total of this model to exactly 1,250.

Outside London, demand for Regents lay largely with municipal operators, many of whom were placing big orders for tramway replacement or expansion of bus services. Among cities and towns which took a majority of Regents for their double-deck requirements in the mid to late 'thirties were Cardiff, Glasgow, Grimsby, Halifax, Huddersfield, Morecambe & Heysham, Nottingham, Liverpool and Leeds, while substantial shares of orders from Bradford, Salford and Sheffield were also obtained. It is noteworthy that list prices for AEC buses were relatively high at this period— a Regent with oil engine (presumably 7.7-litre with crash gearbox) being listed at £1,425 in November 1938 when a Titan TD5 was only £1,210, a Bristol K5G £1,185 and a Daimler COG5 £1,200. One suspects that prices for quantities of vehicles in tenders must have differed much less.

Prominent among cities favouring AEC buses in the late 'thirties was Glasgow. Leyland and Albion had shared most of the orders between 1930 and 1935, but from 1937 to the early wartime period, AEC built an overall majority of the vehicles placed in service with a total of 187 Regents and 30 Regals, all but one with 7.7-litre engines. Typical was No. 578, one of 85 Regents supplied in 1938, in time for the Empire Exhibition held (in Glasgow) that summer, as conveyed by the destination indicator. Weymann built the bodywork on 65 of them, including this one, which also has the lengthened radiator grille introduced at the end of 1937. The BUS registration number series used for this batch of vehicles was delightfully apt, though no attempt was made to exploit its public relations potential.

Several BET companies were regular customers for AEC buses in the late 'thirties, generally favouring the direct injection 7.7-litre engine when it became available. The Rhondda Transport Co. Ltd. took delivery of three Regents with Weymann metal-framed bodywork in June 1937, including No. 149, seen here in the AEC works drive. Note how the poplar trees had grown in the decade since the Southall works were opened. A fleet of 50 similar buses had been supplied to the neighbouring South Wales Transport Co. Ltd. earlier that year.

Company orders tended to be more for Regals, though most fleets also took some Regents. Several of the companies under BET control, such as Devon General, Northern General, Oxford, Rhondda, South Wales and Trent were regular AEC customers, as was the Scottish Motor Traction Co. and the companies then in the Balfour, Beatty group, notably Mansfield District and Midland General. There was also a sizeable flow for independent operators.

The 7.7-litre engine was also used for export vehicles, though more usually the indirect-injection version. These Regents for operation in Adelaide were delivered in 1936. The body styling was typical of Australian double-deckers.

Specifications varied quite widely. AEC publicity put the emphasis on the 7.7-litre engine which was standard from 1935 but in fact several operators continued to specify the 8.8, some in its A165 form, substantially as introduced in 1932, notably Halifax, Salford and Sheffield Corporations. Halifax's General Manager, Mr. G. F. Craven, favoured more power for the undertaking's hilly routes and experimented with supercharging the A165 unit, increasing its output to 170 bhp. Four other Regents in this fleet had a special petrol conversion of the A165 engine, with bore increased to 120 mm, producing a swept volume that was later to

The Scottish Motor Traction Co. Ltd. divided most of its orders for single-deckers between the AEC Regal and Leyland Tiger during the 'thirties. This was one of fifteen Regals with Alexander 34-seat bodywork supplied in 1938. SMT had continued to favour the cutaway rear-entrance for bus bodywork although this was the last batch of Regals of this layout. This view of B188 was taken in New Street Garage, Edinburgh.

(Left) Coals to Newcastle. Although the then Bristol Tramways and Carriage Co. Ltd. had been building most of its own buses since 1908 (and from about 1934 its products were being standardised in almost all companies under Tilling group management), some AEC Regal buses and coaches were purchased in 1937-38. These vehicles were two of a fleet of twenty with Eastern Coach Works bus bodies supplied in 1937 to the Bath Tramways Motor Co. fleet, which had come under Bristol control in November 1936. The Bath concern had standardised on AECs, so this could be regarded as a ''posthumous'' order, but more surprising was the allocation of eighteen Regals with Duple coach bodywork to the main BTCC fleet in 1938.

(Below) The Balfour Beatty group of companies came to AEC for most of its vehicle requirements in the 'thirties and 'forties, usually, as here, with Weymann bodywork. Two of a batch of ten Regals for the Midland General Omnibus Co. Ltd. are seen at Southall before delivery in 1938. As was quite common at that time, the body design was given a touch of coach styling in moulding details.

This photograph of one of thirteen Regals supplied to the Devon General Omnibus and Touring Co. Ltd. in 1938, shows the modified style of front mudguard covering the front dumb irons, large "soup plate" chromium-plated front hub cap and plain bonnet panel (with no louvres) introduced as standard from the November 1937 Earls Court Show. However, as with other similar minor styling changes, these features were by no means universal, tending to be more common on standard chassis with the 7.7-litre engine, as in this case. The Harrington body design evolved for Devon General was an excellent example of the late 'thirties fondness for curved outlines, married in this case to functional straight waistrail treatment and producing an elegant overall effect. The curved-pillar cab windscreen treatment with no break in profile at waist level suited the AEC radiator particularly well. This particular vehicle, 406, was converted to an ambulance for the Royal Navy in 1940 and never returned to Devon General.

Salford Corporation was one of several municipalities which continued to favour the 8.8-litre engine in its A165 indirect injection form after this ceased to be the standard oil engine in 1935. No. 159 (RJ 6632), shown here, was one of ten Regents with Metro-Cammell bodywork delivered in 1936, but the 8.8-litre engine remained standard for AEC buses delivered to this fleet until 1939. The vehicle behind was No. 53 (BA 7387), a Dennis E-type. The picture was taken in Victoria Bridge Street with Manchester Exchange station visible in the background.

become familiar on another unit, 9.6-litres, though the principal use of this petrol design was powering the Vickers Valentine tank as unit A179.

Huddersfield preferred the Gardner 6LW engine and the 1932 installation, with long projecting bonnet, as used for the experimental LGOC Renowns, was revived for 37 Regals and 16 Regents for this operator from 1935 to 1939. From 1937 the vehicles in question had O662G and O661G prefixes to their chassis numbers. These vehicles had fluid flywheels and preselective gearboxes, so were directly equivalent to the Daimler COG6 model, but Huddersfield evidently thought the AEC chassis design preferable.

Conversely, Coventry Corporation specified AEC oil engines in Daimler double-decker chassis. The latter were made in Coventry, and support for local industry was an important factor in their choice. The resulting model was designated COA6 by Daimler and Coventry took the entire production of this model, comprising three with A165 8.8-litre engines and 97 with A171 or A173 7.7-litre units, though Daimler regularly included the model in published lists of types available. AEC was always very coy about non-standard types, and "AEC Gazette" tended to play down references even to the continued availability of the 8.8-litre in the late 'thirties—there was certainly no mention of Gardner engines!

Another user was Midland Red, or to give the company its then full title, the Birmingham and Midland Motor Omnibus Co. Ltd.

Huddersfield Corporation favoured the combination of AEC chassis with preselective gearbox and Gardner 6LW engine for both Regals and Regents in the late 'thirties. Accordingly its buses had a distinct Cyrano de Bergerac look, with the radiator projecting noticeably further forward than was necessary even with the 8.8-litre AEC engine. No. 35 (VH 7892) was the first vehicle to this specification to be delivered, one of three Regals with Park Royal 32-seat bodywork supplied in 1935. The body design on later batches helped to disguise the length of "nose" by placing the cab front panel a few inches in front of the chassis dash, but the bonnet length was still above average.

Like many of the English operating companies, BMMO had been slow to become involved in the operation of diesel vehicles, which was surprising in view of its policy of manufacturing its own vehicles. Howver, it was interesting that after experiments with various units, the choice fell on AEC A171 engines and three pre-production versions of Midland Red's then current ON single-deckers were so fitted and designated DON. Built in 1934, they were followed in 1935 by 50 more units for production DON vehicles, though one engine was diverted to a FEDD double-decker. Although relatively compact, the A171 was appreciably longer than Midland Red's petrol engine and reduced seating capacity from 38 to 36. Midland Red then developed its own

If Huddersfield could be said to have favoured an AEC to Daimler-like specification, Coventry's municipal buses of the same period were Daimlers with a strong AEC flavour. All the double-deckers supplied to Coventry between late 1934 and mid-1939 were Daimler COA6 models with AEC oil engines—even details of their appearance reflected AEC rather than standard Daimler practice in such features as the access holes in the bonnet side and provision of wheel nut guard rings. No. 221, seen here, was one of eleven with direct injection 7.7-litre engines and Metro-Cammell 56-seat bodywork delivered in May 1939. Another Midland municipality to receive a double-decker embodying AEC material was Wolverhampton, for whom the last Sunbeam motor bus built was in reality a Regent chassis with Gardner engine and Sunbeam radiator.

The Northern General Transport Co. Ltd. turned to AEC to help produce its own-design SE6 six-wheeled side-engined single-decker chassis in 1935, when 31 were assembled at Southall. One of the chassis is seen here, with the Hercules side-valve petrol engine only just visible on the far side of the frame in this view. Unlike most six-wheeled bus chassis, this model had separate pairs of springs for each rear axle, with a short balance beam connecting them, a system which gave a better ride than the rather jerky motion typical of the two-spring layout. The front-mounted radiator gave a hint of post-war Midland Red practice, not surprising as the latter's General Manager, Donald Sinclair, had served as engineer with NGT in the SE6 period.

ultra-compact K-type 8-litre six-cylinder engine and reverted to 38 seats with the SON model, but more AEC 7.7-litre engines were bought to convert some of the petrol FEDD double-deckers during the War.

Another user of AEC assistance in building its own buses was Northern General Transport which had begun assembling its SE6 side-engined six-wheelers in 1933-34. These had a layout similar to the Q-type, but used a Hercules WXRT six-cylinder 6.3-litre petrol engine imported from the United States, mainly because this was a side-valve unit and had a sufficently low profile to allow all seats to face forward and giving a seating capacity of 44. This was only possible on the Q if a very high floor level was used, as found on a few of the coaches, but impracticable for a bus version. The high seating capacity was of value to NGT because of bridges limiting the use of double-deckers. When it was decided to build 31 in 1935, production space at the Northern works was inadequate, and AEC agreed to assemble them at Southall. Of these, 25 were buses and six were coaches with the slightly larger Hercules WXLC3 engine of 6.65-litres.

Northern evidently reorganised its production facilities and built further vehicles itself, but AEC involvement in a different form recurred in 1937 when it proved possible to produce an oil-engined model by using a modified version of the AEC engine used in the Regal Mark II. The shorter stroke of this unit helped in keeping the engine height down and by inclining it as far as possible to the right, Q style, it proved possible to accommodate the cylinder head in a box on the edge of the floor. This was used in a four-wheel model, the SE4, of which 25 were built in 1938.

# Trolleybus peak

The trolleybus reached the peak of its popularity during the late 'thirties and formed a sizeable part of AEC's output, justifying the equipping of a special shop at Southall, with facilities for testing under cover. Overhead wires enabled use of a road circuit round part of the factory and including the test hill—claimed to be the only such facility among British trolleybus makers. Prototype four and six-wheeled vehicles were built for London Transport in 1934. The six-wheeler was a 30ft. vehicle with 18ft. 7in. wheelbase, but was given the chassis number 663T076—the trolleybus department at AEC had evidently failed to see that logically these dimensions should have made it a 664T, since they were those of the long-wheelbase Renown from which the trolleybus had been derived. But this was put right in 1935, when a 664T series was started with ten chassis of similar dimensions for Newcastle Corporation. By then, amidships underfloor motors were standard. Thereafter, although Newcastle had further small batches, London Transport became the main 664T user, with 51

Trolleybuses were built in sizeable numbers throughout the late 'thirties. Newcastle Corporation's inaugural fleet of 1935 included the first ten examples of the AEC 664T type, of which No. 9 (BVK 809), one of five with Brush bodywork is seen here soon after entering service. The driver, almost certainly an ex-tramway man, does not appear to have got used to being able to pull into, or near, the kerb even though parked vehicles were beginning to be a problem. The winged motif indicates that the vehicle incorporated English Electric electrical equipment. The bulk of the livery was a similar shade of yellow as still used on Tyne & Wear buses; the non-panchromatic film makes it appear much darker than it was.

London Transport rapidly became the largest trolleybus operator in Britain as conversions of tram routes got under way from 1935. AEC's share of the fleet of 1703 vehicles added to the ex-London United fleet of 61 was rather less than half, even though in addition to the 641 vehicles based on 664T chassis (or in some cases units built into "chassisless" integral-construction vehicles) AEC units were supplied for 24 MCW and two London Transport-built integral vehicles. Here three Weymann-bodied vehicles from the 1938 contract, Nos. 905, 907 and 906 and one with Brush body from the 1937 contract, 602, receive a final checkover before delivery. Note how slight the variations in design from different bodybuilders were. The chassis had 95 hp motors.

(Above) Another group of London Transport trolleybuses on AEC 664T chassis, led by Weymann-bodied No. 950, about to leave Fulwell depot, where they had been equipped for service, for Wood Green where they were to go into operation on route 629. The characteristic appearance of a London trolleybus was quite different from that of a London bus of the same period, both in terms of body design and livery. The choice of good quality metal-framed bodywork and first-class maintenance enabled vehicles such as these to give upwards of twenty years' service with no noticeable deterioration in performance or appearance — the brightwork shone to the end.

(Left) Nominally the same 664T model as the standard London trolleybus, but very different, were the seven vehicles supplied to the Montreal Transport Commission in 1937. These had an extended front overhang to enable the driver to supervise the entrance door ahead of the front axle. Three 663T vehicles exported to Edmonton in 1939 were of similar design, this choice of chassis type number seeming more logical for the 16ft. 2½in. wheelbase chassis. One of the Montreal chassis is seen on test at Southall before going to MCW for bodying.

(Left) The largest single batch of 661T trolleybuses consisted of 76 vehicles with Cravens 52-seat bodywork supplied to Portsmouth Corporation in 1936. Three of them are seen here on the test track at Southall before delivery. Portsmouth had decided to standardise on the two-axle AEC double-deck trolleybus chassis after operation of four as part of its initial mixed fleet, and ultimately built up a fleet of 89, which was also the largest total of this model. The Cravens concern was then at about the peak of its career as a bus and trolleybus bodybuilder.

(Below) Trolleybus inspection facilities at Southall included means of carrying out safety checks on electrical insulation. Here one of the 44 trolleybuses on 661T chassis supplied to Brighton Corporation to take over from trams in May 1939 is seen being tested in this way. These vehicles incorporated Crompton West electrical equipment made in Brighton, with 80 hp motors and regenerative braking equipment— a feature now receiving renewed attention, as the energy recovered from retardation was fed back into the overhead, and thus a trolleybus descending one of Brighton's hills could help in supplying power for another which was climbing. There was a total of six braking systems—air pressure footbrake, handbrake, the conventional rheostatic electrical braking capability (obtained initially on the air brake pedal as standard on AEC trolleybuses), the regenerative system, an electrical runback brake and a coasting brake, both of the latter being independent of the power supply.

supplied in 1935, 200 in 1936, 100 in 1937, 150 in 1938 and 141 in 1939-40, plus eighteen intended for Johannesburg but diverted to London Transport in 1942-43.

The 664T model thus outnumbered all other types of AEC trolleybus, with 831 built. The rear bogie originally introduced for the Renown bus proved well adapted to trolleybus work although many features of this and the other trolleybus models differed from contemporary bus practice, being redesigned to suit electric traction requirements. Compressed air brakes were used, for example, this being a feature standardised on trolleybuses before it became widely used on motor buses.

Of the other trolleybus types, the 661T four-wheeler intended for double-deck bodywork numbered 380 by the time production stopped in the early wartime period, large fleets going to Bradford, Portsmouth, Brighton and Reading. 662T four-wheel single-

deckers built amounted to 28, with Darlington Corporation as the largest user, with eleven supplied in 1934-35. The shorter 663T six-wheelers totalled 89, with only a batch of ten for Grimsby in 1936 and three for Canada after London Transport had pointed the way to the 30ft. version in 1934. AEC trolleybus chassis were also exported to all major continents. Russia received two 664T models, one single-deck and one double-deck, in 1935-36, others went to Montreal and Durban, while another surprising achievement was an order for a 662T single-decker for Milan in 1935-36.

Although not strictly within the terms of reference of this book, mention can hardly be omitted of the diesel railcars built for the Great Western Railway, which made a notable contribution to the development of this form of vehicle, then in its infancy. They were allocated the AEC model number 852, between the 851, an eight-wheel cross-country tractor, and the famous O853 Matador artillery tractor. The reason for the odd-seeming juxtaposition was that development of off-the-road vehicles and the early railcars had been in the hands of a separate concern, Hardy Motors Ltd., which was by then a subsidiary of AEC. The first railcar, the famous streamlined GWR No. 1, was completed in 1933, the side-mounted position of its engine, an 8.8-litre, clearly having echoes of the Q-type, though the rail vehicle's height gave room for it to be below floor level. Three more followed in 1934 and

Only 28 of the 662T two-axle trolleybus chassis intended for single-deck body-work were built and Darlington Corporation took delivery of a total of eleven with English Electric bodywork in the 1934-35 period. This photograph shows No. 34, one of the first two, in the town centre, followed by a slightly earlier English Electric, built when that concern produced trolleybus chassis under its own name, before the link-up with AEC. Darlington favoured extremely conservative body styling, the type of bodywork on No. 34 being based on mid 'twenties practice and retained almost unaltered throughout the mid 'thirties. The livery was dark blue, adding to a sombre overall effect.

(Opposite page) The engine installation of the pre-war railcars had a noticeable resemblance to that of the Q-type, with a vertical engine mounted on the side of the frame. The first cars had single engines but later a twin-engined type was introduced to permit the coupling of a trailer car. In this view an 8.8-litre engine can be seen, with fluid flywheel visible under the frame outrigger in the foreground. Note the shallow sump to minimise the engine's height.

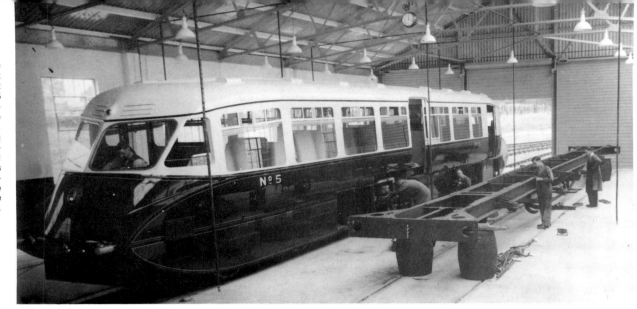

(Right) The interior of the railcar shop shortly after it was opened in 1935. Great Western Railway car No. 5 is seen after return from body-building, together with the frames of two later cars. At this stage the styling retained much of the stream-lined form of the original design of 1933. The factory was conveniently situated along-side, and connected to, the Great Western main line from Paddington to the west.

eventually 38 were built by 1940, of varying designs, most of the later ones having twin engines, latterly of 9.6-litres capacity. I have a vivid recollection of riding in one of the last built when it visited the Newcastle-Wylam branch of the then LNER about 1945 and being fascinated by the mixture of bus and rail sound effects— come to think of it, I still enjoy the sound of the BR diesel multiple units of similar origin.

(Below) The railcar shop shortly after the outbreak of war. Three of the final pre-war design of GWR railcar are visible, with No. 20 nearest the camera. The squared-up lines of the GWR-built bodywork gives an impression akin to that of the wartime "austerity" buses introduced in 1941, but these railcars had been completed before that specification had been introduced. Note the camouflage painting then applied to almost all industrial buildings in a largely unsuccessful effort to make them less easy to spot from the air.

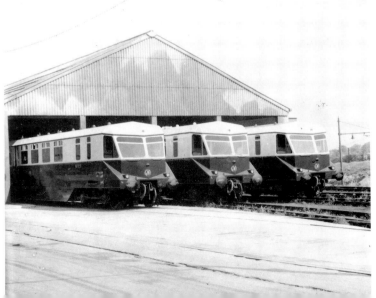

# 8 ORIGINS OF THE RT

Though London Transport was taking delivery of large numbers of STL-type Regents with the medium-sized 7.7-litre engine in the mid 'thirties, its engineers, under A. A. M. Durrant, then Chief Engineer (Buses and Coaches), were coming to the view that a larger engine, more lightly stressed, would be a better proposition for its type of operation. The recently-formed LPTB had immense self-confidence at that time, with an atmosphere which encouraged general progress in the design of buses as it was doing in the spheres of tube trains and station buildings. So a specification for a new double-decker was drawn up, with improvements in passenger comfort and ease of driving as well as reduced maintenance requirements.

The 10T10 Green Line coach on Regal chassis introduced in 1938 gave a clear indication of London Transport's new design philosophy. Instead of the 7.7-litre A171 engine used in the previous year's 9T9 series, a new type of direct-injection 8.8-litre engine, the A180, was fitted, more in a search for durability and flexibility that outright performance, as the engine output to which they were set was well within the capability of the A171. The body design was an excellent example of the highest standards of late 'thirties styling, in keeping with the refined running of the chassis, though it is fair to comment that the deep roof outline looked a little "heavy" even at the time. The attention to detail was characteristic of the period, notable examples being the neat treatment of the nearside front wing, eliminating the usual awkward corner in front of the bulkhead, and the special wheel discs, that at the front matching the rear wheel style as nearly as the different wheel contour allowed. The 266 vehicles, numbered T453-T718, formed the main Green Line fleet from their introduction until replaced by the RF class in 1951-52, although during the war years some were ambulances and others were "Clubmobile" canteens for the US Army.

AEC was requested to begin most of the detailed chassis and engine design work; the project that was to produce the first RT was given the number XU 1631 and put in hand at the Southall drawing office. The new vehicle was to have two key features — a larger-capacity engine derived from the 8.8-litre unit, and an

London Transport's decision to purchase 100 Leyland Titan TD4 double-deckers in 1937, forming the STD class, was to have an influence on AEC engine design policy in the late pre-war period. The then standard Leyland pattern of combustion chamber was adopted for the 10T10 and pre-war RT power units, as well as being incorporated in some engines fitted to buses supplied to provincial customers. However, the influence was not all one way. The London STD buses incorporated AEC worm-and-nut steering gear so as to meet the LPTB specification and Leyland, also influenced in a similar direction by Birmingham City Transport preference for Daimler practice, was to adopt a similar mechanism of its own design on the TD6 and TD7 versions of the Titan. STD 12 is seen here when new — the bodywork was of Leyland's metal-framed design, modified to resemble that on the contemporary STL.

As well as the technically advanced AEC trolleybus, Brighton Corporation's General Manager chose what amounted to a double-deck version of the 10T10 Green Line specification for the 21 Regent buses also chosen for the tramway replacement fleet supplied early in 1939. All the new vehicles had Weymann bodywork of elegant design. Here bus number 71 and trolleybus number 3 are posed with tram number 19 at the Old Steine during the changeover. The municipal fleet carried the same Brighton, Hove and District fleetname and red and cream livery as the buses owned by the company of that title, one of whose ex-Tilling fleet of open-staircase Regents is visible in the background.

air pressure system that would operate the brakes and also the gear-change on the preselective gearbox. A new body design was put in hand at London Transport's drawing office at Chiswick Works and many features of the chassis design were based on joint development work between the two organisations. Much of the original chassis design and the preparation of detail drawings was completed in 1937, in conditions as secretive as had applied to the Q-type.

Development of the engine took an unusual twist. London Transport took delivery of 100 Leyland Titan TD4 double-deckers beginning in April 1937 and it is clear that the smooth running of their 8.6-litre engines made a favourable impression. A new fleet of Green Line coaches on AEC Regal chassis was about to be ordered to replace the 1930-31 petrol Regals and it was resolved that the engines for these would be 8.8-litre units, but with Leyland-style direct injection, using a flower-pot shaped cavity in the piston crown. Thus the 8.8-litre pot-cavity A180 engine was produced. It had seemed that the 8.8 engine was on its way out—AEC publicity material made virtually no reference to it after 1935—and certainly no specific publicity was given to the A180 unit, though this was also produced with toroidal-cavity pistons similar to those in the A173 7.7-litre direct-injection engine.

The 1938 fleet of 266 Green Line coaches, more widely known by the LPTB's engineering code for them, 10T10, than perhaps any other class of vehicles, had A180 pot-type engines (apart from the first six, delivered with A165 units) and preselective gearboxes. They proved to be as smooth-running, except perhaps at idling speed, as the sleek-looking Chiswick-built bodywork (designed by a team led by Eric Ottaway) suggested. The resemblance to the Leyland engine of the time in behaviour was most marked in the medium-speed range. Engine output curves showed a considerable reduction in power from the 130 bhp at 2000 rpm available from the A165, with only 100 bhp at about 1750 rpm, but LPTB, and other operators, were becoming more interested in fuel economy and longer engine life, so this was almost certainly not the maximum output.

Certainly, on the road, quite a lively performance was available. Brighton Corporation chose an almost identical specification for 21 Regent double-deckers which, with 44 AEC 661T trolleybuses, replaced the town's tram system early in 1939. Among the Regents was No. 63, better known by its registration number FUF 63, and later to be preserved by Michael Dryhurst, which I had the pleasure of driving a few times in the late 'sixties. I well recall overtaking two Leyland Atlanteans, then almost new, when climbing hills in the Sheffield area when bound for Halifax in 1968, for example. Gearing was clearly designed to suit hilly routes. but my overall impression was of a beautifully responsive vehicle with well thought-out controls. Writing about it in the August 1968 'Bus & Coach', I said "Overall, it makes one less inclined to be indulgent about the faults of modern buses". London Transport chose the A180 engine for the conversion to oil of most of the remaining petrol powered LT-type double-deckers delivered in 1931, amounting to about 575 units, and these, too, were sweet-running vehicles. The lack of fluid flywheel drag given by the conventional transmission revealed an almost petrol-engine standard of smoothness when idling, and in this respect they were better than the contemporary Leyland engine.

Other users of the A180 engine in Regents during 1938-41 included Aberdeen and Dundee Corporations, Western Welsh Omnibus Co. Ltd. and Johannesburg Municipality. The next step was the A182, of similar design but with strengthened bearings, which appears to have been intended mainly as the basis for the

Both Aberdeen and Dundee Corporations took batches of Regents with A180 8.8-litre engines and preselective gearboxes and Weymann bodywork in 1938. In both cases, the Gardner 6LW engine had established a firm hold in Daimler COG6 buses so the concept of a largish (by the standards of the time) direct injection engine and fluid transmission was well established. Aberdeen's No. 6 (RG 9806) is seen when calling in at Southall before what promised to be a bleak journey north—the absence of the city's name from the ''fleetname'' was standard Aberdeen practice at the time.

engine for the new double-decker. The last three of the batch of Regents supplied to London Transport in 1938, STL 2513-5, are known to have originally had experimental 8.8-litre engines which may have been of this type.

However, the new enlarged engine had a cylinder bore of 120 mm and the standard stroke of 142 mm giving the familiar swept volume of 9.636 litres. This was put into production as the A185 unit, and was the largest-capacity engine used in a British built bus at the time, the nearest rival being the 9.0-litre Albion unit offered in that maker's CX13 and CX19 models. But London Transport deliberately derated it to give 100 bhp at 1800 rpm and the pot-cavity combustion chamber was again chosen, mainly for smoothness.

For the same reason, a new flexible engine mounting system was used. Hitherto, standard front-engined AEC models had used rigid engine mountings, with no more than a thin strip of resilient

These two photographs of the prototype RT chassis, O6616749 (above), and the first production chassis, O6616750 (below), reveal numerous minor differences even though the original overall concept not only remained unchanged but provided the basis for post-war production until 1953. The photograph above was taken in March 1939, after the chassis had completed its brief spell of operation from Hanwell garage (about half a mile away down Uxbridge Road) thinly disguised as an old bus, with open-staircase bodywork and the fleet number ST 1140, and before it went to blossom out with stylish new body as RT 1. The photograph below, taken about six months later, with wartime sandbags and white-painted kerbs evident in the background, shows what was to become RT 2 at nearly the same place. Although some of the differences between RT 1 and RT 2 were trivial, others, notably in parts of the air pressure system, would be enough to make the former somewhat of a headache from a maintenance viewpoint and no doubt contributed to the decision to scrap RT 1's chassis at the end of 1945, sad though that decision now seems from an historic viewpoint. The chassis now bearing RT 1's body is from a later RT.

material to take the edge off vibrations. The Q-type had a more flexible system and some other manufacturers, notably Daimler and Dennis, had used them successfully for several years. The RT was to have a new and very effective system with two ring-shaped rubber mountings, one high up at the front of the engine and the other of large diameter, low down behind the fluid flywheel.

The air pressure system was familiar from trolleybus practice so far as the brakes were concerned, if unconventional to motor bus engineers in Britain, but the air-operated gear change was new, though the vacuum operation on early Q-types had given a similar effect. The powerful spring which closed the brake bands for each ratio of the D132 gearbox (and could cause the pedal to jerk back fiercely if not pressed down to the full extent) was replaced by an air cylinder. Quite a light touch on the gear-engaging pedal would release one gear and lifting one's foot would allow engagement of the next. Pre-selection of the gears was similar in principle to that used previously, but a steering column mounted lever was used, in conformity to the then latest fashion for column-mounted levers on American cars, though the latter had synchromesh gearboxes.

The front-end layout of the chassis was very compact, the

9.6-litre engine being accommodated in almost exactly the same length of bonnet as the 7.7-litre or petrol Regent. A low bonnet level was used, reverting to the practice of the late 'twenties, to give excellent vision forward and particularly downwards to the nearside. A new rather plain-looking radiator shell was specified and was made slimmer on the right-hand side to allow a close fit to the cab front.

Somewhat surprisingly, it was evidently decided to put the first prototype chassis into service disguised as an old bus. So the new chassis, which had a conventional Regent chassis number, 06616749, appeared in November 1938 as London Transport bus number ST 1140 (though it was in no sense an ST-type vehicle) carrying the open-staircase body removed from an ex-independent Leyland Titan, TD 118. It entered service the following month from Hanwell garage, just like the early oil-engine experimental vehicles of 1931-32, continuing until February 1939 without, apparently, attracting any attention from the technical press. It would be difficult to imagine any success with such a ploy today, especially as the vehicle had the then current registration number EYK 396.

A new body was meanwhile being constructed at Chiswick, and its modern lines—again the work of the Ottaway team—complemented the advanced chassis design. Its four-bay construction echoed the Roe body on a conventional Regent chassis for Leeds City Transport exhibited at the 1937 Commercial Motor Show, but the overall impression of modern design in detail as well as the major features clearly marked a big step forward. The completed vehicle appeared in April 1939, attracting favourable

These detail views of RT2's chassis show the snug fit of the 9.6-litre engine in the compact bonnet space. The wooden temporary dash panel was in the same position as the bulkhead of the body. Also visible is the steering column mounted preselector lever, the good steering lock—a London bus requirement and hence characteristic of many AEC buses—and the air pressure brake cylinder mounted on the steering swivel.

reports in both national and technical press, but even the most optimistic could not have foreseen that it was to be over 40 years before the last RT-type buses were retired from public service in London.

However, a commitment had already been made for production to go ahead, for the 150 chassis numbers immediately following that of RT 1 had already been allocated to the first production batch which was in hand at Southall when war broke out in September 1939. In fact the completed chassis did not begin to reach LPTB until January 1940, most being delivered by the end of the year but the last few not arriving until 1941—indeed RT 151, the last, was not delivered until January 1942, well into the era of wartime utility buses. However, the LPTB-built bodies showed no sign of austerity, differing only slightly from that on RT 1. Only one further vehicle with RT-type chassis was built until the end of the War. This was chassis number 06616963, which was delivered to Glasgow Corporation as its No. 723 and registered DGB 371 in July 1940, having been intended as an exhibit at the 1939 Commercial Motor Show, cancelled due to the War. It had a Weymann body, basically of contemporary standard Glasgow style but with cab not unlike the London RT. Another fascinating project that might have been exhibited at the same Show was an under-

Landmark though the body design for RT 1 was, there seems little doubt that some aspects of its appearance were inspired by the "Leeds City Pullman" design built by Charles H. Roe Ltd. for exhibition on the AEC stand at the 1937 Commercial Motor Show, the first such to be held at Earls Court. That had been built on one of the first "1938 specification" standard 7.7-litre Regent chassis, and was Leeds City Transport No. 400. The four-bay body construction and curvaceous front profile was certainly echoed on the RT, but the latter gained immensely from the unbroken lower-deck waistline made possible by its lower bonnet level and shallower windows. One or two details of the RT body were derived from the London STL, notably the concave curves at the rear of both front and rear mudguards and the little staircase window not visible in this view. But overall, it was an all-time classic of bus design.

floor-engined single-decker for Canada, of which the chassis was completed in the early months of the War (see pages 144 & 165).

Meanwhile, in the last year or so of peace, production of "standard" Regents and Regals had continued. "Standard" still covered a variety of engine specifications—7.7, 8.8 and Gardner (Hull specifying 5LW engines for twenty Regents supplied in 1939) and a high proportion of chassis supplied to municipal fleets had preselective transmission. London Transport took delivery of one further batch of 132 STL-type Regents in the summer of 1939, with chassis numbers immediately before those of RT 1-151, having been ordered at the same time. The STL buses looked much the same as those built in 1937-38, but the chassis had direct-

A fascinating picture taken near the experimental department in May 1939. It shows Captain Richard Twelvetrees, a well-known technical journalist of the day, in plus-fours and a somewhat formally dressed Mr. A. S. C. Chattey, AEC's General Sales Manager, discussing an ACLO Regal chassis, one of sizeable numbers then being exported to South America while, in the background, is none other than RT 1, briefly back at Southall after bodying. It is significant that the ACLO had an indirect-injection 7.7-litre engine, by then virtually regarded as obsolete by home market customers.

Hull was a new customer for the AEC-Gardner combination in 1939 when twenty Regent O661G models with 5LW engines were supplied. More were ordered for post-war delivery but standard Regent Mark III models were ultimately supplied. The 1939 buses had bodywork by Massey Bros. to much the same rather flamboyant but attractive style as were then being delivered on Leyland chassis for such operators as Birkenhead and Bolton, suiting the Hull ''streamline'' livery of the period.

injection A173 engines, being the first of this class so fitted, and flexible engine mountings — the latter feature making them noticeably quieter and smoother-running to travel in than standard STL buses. Some 286 of the sloping-front STL buses built in 1933-34 with petrol engines and preselective gearboxes were similarly converted with rubber-mounted A173 engines in 1939.

(Opposite page) AEC had several tries at obtaining orders from Ribble Motor Services Ltd. in the late 'thirties, despite the proximity of the latter's headquarters in Preston to the premises of Leyland Motors Ltd. and although other AEC demonstrators did not remain, this one, KMG 593, was taken into Ribble stock in 1940 and had quite a long career as No. 2380 and then in the fleet of Ribble's coaching subsidiary, Standerwick. The bodywork to the characteristic design of Ribble's Chief Engineer, Captain Betteridge, was by Burlingham. It had an A173 direct-injection engine and an experimental overdrive gearbox — almost all of Ribble's coaches were then petrol-engined.

# The approach of war

About 1,000 more Regents (including the 383 STL and RT buses for London) were produced in the 1939-40 period, bringing the total built to about 7,000, many operators then taking delivery of big fleets for tram replacement purposes. They, together with other

similarly reliable and efficient vehicles built mainly by Leyland and Daimler, stood British city operators in good stead for wartime operating conditions. Heavy passenger loadings and inadequate maintenance facilities due to shortages of staff and materials, and in some cases, bomb-damaged premises, as well as the need to repair damaged buses, combined to put vehicles to tougher tests than had been foreseen when they were built. Among the last

Dundee Corporation No. 112 was a "one-off" Regent apparently built about the time of the outbreak of war. It had one of the few A182 8.8-litre engines with strengthened bearings that formed a stepping stone to the RT's 9.6-litre unit. Little official is known about this vehicle, but the front-end design differed from any of the various AEC styles then in production. The radiator projects noticeably less than usual for an 8.8, a feature also the case on the 10T10. However, the absence of the usual starting handle shaft suggests that it might have had a flexible engine mounting, while the bulge in the bonnet side, just behind the headlamp, is very like the post-war Mark III bonnet's similar feature giving clearance for the dynamo. The vehicle may have been intended as a pre-war "provincial" half-way house to the RT. The photograph shows the registration number YJ 7337, yet it entered service in 1940 as YJ 7586. The Weymann 56-seat body was almost identical to the immediate post-war standard.

Northern General Transport interest in maximum seating capacity prompted the development of a special short-bonnet version of the 7.7-litre Regal built for this operator in 1939-40. The steering column was more nearly vertical permitting the driver to sit slightly further forward and in turn allowing the front bulkhead of the body to be moved forward. The rear of the cylinder block was housed in a metal cowl projecting slightly into the saloon as can be seen from the smaller picture, which also conveys the scant regard paid to passengers' forward vision. In consequence, 38 passengers could be seated, all facing forward on a slightly ramped floor. Although seat spacing was fairly tight, well-designed seats with backrests curved to give a natural posture made these quite comfortable vehicles except perhaps for particularly long-legged passengers. The special body design was another example of the attractive but distinctive styles which were so numerous in the immediate pre-war period. Body construction was split between English Electric, Brush and Weymann, No. 880, being one of the last-mentioned.

exports were six Regents with single-deck bodies supplied to Lisbon in 1940, the first of many AECs for that city.

Regal production during this period just before and after the outbreak of war was mainly concentrated on 7.7-litre engined vehicles. Coach sales to independent operators had dwindled to some extent (the Leyland Tiger having become more universally favoured, perhaps partly because of its quieter gearbox), but some of the company fleets were still taking petrol-engined coaches in small numbers. However, a demonstrator coach for Ribble had an A173 direct-injection engine and was fitted with an experimental D139 overdrive gearbox for a time. There had been experiments with synchromesh gearboxes in 1937, three 1933 STL buses being thus fitted during 1937-39, but nothing more was heard of either

development at that time. A more important innovation was the production of a special short-bonnet version of the 7.7-litre Regal for Northern General Transport, of which the first 53 examples entered service in May-July 1939, and a further 32 in March-June 1940, plus some for the associated Tynemouth fleet. The steering column was more upright and the cab shortened to give more body space, the rear of the engine projecting slightly through the bulkhead and being covered by a cowl. These vehicles thus seated 38 and twenty similar chassis for the SMT fleet had 39-seat Alexander bodies.

In May 1939 South Wales Transport Co. added thirteen Renown single-deckers to the fleet dating from 1933-34. They had Brush 39-seat bodywork having a distinct family resemblance to that on Northern General buses of the period, probably reflecting common initial design in the British Electrical Federation offices in London, even though neither were of the characteristic BEF standard.

Surprisingly, the Renown 664-series six-wheeler had a brief revival in 1939-40. Only one, a petrol-engined single-decker for China General Omnibus Co., had been built since 1936, when Leicester Corporation ordered nine with Northern Counties 64-seat bodies for delivery in 1939 and China General came back for some 26 with Gardner 5LW engines, later followed by fourteen more. South Wales Transport took thirteen single-deckers, and then Leicester took the final sixteen as double-deckers in 1940, bringing

The last Renown six-wheelers to be built were sixteen supplied to Leicester in 1940. Their 64-seat Metro-Cammell bodywork was intended to resemble the Northern Counties products on nine vehicles supplied the previous year, though there were detail differences in cab design, for example.

The British-owned China General Omnibus Co., operating in Shanghai, became a customer for the Renown in 1938-39. This photograph of one of 26 examples with locally-built bodywork obviously influenced by the latest British ideas on styling, and the RT in particular, was taken in November 1939. The chassis, despite what at first might be mistaken for "8.8-litre" appearance, were O664G models with Gardner 5LW engines. Evidently the idea of hand starting was in mind, at least in emergency, for they not only had starting handles but also decompression levers (visible just below the offside headlamp), then available on Gardner-engined vehicles to allow sufficient momentum to be built up before releasing the lever in the hope that the engine would fire. One wonders what the fate of these buses, and fourteen more built a few months later, ultimately was. After apparently surviving the Japanese invasion of China they disappeared around the time of the 1949 revolution.

(Left) The design of units for military vehicles was well under way before the outbreak of war in September 1939. This pair of 6.6-litre six-cylinder engines were the A183 and A184 which, together, powered the Matilda tank. At the end of the war ingenious use was made of similar units by the Northern General Transport Co. Ltd. to convert petrol-engined Midland Red-built SOS 1M6 and SON buses and also the Hercules-powered NGT side-engined buses.

The volume of engineering output of the AEC design office in 1939 seems almost incredible by modern standards. As if the RT was not enough, engines for tanks, a completely new lightweight model and the first underfloor-engined AEC were all produced, quite apart from ''routine'' work on passenger and goods models.

(Right) Although intended primarily as a goods vehicle, this prototype chassis, quite unlike any previous AEC, evidently intended for introduction at the 1939 Commercial Motor Show, had obvious potential in the 26-29 seat class in competition with Bedford, Commer, etc. It was designed to comply with the restriction on an unladen weight of 2½ tons then required to permit operation of goods vehicles at up to 30 mph (otherwise they were still restricted to 20 mph). This view reveals that it had an inclined side-valve six-cylinder petrol engine with coil ignition and hydraulic brakes. The first prototype of the post-war Mercury goods model was of similar semi-forward control layout, though diesel engined (see Chapter 11).

The first AEC to have an underfloor engine was this chassis, built for export to Canada. It is believed to have had a 9.6-litre engine and this was clearly derived from the vertical unit as the AEC motif on the rocker cover was upside down. The transmission was evidently a torque converter, but a small gearbox and clutch pedal were fitted to allow engagement of forward and reverse. Air pressure brakes were incorporated. This photograph was taken in October 1939. The bodywork, believed to have been built by Weymann, was in accordance with transatlantic taste and had the entrance ahead of the front axle (see Chapter 10).

City of Oxford Motor Services Ltd. had been a regular and almost exclusive AEC customer ever since ADC days. Its choice of vehicle design tended to be conservative and at first glance, this Regal, EB 149 (JFC 780), seen in Gloucester Green bus station, Oxford, in August 1940, looks as if it might date from say 1937. In fact it was almost new, being one of five with A173 engines supplied that year, though the Weymann 32-seat bodywork was of a style that had remained almost unchanged since the mid 'thirties; the style of mudguard also gave a slightly dated effect. But Oxford's handsome livery of crimson, maroon and duck-egg looked well, even with wartime white edging on the mudguards. There was no lack of bus travellers in wartime and fuel restrictions meant that almost every bus ran full, even in the off-peak periods.

the total of 664-types built to 345. The Leicester buses had 7.7-litre direct-injection engines, and might have been considered underpowered, but for Leicester's comparatively flat terrain.

On paper, the full pre-war range of models was still available up to early 1940, a **Commercial Motor** list published in February quoting the Renown, Ranger, Regal Mark II and even the Regal 4, of which none had been built since 1937. But production even of Regents, Regals and trolleybuses was drying up as war work became of over-riding importance, and later in the year stopped, on Government orders, though it sometimes took a year or more for chassis to be bodied by concerns who were themselves busy with military work. A couple of A180-engined Regents for Western Welsh delivered in October 1940 were numerically the last chassis completed at this stage, having chassis numbers 06617163-4.

However, pressure from bus operators for new vehicles led to the decision in 1941 to allow manufacture of vehicles for which

parts were in stock or which were part completed. A total of 92 Regents were produced in this way, with chassis numbers beginning 06617173 and ending at 06617289, with several gaps. In quite a number of cases around this time vehicles for which numbers had been allocated were never built. All these 'unfrozen' Regents were to a standard specification, with A173 7.7-litre direct-injection engines and D124 crash gearboxes (though a handful were fitted with 8.8-litre engines from other vehicles by their operator's after delivery) and there were no indications of the chassis having been built to any particular operators' requirements. In fact details of their appearance conformed to what was then the latest standard specification, O661/19. There had been a whole series of these "standards", from 661/2 onwards, but in pre-war days there had been such a variety of specifications to meet operators' requirements that the AEC service department had preferred to record the major unit numbers.

There's plenty of wartime atmosphere in this picture of Western Welsh Omnibus Co. Ltd.'s No. 602 (CKG 124), believed to have been one of the last two Regents built under "normal" arrangements. They had A180 engines and crash gearboxes and were probably the last 8.8-litre Regents produced, though one or two operators converted later "unfrozen" Regents with engines from their own stocks. They had Eastern Coach Works lowbridge bodywork and were the only vehicles from an order for sixteen to be delivered, in October 1940. However, some of the bodies were held in stock and appeared on post-war Regent II chassis.

Bodywork on these vehicles was very mixed. Some received bodies that had been partly completed at various coachbuilders, others were bodied by the operator and others received new bodies of the wartime utility style then going into production. Deliveries were made to some nineteen operators, some being regular AEC customers, but the allocation was by no means always logical. For example, of ten bodies built by Brush to Coventry specification, six went to Midland Red and one to Hull, leaving only three for Coventry, then desperately in need of buses and indeed receiving examples of other makes. Most entered service between September 1941 and the summer of 1942, the largest allocation, 34, understandably going to London Transport, becoming STL 2648-81, though they differed from contemporary LPTB standard in having crash gearboxes. About half received a motley collection of spare bodies from earlier STL buses and the rest a spartan version of the standard STL body.

That was the end of AEC bus production until the end of the War. However, many AEC engines were supplied to convert existing vehicles, numerous operators fitting 7.7-litre units in AEC

The last batch of 661T trolleybuses were ten vehicles for the Notts. & Derby fleet not delivered until 1941-42, though their Weymann bodywork was fully to peacetime standards, though supplied in wartime grey paint. The first to be delivered is seen about to leave the AEC works on tow behind a Mammoth Major eight-wheeler delivering engines, probably for use in tanks, to an unspecified Midlands destination. Regulations permitting towing by such vehicles had just been relaxed.

buses of the early 'thirties in place of petrol engines, some on quite a large scale, and occasionally to other makes of chassis. Moreover, many operators converted indirect-injection engines to direct-injection for better fuel economy, and, in addition to the 7.7, 8.8 and four-cylinder models, conversions were made available for the Q-type engine (used by London Transport and given the unit number A188)—which incidentally cured its overheating problems —and the 6.6-litre A172 Regal Mark II engine, the latter at the

request of Northern General, but providing a basis for further developments about a decade later.

Military vehicle production was the main concern at the factory, the largest single group being the Matador four-wheel-drive artillery tractors, of which 8,612 were built; the total number of military vehicles was 12,896. Production was much more diverse than in World War I for in addition to the variety of AEC-built vehicles, nearly 4,000 tank power units of AEC design were produced.

Engines were also made available for use in new chassis of other makes and in 1943, the A202 unit, a modified version of the A173 7.7-litre unit, was introduced to fit where Gardner 5LW units had hitherto been used, with a minimum of alteration. These were used in ERF and Maudslay goods models, the latter being the first step towards a closer post-war association. Wartime bus production had started in 1942 but AEC's first involvement began in 1943, when Daimler began production of the Daimler CWA6 double-decker, also with 7.7-litre engine but of A173 type as the installation was very similar to that in the pre-war COA6 models built for Coventry. By the end of the War nearly 700 had been built but the model remained in production until 1946.

Then in the summer of 1944, the production of the Bristol K-type double-decker, originally introduced with Gardner 5LW engine in 1937, was resumed but with the AEC A202 version of the 7.7-litre engine, this version being designated K6A. Most of the first W1 series of 150 (a few of which had Gardner engines from operators' stocks) were in service by the end of the War in Europe in May 1945 and the W2 series of a further 100 by early the following year.

No AEC buses were built during most of the war years, but AEC-engined vehicles formed a significant part of the limited numbers built during the latter part of them and such types remained in production for some time afterwards. One of the first of the twenty post-war Bristol K6A buses with the lower PV2 radiator supplied to London Transport in December 1945 is seen outside the Duple works at Hendon when the body, to "relaxed" wartime specification, had been built. The characteristic 7.7-litre style of inclined oil filler is just visible through the hole in the bonnet side, itself an AEC idea adopted by Bristol.

The standard version of the wartime Daimler double-decker was the CWA6. with AEC 7.7-litre engine and Daimler preselective transmission. Its characteristic appearance, with narrow radiator having a wire-mesh grille is well conveyed by this view of Trent Motor Traction Co. Ltd. No. 1111 in Derby bus station immediately after the end of the war, with white-painted mudguard edges but no masks on the diminutive headlamps then standard.

Refurbishing and re-engining old buses was an essential means of keeping the wheels turning in the absence of an adequate supply of new ones. This 1932 Regal of Hanson's Buses Ltd. had completed a million miles when photographed in 1947, but was perhaps a little like the proverbial hammer with new head and handle, for it had been both re-engined and rebodied. Originally an 8.8-litre engine had been fitted but a 7.7 was substituted during the course of a wartime overhaul.

All of these had the original style of tall radiator, but the AEC engine continued to be offered as an option to Gardner and, later, Bristol engines, on the post-war low-radiator series of K-type chassis and the corresponding L-type single-decker until 1950.

These wartime 7.7-litre engines tended to vary individually in smoothness and quite a few had a distinct out-of-balance "thump" which tended to be particularly evident on the CWA6— it seemed that wartime manufacturing standards had been relaxed a little too much.

# Peacetime — production paramount

The return of peace in 1945 found the bus industry with a severe shortage of new vehicles. Wartime production of Guy, Daimler, Bristol and Bedford buses from 1942 had been far below the peacetime total and yet demand for travel was higher than ever, not only for work but also for pleasure—no petrol was available for other than "essential" motoring and, in any case, car ownership was still very limited. It had been announced in March, when even the war in Europe was still on, that small numbers of AEC buses would be available under the wartime allocation system and then that models to be made available would be the Regent Mark II with 7.7-litre engine and later the Regent Mark III RT-type, as it had become known. The reference to Mark III in this context had first occurred about 1941; incidentally the AEC-Ricardo Comet engine had reached a Mark III stage around 1937, but this had nothing to do with the model later known by this name.

The first completed Regent II buses were delivered to British operators in December 1945, but the first chassis numerically were 50 for service in Bombay, with chassis numbers O6617401 up-

The effect of the appearance of sparkling new Regent II buses with Weymann bodywork to pre-war standards of appearance on the streets of Newcastle in January 1946 seemed quite dramatic after the wartime years of drab austerity and lives in the author's memory. By the time the photographer sent by AEC had appeared on the scene the following month someone had decided to remove the front wheel nut guard rings, but even without them, No. 28, in Newcastle's then new version of its pre-war dark blue livery, was a good-looking bus. The conductor, turning to look at the photographer, lets the indicator pause at the oddly-named Two Ball Lonnen before setting it for the return trip to Wallsend on service 13 from the old Croft Street terminus.

Western SMT, not hitherto an AEC user, took both Regals and Regents in the immediate post-war period. These Regal I buses were among the first buses to appear in the post-war red and cream livery. They had Burlingham bodywork—though hitherto largely a coach builder, this Blackpool firm had been one of the main builders of new single-deck bus bodywork for old chassis in wartime and built up a sizeable trade in bus bodies from 1946.

Although it had altered only in detail since 1929, the Regal I chassis' appearance still provided an attractive basis for modern coach body styles. Duple's immediate post-war standard type A coach (also known as FS1) was one of the most handsome of its era, with gently flowing curves which harmonised well with the classic AEC radiator. MMP 171 was one of quite a high proportion of Duple-bodied Regals built in 1946-47.

wards. The gap from the last of the ''unfrozen'' buses O6617289 mostly represented orders which were not fulfilled, though ten numbers from O6617314 had been allocated to Regals rebuilt as double-deckers by Northern Ireland Road Transport Board. From O6617451, supplied to Mansfield District, deliveries of Regent II buses were made to vehicle-starved British operators, mainly company and municipal, most of the first hundred or so having either Weymann metal-framed bodies of the firm's elegant pre-war style with outswept skirt panels or, by contrast, Park Royal bodies of the so-called relaxed utility type, differing little from some supplied on ''unfrozen'' chassis in 1941-42.

The chassis specification, with A173 engine and D124 ''crash'' gearbox, was completely standardised and no alternative was offered, by contrast to the pre-war variety of options. Despite the Mark II in the model name, the specification O661/20 to which these vehicles were built differed only marginally—in the adoption of a revived triple-servo vacuum brake system in the place of the previous vacuum-hydraulic system—from that of the O661/19

models as built in 1941. Even the combination of vertically-slatted radiator and the revival of the louvred bonnet after the plain type used in 1939, had been introduced on the previous model. Differences in the stages of development of previous Regents, now all lumped together as implied ''Mark I'', had been far more important.

Even AEC was confused, for when sales literature for the corresponding Regal single-decker of the type O662/20 appeared, it referred to it as the Regal Mark II. It had evidently been forgotten that there had been a quite different model, the O862, with this designation, and stickers correcting the title of the new model to Regal Mark I were hastily affixed. Deliveries of O662/20 vehicles began about February 1946 and among the first were several batches with Harrington bus bodies of virtually wartime design,

The shortage of new buses led concerns not previously involved in bodybuilding to come into this activity. Air Dispatch was one of a number of firms who were associated with East Lancashire Coachbuilders Ltd. and built bodywork to the latter's design. Cardiff Corporation No. 95 (CUH 371) was the first of ten such buses on Regent II chassis built in 1946, and indeed the first post-war AEC buses with bodies of East Lancs design. Cardiff had been a regular AEC customer in the late 'thirties.

By the time production ceased, nearly 700 of the Regent II and almost 1500 of the corresponding Regals had been built, the latter including quite a number for export to Scandinavia and South America, bringing the original chassis number series to O6618095 and O6625666 respectively. The actual totals of vehicles built since 1929 were 7892 and 5286 respectively, because of the wartime gaps—impressive figures by any standards. However, by this date the Regent II and Regal I were becoming dated in several respects. The rigidly-mounted 7.7-litre engine was not particularly quiet or smooth, though some improvement over wartime had been achieved, but from the passenger's viewpoint, an irritating transmission "grumble" when travelling at certain steady speeds spoilt the effect of what were often attractive-looking vehicles (AEC had returned to pre-war standards of polished aluminium radiators and chromium-plated minor fittings from the first post-war chassis in 1945). In fact the 7.7 engine tended to show up better in other contemporary makes of chassis. The Daimler CWA6 and Bristol K6A or L6A all had even more "solid" engine mountings than the AEC chassis, but the post-war engines were better balanced and neither chassis suffered from transmission roughness—the Daimler benefitting from its fluid flywheel transmission and the Bristol producing rather a pleasant combination of sounds from engine and gearbox. In 1946-47 Daimler also built a number of 7.7-engined CVA6 models, notably for Birmingham and Coventry, the former's 75 being very refined if underpowered vehicles, with effective flexible engine mountings and well-finished bodywork.

Another AEC 7.7-engined model was the Maudslay Marathon Mark III. This was Maudslay's principal post-war passenger chassis and used the A173 engine complete with standard AEC D124 gearbox, but in a reasonably good flexible mounting and here again without transmission rattle. Its success (about 600 were made up to 1950), and that of AEC-engined Maudslay goods models, led to Maudslay's merger with AEC in 1948.

despite the fact that that builder had not been producing PSV bodies during the war period. Numerically the lowest chassis number of a home market vehicle was O6624168, with stylish Duple coach bodywork, one of a number built in the spring of 1946 and delivered in this case to Venture of Hendon. The model was much favoured by independent operators as well as companies, and London Transport took 50 (T719-768) for suburban bus services.

Production of both these post-war Regent and Regal models, well suited in their rugged simplicity to the needs of the time, continued for a couple of years. The last examples entered service in 1948, apart from a few for which bodybuilding had been unusually delayed. Notable among these were some of those for the Midland Red company, which had ordered 100 Regent Mark II models to form its AD2 class during the war. Despite their non-standard appearance (they were designed to conform to Midland Red's own full-width bonnet design), even these were completely standard mechanically and the modifications confined to omitting the standard radiator, bonnet and mudguards, the chassis being delivered with BMMO-designed radiators and the remainder built at the bodybuilders. Brush completed 50 in 1948 but Metro-Cammell was not able to complete its similar number until 1949-50.

# 9 THE MARK III ERA — A GOLDEN AGE

Meanwhile, however, the long-promised Regent Mark III had appeared. One of the 1940 production vehicles, RT 19, had been used as an AEC demonstrator for a year or so shortly after delivery, being temporarily repainted green, and in 1945 the chassis of this same vehicle was updated to resemble the post-war RT standard in 1945.

It was decided that the post-war version would have a toroidal-cavity version of the 9.6-litre direct-injection engine, designated A204. This was not quite so "soft" as the A185, in the nature of the sound it produced and in the performance it offered—at first 120 bhp at 1800 rpm was quoted, later increased to 125 bhp, though London Transport decided to set its engines to develop 115 bhp. London Transport's chassis, coded 3RT, were to have no rear platform extension, the rear of the body being self-supporting, unlike the 1940 2RT version. The AEC chassis type number was now to be O961.

The early allocations of chassis had a somewhat odd pattern, possibly having originally been based on Ministry of War Transport allocations. They were in sequence of sales order numbers in the usual fashion, although not built to order. Numerically the first, and among the first to be delivered in December 1946, were nine vehicles with centre-entrance Roe bodies for West Riding Automobile Co., these beginning the new series of numbers at O961001. However, close contenders for the first deliveries or the first in service were three vehicles for Grimsby, two for Halifax and five for Rhondda, all with chassis numbers over 200. London Transport's first post-war batch of chassis had numbers beginning O961020 and running up to 185, but completion of them was delayed by the decision that bodywork, built by Park Royal or Weymann would be completely jig-built and interchangeable

Early deliveries of Regent Mark III models were on RT-type chassis and although the overall effect was generally good-looking, some of the detail features seemed an odd mixture. Roe built a high proportion of the bodywork on these earliest vehicles and this example was one of eight delivered in 1946-47 to the Halifax fleet, and split equally between the Corporation and the Joint Committee (in which the LMS and LNE Railways were partners), this being one of the latter. The RT-type bonnet top and rear wheel disc were of London Transport style but the front mudguards were more like those on contemporary Regent II buses. The high front bulkhead window deprived the passengers of the excellent view over the low bonnet possible with this chassis.

The 9.6-litre engine in the A204 form used in post-war RT models, complete with fluid flywheel and rear mounting. The RT version of the engine was very "basic", with no air cleaner and no dynamo, the latter being mounted on the chassis and driven from the gearbox.

Transport small-section 9.00-20 size. However, although by no means obvious at the time, this was only a temporary arrangement.

There had been a fair amount of advance publicity about the new model during the war period, some of which referred to the low bonnet level and superb forward vision as among its advantages. I remember getting quite a shock when I saw a catalogue issued around the end of 1946 which referred to a Regent Mark III series 2 and showed a crudely retouched picture of a pre-war Glasgow Regent older than that undertaking's 1940 RT-type. When I first saw such a chassis, its appearance was a good deal better than feared, but I never forgave AEC for abandoning that low bonnet line, both from the external appearance and passenger viewpoints.

So, AEC established the pattern of building, side by side, two versions of the Regent III both based on generally similar 16ft. 4in. wheelbase chassis—the original RT-type, model O961, for London Transport, and the provincial version, originally designated O961/2, for other fleets. It seems clear that behind this lay a difference of opinion between the LPTB and AEC. The RT design had logic on its side in considering the cab design and mudguards as part of the body, but the AEC version provided bodybuilders with most of the cab lower half, as they undoubtedly expected. The higher bonnet line allowed room for an oil bath air cleaner, on the engine, which was of the type A208, whereas the RT, surprisingly for so sophisticated a vehicle, drew air straight into the engine—an indication of dust-free operating conditions in London. Ironically, Leyland, required to build to the RT outline for London Transport contracts a year or two later, showed that it was possible to accommodate a large cylindrical air cleaner alongside the rocker cover.

Another oddity on the RT, again reflecting the "civilised" if intensive London operating conditions, was the absence of shock absorbers or, to use a more precise description, dampers. The provincial Regent III was so equipped and certainly behaved better on bad road surfaces, where the RT version was apt to be very bouncy.

But overall, both models represented a major advance in design with benefits for operator, passenger and driver. Contrary to expectations in some quarters, the complex-seeming air pressure system and, indeed, the whole vehicle, proved exceptionally

Driver's view of the steering-column mounted preselector lever used on Mark III models with fluid transmission. This sectioned view used in early publicity material also shows a speedometer mounted on the other side of the column, but few, if any, vehicles had this arrangement. The drawing makes the selector mechanism look quite complicated, but it merely gave the driver a comparatively orthodox "H" arrangement for gear positions, turned on its side in the manner then becoming fashionable for car gear levers, though lacking the vagueness of many of the latter. The vertical shaft was much longer than shown, of course, the linkage being below floor level.

down to the smallest detail. The first to arrive were RT 402 (Weymann) and RT 152 (Park Royal) in April and May 1947 respectively.

The early post-war RT-type chassis for provincial operators had rather amateurish-looking front mudguards, obviously meant to resemble the contemporary Regent II style, but looking as if they were intended for much larger tyres than the typically London

Several bodybuilders produced special four-bay versions of their standard body designs for the Regent Mark III chassis. Possibly the most successful was the Weymann version with its flowing lines and outswept skirt panels which looked particularly handsome in Sheffield Corporation's livery of cream and blue, with red wheels. No. 260 (KWE 260) was one of fifteen delivered in 1948, the third batch of similar buses for this fleet, to which other examples with Cravens, Roberts and Northern Coachbuilders bodywork were also supplied. The provincial Regent III had a more imposing if less neat appearance than the RT, with chromium-plated radiator and larger headlamps. Note the Regent and Regal Mark III chassis, some left-hand drive, in the background of this picture taken at the AEC works.

reliable. By the time I arrived at AEC, it had been in production for over four years; the weekly quota of about eight RT chassis was always welcomed by the production line workers, who could make good bonus money on them, so familiar was their assembly, and little rectification work was needed before delivery. No significant changes were made to the design and all the 4674 post-war examples had London Transport chassis classification 3RT.

(Opposite page) Not many completed RT buses came back to Southall works once production had got under way, but the publicity department posed RT 2565 for this superb photograph in June 1951. It was a Park Royal-bodied vehicle, but Weymann and Park Royal versions were built to identical London Transport design. The benefit of the front end design being designed and built as part of the body was shown in such details as the nearside front mudguard merged neatly in to the body structure.

Production of RT chassis ended in 1953 and I recall the sense of shock as I saw the "temporary structures" (ie the skeleton cab and mudguards used to deliver the chassis to bodybuilders) being scrapped a few days after the last one had gone—it had seemed that production would go on for ever. They had impressed me when new and my regard for the model, and the pleasure I got from its elegantly functional appearance, and as a passenger from its smooth performance, never flagged.

(Left) The end of a long honourable career. RT 624, 31 years old in terms of original date of registration, about to make the final service run from Barking-side to Barking on 7th April 1979.

(Below left) RT 624 approaching Barking garage after completing the final journey.

(Below) The end of the last duty to be worked by an RT, 40 years after the type first appeared, as RT 624 drives into the garage amid a crowd of enthusiasts.

Going ....

....gone

They were built for a fifteen-year life and so on this basis the last should have gone by about 1969. Admittedly 100 of the last built were stored, proving to be surplus to requirements, for a few years, but no-one could have foreseen when the last one was bodied in 1954 that it would be 7th April 1979 before the last RT ceased normal passenger service when RT 624, new in 1948, made the last run on route 62 to Barking, over 40 years after RT1 had appeared. London Transport overhaul methods meant that units had become intermingled between vehicles of all ages. With-drawals had generally been on the basis of body age or condition,

so in the last few years the surviving chassis, and the units within them, were of varying age. The average was probably not far short of 28-30 years among the final vehicles in service. Yet from a passenger's viewpoint, RT 624's behaviour on the final day suggested that quite a few more years might have been possible, given continued spares availability and London Transports' normal standards of overhaul.

The provincial Mark III did not usually achieve such longevity— nor indeed has any other type of bus— but many gave more than their planned fifteen years. The first examples appeared in

The Regent Mark III soon became a familiar sight in cities and towns all over Britain. This Nottingham example was one of 30 supplied in 1949. They had Metro-Cammell bodywork to a style similar to that supplied on Nottingham's immediate pre-war Regent buses and basically derived from a Metro-Cammell double-deck body standard dating back to 1933. Note the trolleybus overhead and specific reference "motorbus" on the bus stop sign.

service around March 1947, one of the first to be widely publicised being O961629-38 which were Sheffield 527-36, with Weymann bodywork. The series 2 chassis certainly had a more imposing front-end, having a distinct resemblance to the Regal Mark II of the late 'thirties, with chromium-plated radiator shell having vertically-slatted grille, and mudguards with front edge curving gently up towards the full width of the vehicle. However the radiator was deeper and the bonnet had a distinct slope up towards the rear, and the deep top panel being held down by an over-

centre spring and opened by simply pushing upwards on a knob near the front.

Once again John Rackham did some arm-twisting of body-builders and several concerns produced a special four-bay version of their standard body style of the period. The best known and perhaps the most effective was the Weymann version, but the Park Royal metal-framed body of the time, and a Roberts style for Sheffield were other early examples. Roe, which had pioneered the four-bay body on the 1937 Regent Show exhibit and repeated

Operator demand led to the continued production of buses with the 7.7-litre engine, crash gearbox and vacuum brakes but with Mark III appearance, frames and other features. Six Regent III models of type 6811A and hence this specification were supplied to Hants & Dorset Motor Services Ltd. in 1949. They had Northern Counties lowbridge bodywork and were a diverted order originally intended for the Western SMT fleet. AEC vehicles only formed a small proportion of the Hants & Dorset fleet, but AEC-engined Bristol K6A and L6A buses were the company's standard intake in 1948-49.

An alternative approach to fuel economy was the reduction of weight. This lightweight Regent Mark III was based on a virtually standard 9612E chassis with 9.6-litre engine and fluid transmission, yet its unladen weight was only 6 tons 15 cwt. 3 qrs., almost a ton less than usual at the time. Its bodywork was to a special lightweight design by Saunders-Roe, an aircraft-building concern that had entered the bus bodybuilding world in quite a big way in 1946. This vehicle was developed shortly after Saunders had built 250 bodies for RT buses for London Transport in 1949-50. The outward resemblance to the RT outline is obvious, despite the "provincial" chassis, but structurally the design was quite different, with extensive use of aluminium alloy. Unfortunately the Saunders concern ran into financial difficulties and was unable to exploit the possibilities of this venture, which did not give so austere an impression as many of the lightweight buses of the 'fifties. The vehicle, registered OKM 317, has survived, however, and is now preserved after being operated by W. Dodds of the AA Motor Services Ltd. group, based at Troon, Ayrshire, from 1952.

the exercise for later shows, finally got round to a production version in 1950. Sales were brisk and O961-series chassis numbers (which covered both RT and provincial models) of vehicles in service had reached the 1800's by 1948, though chassis were not being built in numerical order, largely because of the congestion at bodybuilders.

Urban operators mostly took to the combination of 9.6-litre engines and fluid flywheel transmission. However, the BET group of companies, after taking a few deliveries for fleets such as Devon General and Rhondda, pressed for the availablility of a version with crash gearbox and vacuum brakes, and this was produced, one suspects with some reluctance, the first customer being the

City of Oxford company, for whom fourteen were built in 1948. It had the now venerable D124 gearbox, with its curious double-sliding third gear, attached behind the A208 engine and a different engine mounting arrangement. Henceforth BET companies tended to favour this version, and some municipalities went over to it.

Other former operators of the 7.7-litre Regent, notably Liverpool Corporation, expressed a preference for its continued availability, again with crash gearbox, and the O681 version of the Regent III was announced, with A173 engine and D124 gearbox mounted in a similar fashion to the Oxford vehicle, in a vacuum-braked chassis retaining the Mark III outward appearance.

The combination of the 9.6-litre engine and crash gearbox was introduced for the BET group but adopted by several municipalities including Liverpool Corporation. This was one of 50 examples of the 9613A model with these features and 27ft. overall length delivered to Liverpool in 1951. The bodywork was by Crossley, which by then had been an associate company of AEC for three years. It was 8ft. wide which, like the length, was generally standard from 1950 although 8ft. chassis were available previously on request. Liverpool already had a large fleet of post-war AEC Regent buses by this date, including 100 Mark II, 125 ''standard'' Mark III with 9.6-litre engine and fluid transmission and 76 of the 7.7-litre crash gearbox version (including the prototype). One of these earlier Mark III buses is seen in the background. The Crosville Bristol on the right of the picture was a K6B model, with Bristol engine, but others of the same batch were K6A buses of similar appearance with AEC 7.7-litre engines, of which Crosville had 118 , plus 97 of the single-deck L6A.

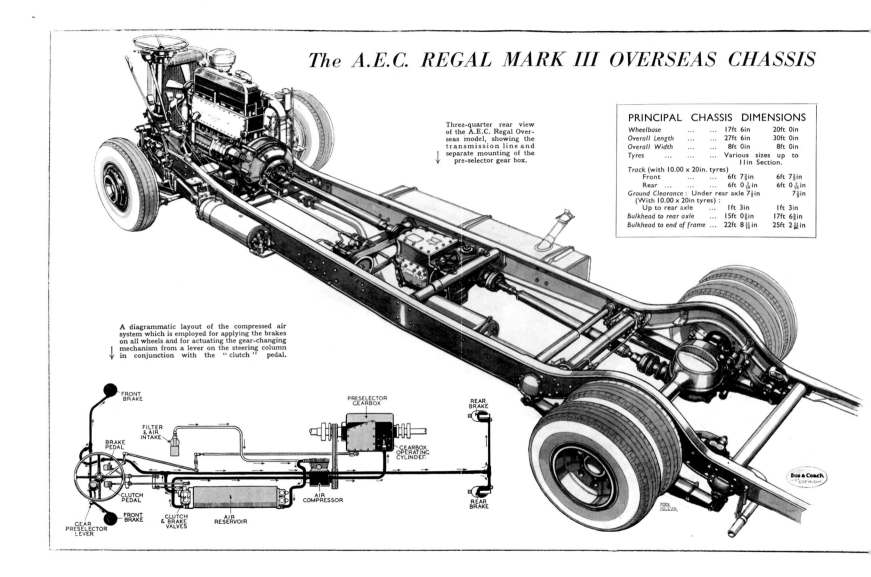

# The A.E.C. REGAL MARK III OVERSEAS CHASSIS

Three-quarter rear view of the A.E.C. Regal Overseas model, showing the transmission line and separate mounting of the pre-selector gear box.

## PRINCIPAL CHASSIS DIMENSIONS

| | | | | |
|---|---|---|---|---|
| Wheelbase | ... | ... | 17ft 6in | 20ft 0in |
| Overall Length | ... | ... | 27ft 6in | 30ft 0in |
| Overall Width | ... | ... | 8ft 0in | 8ft 0in |
| Tyres | ... | ... | Various sizes up to 11in Section. | |
| Track (with 10.00 x 20in. tyres) | | | | |
| Front | ... | ... | 6ft 7¾in | 6ft 7¾in |
| Rear | ... | ... | 6ft 0⁷⁄₁₆in | 6ft 0⁷⁄₁₆in |
| Ground Clearance : Under rear axle 7½in | | | | 7½in |
| (With 10.00 x 20in tyres) | | | | |
| Up to rear axle | ... | | 1ft 3in | 1ft 3in |
| Bulkhead to rear axle | ... | | 15ft 0⅜in | 17ft 6⅜in |
| Bulkhead to end of frame | ... | | 22ft 8¹¹⁄₁₆in | 25ft 2¹¹⁄₁₆in |

A diagrammatic layout of the compressed air system which is employed for applying the brakes on all wheels and for actuating the gear-changing mechanism from a lever on the steering column in conjunction with the " clutch " pedal.

FRONT BRAKE

FILTER & AIR INTAKE

BRAKE PEDAL

PRESELECTOR GEARBOX

REAR BRAKE

GEARBOX OPERATING CYLINDER

CLUTCH PEDAL

FRONT BRAKE

GEAR PRESELECTOR LEVER

CLUTCH & BRAKE VALVES

AIR RESERVOIR

AIR COMPRESSOR

REAR BRAKE

(Facing page) This drawing of the left-hand drive Regal Mark III model O963 chassis first appeared in the July 1946 issue of ''Bus & Coach''. It shows that not only the steering but the complete chassis was of opposite-hand layout to that used in Britain. On the driver's side of the engine only the starter was likely to need attention between overhauls and this could be reached from below, as on home-market chassis.

(Right) South America, a major market for AEC vehicles (sold under the ACLO nameplate) since the 'twenties, became of renewed importance in the late 'forties and was particularly in mind when the left-hand Regal III was designed. Montevideo, in Uruguay, was one of several cities where it was popular. This example was delivered in 1948 to Compania Interdepartmental de Transportes Automotores SA, a small concern operating nine Regals. Note how the local body style retained characteristics of much earlier vehicles.

Meanwhile single-deck Mark III passenger models had been introduced, the first to be publicised following building of a prototype being a left-hand drive export model, type O963. AEC saw a major export market in South America in particular and decided to offer a completely ''handed'' chassis. Thus the A207 engine was a mirror image of the home-market version, with auxiliaries on the right. It thus had a major advantage over left-hand export versions of competitive chassis, notably the Leyland Tiger, on which it was necessary to grovel down by the side of the driver's seat to adjust the fuel pump, for example. This certainly paid off and sizeable export orders for the O963 came in, not only from South America, where an order was soon received from Sao Paulo for 50 and then a further 100 vehicles, for example, but also such countries as Norway and Finland. A left-hand Regent version was also produced and this also used the O963 chassis number series, early customers including Barcelona.

The right-hand Regal III, the O962, was also largely an export vehicle at first, both being available in wheelbase lengths of 17ft. 6in. and 20ft. The first home market examples were mainly for independent operators, and later an O682 version with 7.7-litre engine was offered.

In 1948 it was decided that the system of issuing type numbers to alternative standard versions of the same chassis was becoming

By contrast, some South American Regal III models received bodywork in the then latest streamlined idiom. This example for El Condor S R L of Buenos Aires, Argentina, also new in 1948, showed clear evidence of American car influence. The bodywork was in fact based on framing supplied from Britain by Metal Sections Ltd. and completed by a local firm, Los Andes. It was the first of twenty for service on two routes of 420 and 470 kilometres to holiday resorts.

(Above) The export of six Regents with single-deck bodies to Lisbon Electric Tramways Ltd. in the early wartime period laid the foundation for a long association with AEC. This is one of 102 Regal Mark III buses supplied in 1948. Weymann supplied the bodywork on 32, including the vehicle shown, and Saunders that on 50. At that stage Lisbon had no double-deckers but later fleets of buses were Weymann-bodied Regents.

(Top left) On the home market, the Regal Mark III was often used as a coach chassis. This vehicle, one of two Burlingham-bodied examples on the 9621A chassis with crash gearbox for Eatonways Ltd. of Birmingham supplied in 1948, was typical. Seating capacity was 33, equally characteristic of the period.

(Centre left) On the other side of the world, this scene showing a Regal III supplied to Wellington Tramways, New Zealand, has a decidedly British atmosphere.

(Bottom left) A little under four years after the Battle of Arnhem, with its heavy losses to the British paratroops attempting to establish a bridgehead for the advance towards Germany, the local operator Geldersche Tramwegen placed this Regal III with characteristically Dutch bodywork in service.

confusing. So a new system of four-figure numbers with a letter to indicate transmission type was introduced. The first three figures were the basic type as before and the fourth a series number, similar to the old "stroke" number. Thus a standard provincial Regent III, previously O961/2, became 9612E and the corresponding Regal O962 became 9621E, while crash gearbox versions became 9612A or 9621A and the 7.7-litre models 6811A and 6821A. This was introduced immediately, some batches of chassis having a mixture of old and new-type numbers; the only model to remain unaffected was the RT, which remained O961. Many chassis were being produced out of order and so sometimes early-number chassis had new-style numbers, being built in 1948 or later. No 7.7-litre Regents had been built with the old numbers, so Liverpool's order for 75 began the series at 6811A001, but the 682 series was very mixed in this respect.

The overall picture for the Mark III range was of immense success, and its influence on British PSV design was far-reaching. Leyland, who had adopted a smaller-engine policy for its immediate post-war PSV models, hastened to introduce the 9.8-litre PD2 by 1947 and other makers followed suit with 9-10 litre models in 1948-49. Many cities and towns largely built their post-war replacement and expansion programmes round the Regent III, and if the Regal III was less widely used at home, it played a big part in the export drive needed to help balance the country's books after the financial damage done by the war. In 1950 new 27ft. versions of the Regent were introduced to take advantage of the increase in length from the previous 26ft. and the 9.6-litre models became 9613E or 9613A, while the 7.7 version became 6812A. The later Mark III models, from 1951, mostly reverted to polished aluminium radiators, the chromium-plated shell type used previously having proved less robust. However, some operators preferred the chromium type and it remained available on request.

It would be wrong to give the impression that these models were fault-free, however, and various changes in design were introduced. The water circulation within the "provincial" engines was modified and the unit numbers became A217 and A218 for left and right-hand versions. A curious fault was brought to light by the supply of sets of fluid flywheels and preselective gearboxes (some of the latter, incidentally, being converted and overhauled pre-war D132 units from STL-type buses) to Leyland for incorporation in the RTL and RTW buses that were being built by that firm

(Opposite) Among the lowest chassis numbers in the 962 series to be allocated to home market vehicles were given to a batch of vehicles for the Halifax fleet. However, they were not built until 1949 and thus received 9621E chassis numbers. This one was 9621EO57. Attractively functional Roe 32-seat rear-entrance bodywork was fitted, but within a couple of years or so, such vehicles had become completely outdated by the swing to underfloor engines.

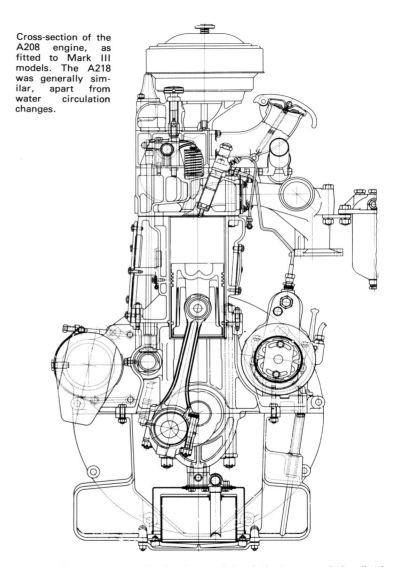

Cross-section of the A208 engine, as fitted to Mark III models. The A218 was generally similar, apart from water circulation changes.

for London Transport. Leyland complained that some of the fluid flywheels were out of balance. Investigation revealed that this was so and thus the cause of a curious "shiver" that had also plagued some Mark III buses was found, firm instructions being given to balance them henceforward.

BUT trolleybuses were a joint enterprise between AEC and Leyland, set up some sixteen years before the merger between the two concerns took place. The double-deckers, intended principally for the home market, were of AEC design. This was the last vehicle of two batches of 9641T models supplied to Newcastle Corporation, photographed at the turning circle at the end of the AEC works drive. It was exhibited at the 1950 Earls Court Show and proved to be the last Newcastle trolleybus. The bodywork on all the six-wheel BUT trolleybuses supplied to Newcastle was built by Metro-Cammell to a London Transport design, the first twenty supplied in 1948 being identical even in destination blind and opening window specifications, but the fleet of 50 supplied in 1950 had Newcastle standard equipment in these respects, as shown here. A left-hand drive 9651T was also produced in small numbers and other AEC-design export models were the 9711T and 9721T.

Crossley Motors Ltd. came into the AEC empire in 1948, and with the similar purchase of the Maudslay Motor Co. Ltd., this led to the formation of the ACV group. A typical Crossley product was this DD42/8, one of two supplied to Southport Corporation in 1950 and among the last built. It originally had Brockhouse turbo-transmitter fully-automatic transmission, a feature found on a small proportion of Crossleys from 1946 but almost invariably as in this case, soon replaced by a standard gearbox. The bodywork was also by Crossley and this aspect of the firm's activities continued for several years after the manufacture of Crossley designs of chassis ceased. The Crossley works was also the home of BUT trolleybus production during the early and mid 'fifties. Crossley Motors Ltd. had begun as an offshoot of Crossley Bros. Ltd., gas and oil engine builders, and Crossley buses had generally had their own designs of engine, latterly an 8.6-litre six-cylinder diesel.

# 10 A TIME OF CHANGE

Meanwhile there had been major developments in other directions. In June 1946, it was announced that a new company was jointly to be set up by AEC and Leyland to design, build and market trolleybuses. British United Traction Ltd. operated from an office in Hanover Square but in practice Leyland's works at Kingston on Thames, used before the war to build Cub models, was the first factory. AEC looked after the double-deck models and Leyland the single-deck range from the design viewpoint and in practice the 9641T six-wheeler and 9611T four-wheeler were developed from existing AEC models. Later BUT's activities were extended to include railcars, though more AEC railcars, for the Great Northern Railway of Ireland, were yet to be built. Any expectation that this association was to lead to a complete merger of AEC with Leyland was not to be fulfilled for sixteen years.

Although British United Traction Ltd. was a separate concern, its trolleybus manufacturing policy was such that AEC and Leyland contributions were quite separate and easily distinguished. In theory, AEC looked after the home market and Leyland built export models. The model designations made the origins of the three basic models quite clear. The 9611T was a two-axle trolleybus, based on the Regent III 9612E bus chassis; the 9641T was a six-wheeler again with Regent III similarities but inheriting its rear bogie very largely from the successful pre-war 664T, while the export two-axle ETB1 was a Leyland-designed model intended to meet overseas requirements for a vehicle with entrance ahead of the front axle.

Though the first signs of decline—notably London Transport's indication that no further trolleybus conversions were planned— occurred in the early post-war period, BUT had considerable success with its post-war AEC-designed range. The 9641T orders started, ironically enough, with an export order for 60 for Durban. A home market order followed for Cardiff and then came London Transport's first post-war order for 77 vehicles, classified Q1 with Metro-Cammell 8ft. wide bodywork to a post-war version of this operator's characteristic style. To simplify production, both Glasgow and Newcastle Corporation took vehicles of almost identical design and LTE then received a further batch, the series ending with more vehicles for Belfast and some for Huddersfield. A total of 598 vehicles was built, of which a few for Cardiff and two Spanish fleets were single-deckers.

Meanwhile, the 9611T made only slightly less impressive progress, with 182 built for a variety of operators, including Bradford, Brighton, St. Helens, Nottingham, Notts & Derby, Reading and, abroad, Pretoria and Colombo, all in the 1947-51 period. Then the model designation was altered to 9612T to take account of a change to 27ft. length and an order secured from Manchester for some 62 vehicles delivered in 1956, the first for AEC-designed chassis for that municipality since the 'twenties, and eight for the neighbouring Ashton-under-Lyne fleet. Finally Glasgow Corporation ordered 90 of a 30ft. version, the 9613T, delivered in 1957-58.

In 1948 there came the purchases of the businesses of Crossley Motors Ltd. and the Maudslay Motor Co. Ltd., followed on 1st October by a change of title to Associated Commercial Vehicles Ltd. for the parent company of the group. The AEC manufacturing side then came under a new company with the official title AEC Ltd., thus recognising the initials by which the products of the Associated Equipment Co. Ltd. had been known almost from the beginning. Mr. C. W. Reeve, who had been Chairman of the latter company since 1933, became Chairman of ACV and Lord Brabazon became the first Chairman of AEC Ltd., of which the Board now included John Rackham. Park Royal Vehicles Ltd., the body-builders, also came into the ACV empire the following year, bringing with it Charles H. Roe Ltd., which had been a Park Royal subsidiary since July 1947. For a time Crossley and Maudslay continued to produce their own designs of vehicles.

# Engines under the floor

At this time interest was growing in underfloor-engined vehicles, and the experience gained in the development of the 1939 prototype for Canada went into a new venture. This was the Regal Mark IV single-decker, announced at the end of 1949, though volume deliveries to operators did not begin until almost a year later. AEC could not claim to be pioneers of this type of vehicle, but the Canadian vehicle pointed the way so far as the generally accepted layout was concerned, with entrance opposite the driver, both being ahead of the front axle.

The Regal Mark IV was really an underfloor-engined equivalent of the Mark III model, with horizontal A219 version of the 9.6-litre engine and air-operated preselective gearbox, and air-pressure brake operation. Officially, the power output of the engine was unchanged at 125 bhp but the uneven injection pipe lengths from the injection pump mounted accessibly at the front of the engine had the effect of cutting output to about 120 bhp. The gearbox was separately mounted and the underslung worm rear axle, unusual on an underfloor-engined model, was very similar to that on the Mark III series.

When designed, the home market maximum length for a two-axle single-decker was still the 1931 figure of 27ft. 6in., so the first home market model was a 15ft. 8in. wheelbase version and an export version with 17ft. 6in. wheelbase was intended for bodywork about 33ft. long. Prototypes of these lengths, respectively right and left-hand, were built and bodied by Park Royal. These

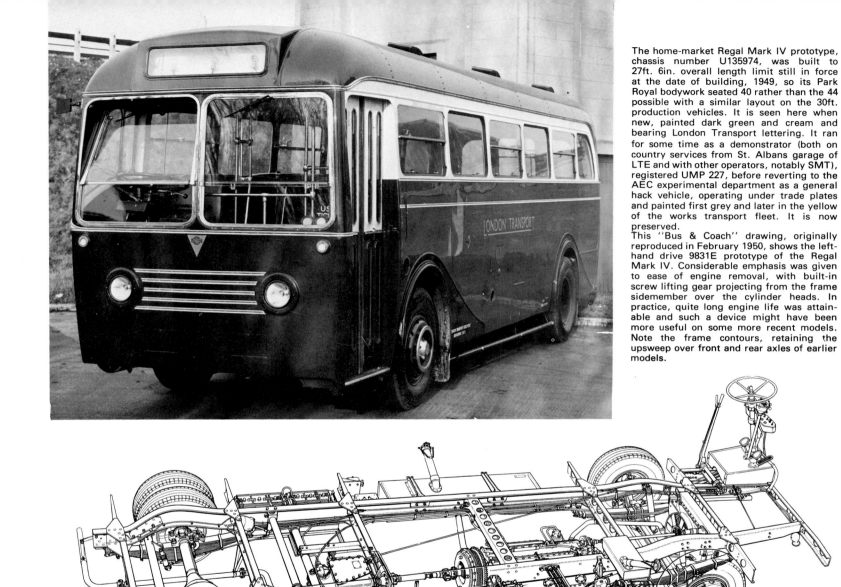

The home-market Regal Mark IV prototype, chassis number U135974, was built to 27ft. 6in. overall length limit still in force at the date of building, 1949, so its Park Royal bodywork seated 40 rather than the 44 possible with a similar layout on the 30ft. production vehicles. It is seen here when new, painted dark green and cream and bearing London Transport lettering. It ran for some time as a demonstrator (both on country services from St. Albans garage of LTE and with other operators, notably SMT), registered UMP 227, before reverting to the AEC experimental department as a general hack vehicle, operating under trade plates and painted first grey and later in the yellow of the works transport fleet. It is now preserved.

This "Bus & Coach" drawing, originally reproduced in February 1950, shows the left-hand drive 9831E prototype of the Regal Mark IV. Considerable emphasis was given to ease of engine removal, with built-in screw lifting gear projecting from the frame sidemember over the cylinder heads. In practice, quite long engine life was attainable and such a device might have been more useful on some more recent models. Note the frame contours, retaining the upsweep over front and rear axles of earlier models.

had chassis numbers in the U series of numbers used for experimental parts, a practice that became usual for subsequent prototypes or experimental vehicles, though the production type numbers were 9821E and 9831E for right and left-hand versions.

The home market vehicle was registered UMP 227, painted in an approximation of Green Line livery and used for demonstration before becoming an experimental department hack. The left-hand vehicle, in blue livery, went to Holland for a time before returning and being sold during the mid 'fifties.

London Transport had delayed its main post-war single-deck replacement programme but now ordered some 700 Regal IV vehicles, which were to be of semi-integral design with their Metro-Cammell bodywork and had many special features to the operator's requirements, so were given the chassis numbers 9821LT001 upwards. By then the overall length limit had been increased to 30ft., but the first 25 vehicles were too far advanced to alter and were the only 27ft. 6in. Regal IV models delivered to any operator. These were sightseeing coaches, and the following 263 were Green Line coaches, almost directly replacing the 1938 fleet. The remainder were buses, the whole 700 being delivered in 1951-53.

The London Transport RF-class vehicles on Regal Mark IV chassis of 1951-53, bodied by Metro-Cammell to LTE specification, lacked the stylish curves and long window bays of the 1938 10T10 class of Green Line coaches but were to proves exceptionally long-lived. This was the first of the Green Line series, most of which covered well over a million miles before being withdrawn. The last few examples of the bus version, of almost identical appearance, survived in service until March 1979. In terms of comfort, they set higher standards than many later vehicles.

These were to prove nearly as long-lived as the RT buses to which they were so directly related. Indeed in terms of miles, the Green Line RF coaches were possibly the longest-running fleet of AEC models ever built. Most of them had exceeded a million miles by August 1968, when in an article I wrote for "Bus & Coach" I reported that failures in service remained lower than on many more recent types, averaging one per 70,000 miles. Overhauls of units were carried out on an "as required" basis, averaging about 200,000 for engines and 300,000 miles for gearboxes—the latter being particular noteworthy, bearing in mind the traffic congestion involved in travelling on Green Line routes across London. Many of the Green Line RF coaches were given a face lift in 1966-67 and it was one of these, with an estimated 1,140,000 miles behind it, that I drove before writing the article, concluding

Once again, South America, and Montevideo in particular, figured prominently among export customers for a new model. This early 9831E-type Regal IV supplied to the C.U.T.S.C.A. fleet was photographed near a recently-built hospital in 1951. Note the use of the winged mounting for the triangle badge, in this case bearing ACLO lettering as usual for this market.

(Bottom left) In the home market, the Regal IV made an impressive coach chassis. Styling of bodywork for underfloor-engined chassis was still in an experimental stage and this Windover design was one of the more striking, inspiring strong reaction, either favourable or unfavourable. This example for the Timpson's fleet was photographed at Harrow school.

that it handled as if about six months old. The only fault that sticks in my mind was a characteristic slight steering kick that resulted from incorrect steering geometry when the driving position had been moved forward as compared to the Mark III design.

The Regal IV was no lightweight and inevitably fuel consumption was fairly heavy by contemporary single-deck standards, the Green Line examples giving about 8.2 mpg despite their modest 30ft. by 7ft. 6in. dimensions. By the time the model was in production operators were beginning to pay renewed attention to fuel economy, as wage costs tended to rise and the first signs of a fall in the numbers of passengers carried was noted. This undoubtedly had an effect on the model's sales outside London. Manufacturers had tended to over-estimate the possibilities of a swing from double to single-deck vehicles, and only small numbers of Regal IV models went into municipal service.

As a high-grade coach chassis, it did better, and the fleet of coaches placed in service on the Edinburgh-London service by

The solitary Regent IV built in 1950. It was sent out on a tour of potential customers and this photograph shows it in Brighton. No doubt the industry's thumbs-down reaction to the Q-type in the 1933-35 period prompted a conservative attitude to body layout—the rear entrance layout was in almost universal favour. The Crossley body was a curious mixture of London RT (especially the interior) with a touch of contemporary Crossley and even Birmingham City Transport practice. The seating capacity of 60 (30 up, 30 down) was no better than several operators' conventional double-deckers and may have indicated weight problems.

The **second attempt at a body design for the Regent IV, by Park Royal, was** more attractively proportioned but retained rear-entrance layout. It was in Leeds City Transport livery and bore the fleet number 800, later carried by a conventional Regent III at the 1952 Commercial Motor Show. However, the vehicle shown barely saw the light of day before the project was abandoned and the bus scrapped. Would a more courageous return to a Q-type body layout have been more successful?

Scottish Omnibuses Ltd., then still using the SMT fleetname, was to remain a familiar sight on the Great North Road for many years, while Sheffield United Tours Ltd. helped to build up its reputation as an operator of international repute with Windover-bodied examples of eye-catching if controversial design. Overseas orders were also encouraging.

The continued preference for double-deckers for urban service in Britain prompted AEC to build an equivalent to the Regal IV with double-deck bodywork in 1950. The engine position of the Regent IV was as on the single-decker, but in other respects the layout followed conventional double-decker practice of the time, catering for a rear-entrance platform and having the driving position over the front axle. The frame height was about midway between that of the standard Regent III and Regal IV models, with a slightly raised portion over the engine. The 9.6-litre engine and air-operated preselective gearbox were standard as on the Regal IV.

Chassis of the Regent IV outside the experimental department at Southall. Note the stepped sidemember over the engine. The short exhaust system, with outlet ahead of the rear axle, was unusual on an AEC passenger model of this period.

A rather odd-looking body was built for it by Crossley Motors and it was sent out to a number of operators to seek their reaction. This was not enthusiastic since the layout gave only a slight increase in passenger space, as compared to the conventional

169

front-engined double-decker of the time. A trolleybus-style full-width cab was provided for the driver and the only gain in useful space was due to the fact that this cab was somewhat shorter than that of the Regent III because it did not have to accommodate the length of the engine.

The weight was said to be somewhat excessive and a lighter body was produced by Park Royal but did not affect the outcome, which was simply that the project never received any publicity from AEC and was quietly dropped, the prototype being subsequently scrapped.

(Top left) One of the most attractive of the early coach body designs for underfloor-engined chassis was the Burlingham Seagull. This example, supplied to Mulley's Motorways of Ixworth, Suffolk in 1952, has the original centre-entrance layout. It is on a Regal Mark IV chassis with preselective gearbox and is now restored—this photograph was taken at the Southampton Transport Centenary Rally in 1979.

(Below and left) The bus that never was. The Regal IV with Willowbrook 42-seat body in the livery of City of Oxford Motor Services Ltd., seen below, was exhibited at the 1950 Commercial Motor Show. It was based on a 9821E chassis with preselective transmission and was not taken into stock by the Oxford company despite being numbered 730 and registered OJO 730, being subsequently sold to Douglas Corporation as that undertaking's No. 30 and re-registered NMN 201. However, Oxford did receive the almost identical-looking Regal IV also numbered 730, seen left, in 1952 as the first of a fleet of ten vehicles on the synchromesh 9821S chassis, though that was registered SFC 730. Oxford's resistance to the preselective gearbox seems ironic in retrospect as that concern had been among the earliest to order a fleet of six Regents so equipped in 1932. Despite its success elsewhere, it seems that the increase in fuel consumption of possibly 10 per cent was enough to deter Oxford from adopting any form of fluid transmission until the era of rear-engined buses in the late 'sixties. The photograph shows it being reversed into the running shed at Southall in May 1952. Note the trolleybus overhead.

John Rackham retired in the summer of 1950, being succeeded by his assistant, Mr. G. D. Robinson. So the Rackham era came to an end, with the Regal IV as the last major model for which he had been responsible. Just how far he had been involved in the decisions behind the abortive Regent IV episode is not clear—he told me that the object of the design was to standardise on components between double and single-deck models, and to give increased seating capacity. But as no more than two or three extra seats could have been accommodated the gain was marginal. Certainly the vehicle lacked the logical basis of previous designs and I find it hard to imagine that he would have been happy with the appearance of the original body on the prototype, though I regret not asking him about this.

There was no immediate change of policy on his departure—major changes would, in any case, have been a matter for decision at board level, but gradually changes in emphasis became apparent during the following two or three years. I arrived in the drawing office as a junior draughtsman in the autumn of 1951, so did not have the experience of working under him, but his influence was still very evident.

The BET group's preference for a conventional gearbox was causing more emphasis to be put on this and less on the preselective transmission, even though the majority of passenger vehicles being delivered were then still of the latter type. Experimental work on synchromesh gearboxes had been going on for some time and, indeed, three STL-type Regents dating from 1933 had been experimentally so fitted in 1937 before reverting to standard in 1939. The Trent Motor Traction Co. had also specified Crossley synchromesh gearboxes in twenty Regal 7.7 and ten Regent 9.6 models in 1950, these being designated 6821X and 9612X respectively.

The first AEC model to be offered with a synchromesh gearbox as a production option was the Regal IV, designated 9821S in this form. The gearbox, four-speed with synchromesh on all forward gears, was mounted separately from the engine—a reversion to pre-1929 practice for a "conventional" AEC gearbox, even though all preselectors had been of this layout. Despite its seemingly modern all-synchro specification, the D159 gearbox had straight-toothed gears and sounded very like an AEC crash gearbox.

Few 9821S models were built because an increase in frame depth for all but LT models caused the model designations to be changed to 9822E or 9822S, according to transmission. City of Oxford Motor Services Ltd., however, did take into stock ten of the 9821S version in 1952, after not taking delivery of a 9821E

The BET requirement for conventional transmission resulted in the specification of crash gearboxes for virtually all Mark III vehicles for this group's companies. This vehicle was one of eleven Regents of the 9613A type originally ordered to replace Llanelly District Traction's trolleybuses but delivered to South Wales Transport Co. Ltd. which had acquired the undertaking in March 1952. They had gearboxes of the "wide-tooth" D162 type introduced as an attempt to overcome failures that had been experienced with the original 1931-design D124 when mounted behind the 9.6-litre engine. The Weymann body was of an interim medium-weight design retaining most features of that firm's handsome post-war standard but of lighter construction—the figure of 7 tons 6 cwt. 3 qrs. being creditable for a 27ft. by 8ft. bus lacking the crudity of finish associated with many light double-deckers of the 'fifties. The RT-style built-up nearside mudguard was an unusual feature. The radiator was the cast aluminium type

exhibited in Oxford livery at the 1950 Show, apparently because of a deep-rooted aversion to preselective transmission.

The crash gearbox version of the Regent III had meanwhile been in service in some numbers for two or three years, and a number of failures of the D124 gearbox had indicated its limitations when transmitting the torque of the 9.6-litre engine. A stopgap measure was the introduction of a version with wider gears, the D162, but the synchromesh gearbox, as used on the Regal IV, was clearly a longer-term answer to this problem. It would also produce a vehicle capable of competing directly with the Leyland Titan PD2 which had been introduced with a synchromesh gearbox as standard in 1946-47. (Ironically, Leyland was at about the

Bradford Corporation set the ball rolling so far as new front end designs for the Regent were concerned by specifying the Birmingham-style "new look" front on 40 of the 9613E chassis supplied in 1952. Crossley was at that time producing vehicles of this style for Birmingham and the chassis went to the Crossley works to be fitted with the front-end sheet metalwork before bodying by East Lancashire. Chaceley Humpidge, then Bradford's General Manager, also specified the Birmingham-style recessed windscreen. Note that this version of the design bore Bradford's coat of arms at the top of the grille and the AEC badge at the bottom.

Kingston-upon-Hull Corporation followed Bradford's example with six Regent III 9613E models delivered in 1953. However, these had Weymann bodywork of much the same style as that shown on the previous page, and followed a total of 80 earlier Regent III buses with preselective transmission and Weymann bodywork then comprising the main post-war strength of the Hull fleet.

same time seeking more effective competition with the AEC, Daimler and Guy models with preselective transmission and purchased the Self-Changing Gears concern to this end.)

A version of the synchromesh gearbox suitable for mounting directly behind the engine was developed and introduced as the D166. The 9613S version of the Regent III was, in effect, the 9613A with the new gearbox. It was immediately adopted for BET-group orders from its introduction in 1952 and gearboxes were also supplied to replace the crash gearbox units in some existing chassis. In fact the first prototype unit was fitted to the Devon

After successful operation of the prototype D166 synchromesh gearbox in a 1952 Show-model Regent III originally built as a 9613A-type chassis, the Devon General Omnibus and Touring Co. Ltd. specified the 9613S model with D166 gearbox for twelve more Regents in 1954. They also had the "new-look" front of the 1952 vehicle, but the Weymann bodywork was of the austere lightweight Orion type by then standard for MCW bodywork built by either Metro-Cammell or Weymann. DR 726 is seen here.

General 9613A exhibited at the 1952 Commercial Show, which gave no trouble in operation on that concern's hilly routes. Some of the early production examples were not so satisfactory and it emerged that some of the problems could be traced to the differences between the painstaking machining and assembly of the prototype by the skilled staff in the experimental department and methods used for volume production. However, this was subsequently sorted out.

That same Devon General vehicle had been a stepping stone in the development of major changes in appearance for the Regent. In 1950, Birmingham City Transport had introduced its famous "new look" design for double-deckers, with a wider bonnet and having the radiator concealed by a somewhat bulbous cowl with a coarsely-slotted front grille lacking any of the usual makers' identity features. It had been applied to Guy, Daimler and Crossley buses for that City and although much of the development work was done by Guy, some Crossley examples had been the first to appear. The style caught on, possibly because of publicity connected with the Festival of Britain in 1951, though personally I thought that the same basic idea had been produced more neatly by both Midland Red and Foden several years earlier.

Bradford Corporation resolved to apply the new-look design to 40 Regent III buses for delivery in 1952 and their 9613E chassis were built without radiator grilles, bonnets or wings, and then sent to Crossley's works at Stockport for the new-look front-end structures to be fitted, before bodying at East Lancashire's Blackburn works. The Devon General vehicle, also with new-look front, was exhibited with a new "Aurora" style of Weymann body (the only example built) at the 1952 Commercial Motor Show. Hull followed suit with standard Weymann-bodied 9613E chassis and Devon General had further examples on 9613S chassis in 1954.

That Show signalled increased interest in lighter vehicles, and although AEC had nothing new on display in this line, development work on new ranges of vehicles had already been in hand for some time. Most of the story belongs to the next chapter, but reference should be made here to the lightweight version of the Regent III chassis, which, though only produced in very small numbers, indicated one future line of development. This was the 6813S, which as its designation indicated, was a 7.7-litre model with the D166 synchromesh gearbox. Chassis weight was pared down by minor changes in design, and the U-numbered prototype chassis fitted with an attractive lightweight body by Park Royal was sent round the country as a demonstrator, registered 7194 H. However, its function was perhaps more to size up demand for lightweight double-deckers than as a sample vehicle for which orders were directly sought, though Rhondda took ten examples.

The 7.7-litre was about to be phased out of production, together with the Monarch goods model which was its principal application by that date.

Reference must also be made to two aspects of co-ordination of AEC activities with those of the other members of the ACV

Nine Regent Mark III models for Coventry Corporation were delivered as Maudslays and received Maudslay chassis numbers 50001-9 in addition to their AEC numbers 9612E4639-47, having been assembled at the Alcester works. They had Metro-Cammell bodywork of that maker's sloping-front style as standardised for this chassis. They entered service in January 1951 along with one of the immediate post-war RT chassis, O961217, which had been delayed until Metro-Cammell could accommodate it as part of the programme to build bodies for RTL-type buses for London Transport.

group as it then was. For a year or two production of Crossley and Maudslay vehicles of those concerns' own designs had continued largely unaffected by the take-over, though I believe AEC engine designers sought to "blow some of the cobwebs out" of the final versions of the Crossley diesel engine. Conversely Crossley had supplied not only synchromesh gearboxes for AEC Mark III chassis for the Trent fleet before AEC's own synchromesh unit was ready, but also a five-speed overdrive constant-mesh gearbox supplied in left-hand drive Regal III chassis designated 9631R for use on the trans-continental Europabus coach service by the Swedish Linjebuss concern.

However, as Crossley and Maudslay production wound down, a curious pretence of continuing their names on otherwise standard AEC-designed vehicles was begun. At the Commercial Motor Shows from 1950-56, some vehicles that had never been near Errwood Park or Alcester carried Crossley or Maudslay nameplates, only to have them removed before delivery to the operator. Possibly the most ludicrous was the "Crossley" Regent III with Roe body for Leeds at the 1950 Show, which formed part of an unbroken tradition of Roe-bodied Regents for Leeds that had begun at the 1935 Show. Sales leaflets were produced referring to Crossley Regents and Maudslay Regals, etc. A very few examples were delivered to operators and a batch of nine Maudslay Regent III buses for Coventry did at least have the justification of having been assembled at the Maudslay works, and hence within Coventry's home county, Warwickshire. But the "badge engineering" phase of the ACV regime did nothing to improve the AEC image and, indeed, must have been embarrassing to senior staff.

A short-lived episode in the AEC story was the "production" of AEC vehicles carrying Crossley or Maudslay badges. This was a ploy designed to allow more vehicles to be exhibited at Motor Shows. The SMMT effectively put a stop to the scheme after protests from others of its members! This explains the "disguise" of these two handsome examples of the bodybuilders art. The Regal III, a 9621E with fully-fronted Duple body, was registered in Coventry in 1948 as a Maudslay demonstrator before being acquired by Greenslades of Exeter. There had previously been "genuine" Maudslay Marathon III demonstrators with similar bodywork. The Regent III was the 1950 model 9612E Show exhibit with Roe bodywork for Leeds City Transport, No. 700, which, like most such vehicles, lost its Crossley badges before entering service, and incidentally remained in the Leeds fleet until 1969.

# Production methods

Before continuing with the next phase of development, it may be of some interest to give an indication of AEC's methods and the general atmosphere in the factory at that date. It had been laid out to give maximum efficiency of production when first opened in 1927, and although various peripheral additions had been made, it largely retained the original concept. The "goods inwards" department was at the side of the factory alongside the Western Region (ex-Great Western Railway) main line, and some new materials came in via a siding from that line, though most by road, even at that date.

Although relatively few complete proprietary units were bought, **numerous AEC-designed components came in from specialist**

This aerial view of the Southall works looking east was taken at about the time the author worked there. The Western Region main line can be seen on the left of the picture with Uxbridge Road just visible at the top left and Windmill Lane running across the top. The drive from the main entrance ran parallel to the main line, leading directly into the goods inwards department occupying the long building adjacent to the railway in the bottom left-hand corner of the picture. From it, material progressed through the various machine shops and sub-assembly sections to reach the chassis assembly line which at that time ran "upwards" just left of the centre of the picture. The row of poplar trees running across the middle distance led past the single-storey senior management and sales building (originally the Associated Daimler offices) and the two-storey chief engineer's department, with experimental department downstairs and the drawing office (in which the author worked from 1951-55) above. The longer bays in the bottom right corner of the site held the chassis finishing and inspection departments, railcar shop, etc.

At the top right of the picture was the service department. Later the remaining frontage on to Windmill Lane was occupied by new spares, service and inspection departments opened a decade later and incorporating the offices latterly used by the Leyland Vehicles Passenger Vehicle Department.

suppliers. This applied to all castings, stampings and major pressings, the factory having no foundry, and only limited forge and pressing facilities. Specialist items such as electrical equipment, batteries, wheels, tyres and fuel injection equipment were "bought out" complete, as were such parts as pistons and engine bearing shells where design was initiated at AEC but also involved the specialist know-how of firms in those fields.

Despite these reservations, a great deal of "manufacturing" as opposed to mere assembly was done. All machining of such items as cylinder blocks, crankshafts, gearbox and axle cases, gears of all types as well as the numerous smaller parts was normally done within the works, as was the assembly of these parts, first into the major units and then into the complete chassis.

The works were laid out so that, for the most part, items flowed in a logical sequence of machining and unit assembly from the goods inwards unloading bays to the "track", where chassis were assembled, on a slow-moving conveyor belt. Thus the gearbox

assembly section drew its parts from the machine shop and was designed so that completed gearboxes were produced at a point near the part of the track where gearboxes were fitted to the chassis.

The vehicle was intended to be complete so far as main units were concerned at this stage, but not yet self-propelling, so it was towed to the chassis finishing department where the wiring and piping were assembled before the chassis was handed over to the department of the Inspection and Dispatch Manager. At an earlier stage, chassis had, I gather, been driven off the track and the department I knew as "chassis finishing" was then devoted to inspection, though trolleybus chassis had always been finished in the latter.

In my day, the IDM was George Skinner, who was quite a character. He had been in charge of AEC Service in Canada and knew all about keeping vehicles in service when there wasn't a factory round the corner to get the operator out of trouble. He set high standards for his inspectors who kept an eye on production at the various stages. Every two or three months, he would pick on a chassis at random and personally go round it item by item, marking any inadequately tightened nuts or other faults with chalked rings. He would then assemble the inspection staff responsible

Interior of the main drawing office at Southall. This photograph was taken in 1933, but the appearance of the office had not greatly altered up to the time I arrived in 1951, though drafting machines, greatly facilitating the work, were beginning to appear. The offices visible in the background housed respectively the Railcar Engineer, the Chief Draughtsman, Chief Designer, Assistant Chief Engineer and Chief Engineer. In 1955 the office was approximately doubled in size, though the end shown was not greatly altered in layout. Whether the expansion of staff that this allowed was justified in relation to what had been achieved previously is perhaps open to doubt.

The author with his section leader, Ray Martin (in white coat), about 1952-53. The window in the background overlooked the engine experimental test house and was about half way along those visible on the left of the view of the office as a whole. The atmosphere in the office was generally as cheerful as indicated, though the more senior management appeared somewhat remote. What is more, there was a sense of confidence in the firm's ability to compete effectively at home and abroad.

and tell them that the customer for this chassis had probably saved up all his life to buy an AEC, and deserved it being put together properly. Sob stuff, maybe, but there is no doubt in my mind that it helped to keep up the firm's reputation. All chassis were road-tested, concrete blocks being used to simulate normal loads. Overhead wires had existed for trolleybuses to be taken round much of an internal test track, complete with gradient, but this was disused during my days at AEC.

There is perhaps a tendency to become starry-eyed about a concern after it has ceased business. However, in my four years at AEC from 1951-55, I can not recall any instance of deliberate lowering of quality or design standards. Ways of saving manufacturing costs were constantly in mind and one of our main duties as draughtsmen was always to consider any new item from this angle. My job in those days was on what was called the production side of the drawing office, where our duties included turning the design side's U-number drawings into a fit state for volume manufacture. Another sizeable and regular task was the conversion of operators' requests for special features, received in typewritten form from the technical sales office, into specific drawings and part number lists. Making alterations to drawings, always the first task to be given to newcomers, and although sometimes boring, gave an excellent grounding into the way the factory worked, particularly as quite an elaborate system was used to record the precise details and inform all departments concerned.

I remember going into the production control department and seeing how the ordering of parts was based on programmes for future models derived from the sales department's estimates of what it could sell. Thus a typical Mark III passenger programme might provide for say 500 basic sets of parts, made up of 400 right-hand and 100 left-hand chassis, split up into 300 Regents and 200 Regals, with 250 preselective gearboxes and 150 crash, or later, synchromesh units. This was all an inspired guess, though very large or long-term orders could be built into the programme, as was the case with London Transport's orders. Not infrequently it would prove to be inaccurate and, say, more sets of one type of transmission put in hand and the balance of the other held over to the next programme, perhaps with a feed-back to the sales department to drum up more orders, using them up by offering better delivery. It was particularly difficult to allow for changing demand, such as the virtually complete switch from front-engined to under-floor-engined single-deckers between 1950 and 1952, and then the further switch to lighter models in 1953-54.

Some design improvements would be brought in when stocks of parts were used up, but others of a more urgent nature were put in hand immediately and any involving safety would call for a "campaign change". In the last-mentioned case, arrangements were made for all vehicles in service considered liable to suffer from the defect to be modified as soon as possible. This happened rarely—I recall about three—but when it did could involve vehicles in Sydney just as much as any operating just outside the factory.

The design of single-deckers and, especially in regard to styling, coaches, was in a state of flux in the early 'fifties, with the well-established and often elegant old order giving way to new uncertainties. NXL 847 was first registered in the summer of 1953 and was one of the last half-cab Regal coaches, being placed in service by Eastern Belle Motor Coaches of London E3. It was based on the home market 19ft. 3in. wheelbase version of the Regal Mark III chassis produced in small quantities from 1950 to take advantage of the 30ft. overall length then permissable (the overseas 20ft. wheelbase was unsuitable because of the British turning circle requirements). In this case the 7.7-litre engine was specified so the chassis type was 6821A. The Duple body was a suitably extended version of that firm's immediate post-war standard design and with the relatively low build typical of that period, looking longer than its 30ft. The vehicle has been restored and is seen at the 1979 Southampton Centenary rally.

The other side of the coin was represented by this "Maudslay" Regal IV, one of the exhibits at the 1952 Earls Court Show. Its Strachans 41-seat bodywork had a distinctly unhappy expression. It was for A. F. Braybrooke & Son of Swaffham, Norfolk, operator of a number of AEC Q-type coaches.

# 11 RELIANCE RENAISSANCE

AEC had been interested in breaking into the market for lighter vehicles since the 'thirties. The Regal Mark II of 1935-39 had only represented a mild move in this direction. A prototype vehicle evidently intended to compete in the under 2½ ton unladen weight goods category had been produced in 1939 and photographs taken at the time suggest that it was to have been exhibited at the Commercial Motor Show due to be held in November of that year but cancelled because of the war.

No details were published, but it is known from comparative studies that it was intended to compete not only with the Leyland Cub and Lynx ranges but also the Bedford. The photograph shows that it had semi-forward control and a six-cylinder petrol engine, remarkably of side-valve layout—not used by AEC for any production model introduced after 1928. It seems very likely that a passenger version would also have been offered and hence there would

This photograph of a prototype chassis for the Reliance underfloor-engined range was taken on 5th March 1953. It was similar to the initial production MU3RV model announced the following Autumn in terms of the units used and their design features, though there was some re-arrangement of layout. In particular, the engine on this prototype was arranged with cylinders on the left of the chassis and the sump on the right; this was reversed for the production model. However, the basic concept of a somewhat simpler and considerably lighter vehicle than the Regal Mark IV—the production chassis weight was about 3¾ tons as compared to 5 tons—was in tune with the industry's changing requirements.

have been an AEC competitor to the much-beloved Bedford OB. Whether AEC could have got the price down to a comparable level is perhaps doubtful.

However, nothing came of the project, though it is significant that the first prototype of a new medium-weight goods range produced by the experimental department around 1951-52 was of the same layout. This was a diesel, with an updated version of the Regal Mark II's ''bootlace'' engine. Then a corresponding underfloor-engined passenger chassis was produced early in 1953. Internal references were at first to model X—an interesting throwback to 1909— but it was later revealed as the new Reliance. At the same time work was going ahead on an integral construction

version in conjunction with Park Royal, called the Monocoach. This was somewhat illogical as the vehicle was decidedly a bus, though there had at one time been a proposal to call one version Monobus.

Both were officially described as medium-weight models and indeed the initial M type letter of the whole new passenger and goods range signified this. The new Reliance was designated MU3RV in the form at first standard for the home market, this new system indicating "medium-weight, underfloor, synchromesh, right-hand, vacuum brakes". In other words, letters were used in place of figures except for the one item hitherto signified by letter—all very confusing. For the first time since 1929, the chassis as a whole could be described as all-new (except possibly for the Regal II origins of its engine), not only in regard to axles but also many smaller parts. The layout was of the by then conventional straight-framed amidship underfloor-engined single-deck type,

The first Reliance to be completed was sent on a demonstration tour beginning in the summer of 1953. Here 50 AMC, which had chassis number U163452, is seen in Torquay operating for Devon General. The Park Royal 44-seat body design was peculiar to this vehicle and, so far as the appearance was concerned, the corresponding integral-construction Monocoach prototype shown below. Though nothing about it could be regarded as objectionable, it had a somewhat bland "characterless" look. This vehicle was painted red and cream in an unusual layout. Its weight was 5 tons 7 cwt 3 qrs., a remarkably low figure by any standards.

The corresponding AEC-Park Royal Monocoach was decidedly a bus and even the use of a Green Line fleetname on the prototype vehicle had an element of wishful thinking, though it performed a spell on route 711. Unusually, for an AEC demonstrator, it was registered in London rather than Middlesex (which prior to the formation of Greater London had separate series of index marks), receiving a number from a series reserved by London Transport, NLP 635. It is seen here at Reigate on LTE country bus service 447. LTE's single-deck fleet had been almost completely renewed so tests on these relatively light underfloor-engined single-deckers—the other vehicles were a Bristol LS and a Leyland Tiger Cub—were somewhat academic.

The new engine design introduced for the medium-weight range, shown here in the AH410/470 horizontal form used for the Reliance and Monocoach. The design was simplified by the use of one-piece "monobloc" construction for the cylinder block and crankcase, but the "wet" cylinder liners, in direct contact with the cooling water, proved a source of trouble, particularly in regard to cylinder head gasket failures, if the engine was driven hard. But for many types of operation, particularly in pre-motorway days, this was not a problem, and good all-round performance was given.

with 16ft. 4in. wheelbase, as on the Regal IV, but lighter than that model in almost every respect.

The engine was offered in two versions, AH410 or AH470, the H signifying horizontal as opposed to the corresponding AV vertical versions used in the new Mercury goods range. The figures, as on all subsequent AEC diesels, referred to the swept volume in cubic inches, this form of designation being a nationally agreed standard for diesel engines at that time, evidently with American practice in mind. Incidentally, and ironically in the light of subsequent events, AEC was at that time changing **from** metric dimensioning of drawings to the use of dimensions in inches, for the same reason. Metric dimensions had been standard since the early days and for many years complications continued as new and old practice co-existed side by side, even on the same drawings — sometimes metric dimensions had to continue to be used for new parts because of the availability of serviceable jigs. Yet by 1968 AEC, by then part of British Leyland, had reverted to metric dimensions for new designs, again in line with national policy. If only they had left things alone .....

The AH410 retained the exact 105 x 130 mm cylinder dimensions of the pre-war A172 Regal II engine, while the A470 had an increased bore size of 112 mm. So the respective swept volumes were 6.754 and 7.685 litres. The standard gearbox was a new five-speed direct-top synchromesh unit, the D171 but for some reason advantage was not taken of the possibility of using a high top gear to give an overdrive effect and I suspect many early Reliances eventually went to the scrap heap with first gear virtually unworn as it was unnecessarily low. The actual gears were still of AEC's typical straight-cut form and characteristic sound effects

The remainder of the chassis was quite orthodox, though the spiral-bevel axle was a departure from previous AEC practice. AEC, despite having pioneered air brakes, did not at first offer them as standard on the synchromesh Reliance. This was slightly odd, because Leyland's chassis in this class, the Tiger Cub, had standardised on them when introduced at the Earls Court Show in 1952. Inevitably, though design of the Reliance was then virtually complete, it was seen as AEC's answer to the Tiger Cub when publicly announced nearly a year later.

There was, however, an alternative version with a new form of air-operated epicyclic gearbox and air brakes, the MU2RA. This

departed from the preselective principle in that the driver simply moved a small lever, and the ratio desired would then be engaged. There was no "clutch" pedal and the system was variously described as "direct-acting", "two-pedal" or "semi-automatic". The principle had been developed by the Self Changing Gears concern (by 1954 under Leyland control) though AEC's version, using electro-pneumatic control from a steering column mounted switch, had been devised in conjunction with CAV Ltd., and was given the name Monocontrol.

Two prototypes had been built, the synchromesh Reliance, 50 AMC, touring mainly company operators, while NLP 635, a Monocoach with epicyclic transmission, spent a period with London Transport. At first it had air-operated preselective transmission as on RT and RF models, but was converted with a Monocontrol unit when this became available. However, LTE did not require further single-deckers at that time, being still in the process of replacing virtually its entire fleet of such vehicles with the RF class on Regal IV chassis.

Orders began to come in steadily if not dramatically. Leyland had the benefit of a bulk order for 500 Tiger Cubs from the BET group, whereas the Reliance and Monocoach were given no similarly headline-catching send-off. But independent operators and traditional customers for AEC single-deckers placed early orders, the latter including Northern General, which perhaps could be

A new Monocoach demonstrator was built for the first public display of the new model at the Scottish Show held in Glasgow in November 1953. It was of revised appearance and set the standard both for production Monocoach vehicles and, so far as the upper part of the body structure and external appearance were concerned, production Park Royal-bodied Reliance models. It was also sent on a demonstration tour and is seen here when on hire to the East Kent Road Car Co. Ltd. in Canterbury, the vehicle on the left being a pre-war Leyland Titan TD4, JG 7017, with post-war bodywork by Eastern Coach Works. East Kent, not hitherto an AEC customer, soon began to place regular orders for Reliance single-deckers and, later, Regent double-deckers to the virtual exclusion of other makes until the end of the 'sixties.

Scottish Omnibuses Ltd., as the old SMT concern had become (though it was to retain the latter as a fleetname for a time), was the first and largest customer for the Monocoach, taking delivery of the first six production vehicles, numbered MC3RV001 upwards, and then a further 50 delivered in 1954-55, including B504 (LWS 908) seen here in Edinburgh when new. All had the smaller-capacity AH410 engine. The Alexander concern also took 50 Monocoaches as well as Park Royal-bodied Reliances of directly comparable specification, revealing that the alleged weight-saving advantage of integral construction amounted to a mere 2¼ cwt. as compared to the Reliance unladen weight of 5 tons 16¼ cwt. As S.O.L. was experiencing trouble with the spring mountings on the Monocoach, future orders were for Reliances and, after a decent interval, the Monocoach was dropped, while the Reliance went from strength to strength.

regarded as godfather of the model since its NGT SE4 buses of 1938 had basically the same engine. Significantly, NGT had taken no AEC buses since the immediate post-war period, and the Reliance soon began to pick up other orders from companies not hitherto regarded as AEC customers, such as North Western Road Car Co. Ltd. and Aldershot & District Traction Co. Ltd.

At first a few quite impressive orders were taken for Monocoaches, notably for the Scottish Bus Group and NGT, but soon the separate chassis Reliance had become far more popular, even though identical-looking Park Royal bodywork was quite often specified. The claimed weight advantage for the integral vehicle proved to be only about 2 cwt. A standard 44-seat Reliance bus came out below 6 tons, and as the Monocoach began to suffer from

A noteworthy Reliance success was the virtually complete standardisation of this model for the single-decker needs of the Aldershot & District Traction Co. Ltd. soon after its introduction until the mid 'sixties. Hitherto this concern had almost exclusively relied on the products of the Dennis concern, based at Guildford within its territory, but Dennis withdrew from the market in full-sized single-deckers in the mid 'fifties. No. 302 was one of 30 Reliances with Weymann bodywork of a type that was to be particularly associated with A & D, delivered in 1957 and was photographed when new at Horsham. The livery of two shades of green and cream was nicely set off by the distinctive style of fleet-name lettering.

structural weaknesses near the spring mountings, the benefit of a conventional chassis became almost universally preferred. The Monocoach underframes complete with engines, running gear and temporary reinforcement, could be driven to the bodybuilders, some going to concerns other than Park Royal, notably U.T.I.C. in Portugal and, in a very few cases, Willowbrook and Alexander.

Within a year about 300 Reliances had been sold and the 1954 Show seemed to be full of them. There was a total of eighteen, though some were masquerading as Crossleys or Maudslays, and almost the same applied to 1956, with fourteen examples. By this date it was clear that the Reliance was the most successful single-deck passenger model AEC had produced since the original Regal, and by the early 'sixties even that record had been broken.

The later story of the Reliance is told in subsequent chapters, but it is significant that the model's success was not tied to any operator or even one group, though BET companies were very prominent among the biggest customers. The original 30ft.-long chassis were very much in tune with the needs of the times. The return of private motoring and the large-scale advent of television had cut numbers of passengers being carried and, with the beginning of the regular pattern of wage increases, had made operators more cost conscious. Lightweight vehicles were very much in

A photograph posed with a pretty girl has always been an effective way of attracting attention to a new vehicle design. This Duple-bodied Reliance supplied to Samuelson New Transport Ltd. in 1958 was typical of sizeable numbers of Reliance-Duple coaches supplied to a wide variety of independent and company operators in the late 'fifties. Samuelson's was a BET subsidiary based at Victoria Coach Station, London. Its main duties, apart from general hire work, tended to be the provision of standby coaches for some of the principal express service operators who ran routes into Victoria.

fashion and yet the Reliance was also capable of giving good performance and fuel consumption even when fitted with well-appointed coach bodywork; if not as refined as a Regal IV, it was usually quieter than a Tiger Cub. Many independent operators thus became AEC customers for the first time, some no doubt influenced by the pleasant handling characteristics, and others returned to the fold. Municipal orders were more modest, but those operators who were favouring single-deckers, sometimes later in conjunction with one-man operation, often chose the Reliance for such vehicles.

Substantially, the AH470-engined Reliance retained its main basic design features until the model was superseded by the AH505 version at the end of 1964. The AH410 version had been favoured by some BET and Scottish company fleets when the Reliance and Monocoach had been first introduced, but little fuel economy was gained and orders for this version tailed off almost completely after a year or so. The Monocoach itself had fallen out of favour after some initial success and was similarly discarded from the range. Heavier-duty axles were the main feature of export models, designated by an L in place of the R in the type code if having

The familiar outline of the standard Park Royal-bodied Reliance was also to be seen in some export markets. This example was in the fleet of Trinidad Bus Service Ltd.

left-hand steering or by a final E added to the designation of right-hand. The combination of synchromesh gearbox and air brakes was made available (model MU3RA) and was standard on export chassis. "Series 2" versions replaced the original from 1959, designated 2MU3RV, etc. and incorporated minor improvements. A version with air suspension, the 3MU3RA, was also introduced but few were built. About 4,000 had been produced by 1962, the majority of home orders still being for the synchromesh, vacuum brake model. The Reliance had thus overtaken all previous single-deck AEC models in popularity, as well as its direct competitors, putting the Company in a very strong position in this market in the last years of the 30ft. limit on overall length.

The Regal Mark IV virtually became an export-only model upon the introduction of the Reliance. It was officially still available in 9822E and 9822S forms for home market operators until 1955 but only a handful were sold after 1953-54. The longer and heavier-duty export models continued to sell quite well, notably to the larger Australian operators, whose orders were large enough to justify special versions of the chassis. Thus the original 9821E and 9831E designations for these models in export right and left-hand form were supplemented by versions with higher series numbers such as those with a heavy-duty Kirstall front axle (9825E and 9834E) and then a heavy-duty AEC 7-ton front axle and dual-

The Reliance brought new customers to AEC, including many who had hitherto standardised on other makes of vehicle. Barton Transport Ltd., one of the largest independent operators, had been a consistent Leyland customer since the early 'thirties but favoured the Reliance from soon after its introduction. No. 740 (SNN 740) was the first, based on chassis number MU3RV027, placed in service in 1955. Alexander, then emerging as a builder of bodywork for operators in all parts of Britain, built the 45-seat bodywork.

Grimsby & Cleethorpes Transport Joint Committee, then recently set up to take over the municipal transport systems of the two towns, was one of the pioneers of one-man operation of full-sized single-deckers. No. 31 (KJV 996) was the first of four Reliances with Willowbrook 42-seat bodywork which entered service in February 1958. At that time it was considered desirable to provide separate entrance and exit doors if undue delay was to be avoided on such a vehicle, where the driver collected fares on an urban service. Other operators with similar vehicles included Chesterfield Corporation and, briefly, London Transport, which had three examples in 1960 for country service operation.

Johannesburg Municipal Transport had been a major AEC customer since the 'thirties and fourteen Regent III models of the 9613E type were added to the fleet in 1952. This line-up outside the imposing JMT premises shows how South African double-decker body designs of that period could be regarded as derivatives of British practice. No. 433, nearest the camera, had BMS bodywork of a design based on an earlier post-war Park Royal standard, while Bus Bodies (South Africa) followed MCW practice, with touches of both Weymann and Metro-Cammell evident in the lines of the remaining vehicles. In both cases, the South African concerns were associated with the British companies in question.

A familiar sight at Southall during the early 'fifties were left-hand drive Regent III buses for the Lisbon fleet. They had been bodied at Weymann's works at Addlestone and painted in grey undercoat but were in some cases stored at the AEC works for quite long periods pending shipping. The body design was basically very similar to the early post-war Weymann standard, complete with outswept skirt panels, but the deep louvres and numerous opening windows gave an indication of the sunnier climate for which they were intended.

circuit brakes (9826E and 9835E). Versions with ZF six-speed gearboxes imported from Germany had similar numbers but S suffix letters—the beginning of a long association with ZF.

Many of these vehicles had the optional 11.3-litre A220 version of the originally standard 9.6-litre A219 horizontal unit and indeed, the 9826 and 9835 had the larger unit as standard. The 11.3-litre swept volume was obtained by increasing the cylinder bore size from 120 mm to 130 mm, the stroke remaining at the traditional 142 mm. This larger size engine had originally been introduced in vertical form in 1949, principally as an export option at first used mainly on goods vehicles, and giving 150 bhp at 1800 rpm, though examples for Johannesburg used the extra capacity to compensate for the loss of power due to that city's altitude and were designed to give a performance roughly equivalent to that of a 9.6-litre engine at sea level.

# 12 THREE-WAY POLICY ON DOUBLE-DECKERS

Although AEC's single-deck passenger model policy was very effective in the mid to late 'fifties, the lack of unity on double-decker design was reflected in a splitting of effort which probably helped to weaken the firm grip of the market that AEC had held in the "Mark III" period up to 1953. In fairness, there was some diversity of thought in the operating industry, too. The cold wind of economic pressure and drop in demand for bus travel made some people think that the day of the double-decker was largely over. Others favoured the use of lightweight vehicles with small engines and relatively simple specification. London Transport agreed about the need to save weight but was looking for more refinement in comfort and ease of driving, building on its experience with the RT. Another line of thought, particularly for company fleets operating in areas where low bridges were a problem, favoured the development of a vehicle with similar layout to the Bristol Lodekka, which had impressed many operators when introduced in proto-type form in 1950, but which was not available outside the State-owned part of the operating industry.

This diversity of thought was reflected within AEC. Much of the design initiative of the successful Reliance range had stemmed from Mr. R. A. (Bob) Fryars, who was then Assistant Chief Engineer. He was the son of the Robert F. Fryars (later Sir Robert) whose name had often appeared on the side of demonstration vehicles as the Company's Secretary, but his own engineering ability was established at an early age when he became a Whitworth Scholar, an award made as the result of outstanding merit in competitive examinations. He tended to favour the single-decker, but there was interest from the BET group in particular in a relatively light and simple conventional double-decker with an engine similar in principle to that in the Reliance.

London Transport was seeking AEC co-operation in its development of the successor to the RT and this was clearly to be an advance on the latter in terms of sophistication—A. A. M. Durrant was still in charge of its team of engineers. Adding another strand was the appointment of Mr. A. J. Romer as Managing Director in August 1950. Hitherto, I have made little reference to the

A considerable amount of drawing office time was spent on developing the radiator grille for the Regent V. The end result had a recognisably AEC character, though the top half would probably have looked better had it been a more direct copy of the traditional AEC radiator outline. This example was on one of the first bulk orders to be received, comprising twenty of the MD3RV lightweight model with Weymann bodywork for South Wales Transport Co. Ltd., delivered in 1955. This view also conveys the noticeable overhang of the front mudguards beyond the slightly narrower-tracked front axle and narrower-section 9.00-20 tyres used on this model.

(Opposite) Maidstone & District Motor Services Ltd., an intermittent customer for AEC double-deckers though a more regular one for single-deckers, took 22 of the Regent Mark V lightweight MD3RV model in 1956. All had Park Royal bodywork, eight, including the vehicle shown, being of the lowbridge type. The curvaceous front-end styling of both body and chassis produced quite an attractive appearance, enhanced by M & D's distinctive dark green and cream livery of the pre-NBC era.

holders of the topmost jobs at AEC because their influence on bus design appeared to be more indirect. For example, C. W. Reeve, who began his specific association with AEC in 1928 as assistant to Lord Ashfield (who was then Chairman), became Managing Director in 1929 and Chairman in 1933, continuing as Managing Director until 1944, tended to concentrate on factory administration and export development though he must be given credit for the highly successful overall policy of the Company. However, Romer had been trained as an engineer and had been involved with the development of the Lodekka when General Manager of the Bristol works before his appointment with AEC.

It was not until 1954 that AEC's double-decker range reflected the changes in thinking. A hint had been given by the lightweight 6813S version of the Regent III and it was a model directly succeeding this that was presented as the centre-piece of the new Regent Mark V range. This was the MD3RV, having the vertical AV470 equivalent of the Reliance's power unit in a chassis mechanically very similar to the 6813S but having, as standard, a new front-end, clearly influenced by the "new look" design, with this time a recognisable "AEC" style of radiator grille. I recall that about seven successive designs were produced in the drawing office

The new style of front end was not universally popular, operators' most common objection being the severely practical one of reduced engine access—somewhat amazingly, the wide front panel became a permanent fixture once built into the body. So some operators took up the option of continuing with the Mark III front-end on the Mark V chassis. Both at the time and in retrospect, the author thought that a more harmonious appearance resulted. This is a City of Oxford Motor Services example, on the first batch of MD3RV models to be supplied to this company, of which the chassis numbers immediately followed the South Wales buses illustrated on page 186. This is L184 (WJO 184), one of three with Park Royal lowbridge bodies designed to have enclosed entrance platforms but, as seen here, delivered without doors, which were added shortly after delivery. The light front axle was again an indication of the chassis type; the unladen weight was 7 tons.

(Below) Front-end designs and their variations were a source of considerable confusion on AEC Regent models during the early 'fifties. The confusion was ''worse confounded'' by individual operators' idiosyncracies. It seemed at times that each fleet would want its own design. Liverpool Corporation had two goes at ''own-design'' versions. The first 100 were based on Mark III 9613S chassis and were placed in service in 1953-55, though this first vehicle, A1 (NKD 501), was displayed at the Commercial Motor Show in 1952. Crossley 56-seat bodywork, very similar to that on the vehicles supplied in 1951, was fitted, but the chassis front-end, also produced by Crossley, was of a full-width bonnet style quite like that favoured by Midland Red.

Liverpool's second-generation new-look front-end was applied to Regent V chassis of the D3RV type, mechanically almost identical to the 9613S, beginning in 1955 with 67 chassis with Crossley bodywork. The front-end, built on the chassis by AEC, had the ''three-quarter width'' style of bonnet, basically as on the standard Regent V, but with a built-up section over the nearside mudguard and having a slatted radiator grille very similar to that on the Glasgow Gardner-engined chassis shown on page 191. This photograph shows one of the second batch of 100 with Metro-Cammell bodywork (though as with the Crossley bodies, assembly was in some cases by Liverpool). The body design was a modified four-bay version of the Orion style.

for that grille before it was decided to adopt what amounted to a slightly modified version of the first one, inspired largely by the contemporary Rover car design. The MD3RV had a four-speed synchromesh gearbox, also derived from the Reliance, and vacuum brakes, but the MD2RA, introduced slightly later, was the corresponding model with Monocontrol epicyclic gearbox and air brakes. Both versions were usually ½ ton lighter than most heavy-duty double-deckers of the period, weighing under 7 tons with suitable bodywork.

For those who wanted a heavier-duty type of chassis, the A218 9.6-litre engine continued to be offered in the D3RV and D2RA chassis (synchromesh and Monocontrol respectively). Significantly, for the first time on an AEC, direct reference was made to the availability of the Gardner 5LW or 6LW engine as an alternative to the AEC units, though only in small print in the catalogue in relation to the D2RA. A specification was also prepared for a 5LW-engined synchromesh version, but this was not publicised.

By no means all operators wanted the wide-bonnet front end, the main objection being the greater difficulty of access to and removal of the engine. So the Mark III style of radiator, bonnet and front wings remained available as an option.

The MD3RV model was, for a time, adopted as standard by several BET companies, notably Devon General, Oxford, Rhondda and South Wales, and batches were also taken by the Newcastle and Doncaster municipal fleets, among others. Leeds was the principal user of the Monocontrol version, with some 80 in its first order and 55 in the next, all of these having exposed radiators. About 500 of the MD-series Regents had been built by 1958.

Leeds City Transport was the first and principal user of the MD2RA version of the lightweight AH470-engined version of the Regent V, and the first of the initial batch of 80 buses, No. 760 (WUA 760), is seen here in City Square when new in 1956, alongside one of the "Horsfield" batch of trams dating from 1931. The Roe bodywork on this batch of buses differed only slightly in appearance from that on most of the later Leeds Regent III buses, and as the Regent V models retained the exposed radiator styling, the overall visual effect was of only slight change.

Just to confuse the issue even more, not far away in Sheffield, the municipal fleet was at about the same date taking delivery of some buses which appeared to be Regent V models but were, in fact, Regent III 9613S type having the Mark V style of front end. No. 745 (WWB 745) was one of 36 having Weymann Orion-type 58-seat bodywork.

The standard 9.6-litre synchromesh version of the Regent V is represented by Eastbourne Corporation No. 49 (DHC 649), one of seven D3RV models with East Lancashire 56-seat bodywork delivered in 1956 and seen here soon after delivery. The 11.00-20 front tyres gave this version a more substantial appearance, which was in keeping with the durability of the A218 engine. In the background is the famous 1939 Leyland Lion No. 12 (JK 8418), subsequently preserved, but then still in service.

(Below) AEC had conducted comparative tests between the Gardner 6LW engine and its own A218 9.6-litre engine in 1951. This photograph of the experimental department's "hack"—basically a shortened Regent III— was taken in September of that year, when it was running with the 6LW. The installation gave an appearance reminiscent of a pre-war 8.8-litre Regent, with the radiator projecting forward by about 3in., and was noticeably neater than pre-war 6LW-engined Regents.

The 9.6-litre engined model tended to be favoured for municipal fleets, notably Sheffield (which undertaking also took some late Mark III 9613S models which, confusingly, had Mark V style front ends), Liverpool (with a further style of front end peculiar to this fleet) and Nottingham (with Mark III-style exposed radiators). All these were D3RV models, with synchromesh gearbox, which were the closest of all the Mark V range to their Mark III predecessors. In fact the only difference of any consequence between the version with exposed radiator and previous standard 9613S models was an increase in the width of the front springs from 3½in. to 4in.—this apparently trivial item was the key feature that distinguished the two series of models amid all the confusion of varying specifications (the wider spring bracket was visible on exposed-radiator models).

The D2RA, fluid flywheel epicyclic gearbox successor to the principal Mark III model, was at first quite rare, but three municipalities took up the option of Gardner-engined Regent Mark V models with this form of transmission in 1955-56. The first was Glasgow Corporation, which laid down a specification for 75 chassis which cut right across any AEC standard of the period, and was designated D2RV6G. Not only did it call for the 6LW engine but

coupled it with the pre-war type of spring-operated preselective gearbox, of the type used in pre-war models, and vacuum brakes—again a feature not found on post-war fluid transmission models. Because of this combination of features, scarcely a unit on the chassis was standard, even though most were adaptations of production items. I happened to have the job of ''productionising'' the drawings as they came across from the design side of the office.

In line with standard AEC practice, I took out new unit numbers as required, including what I believe was the last bus engine number in the old series starting at A101 that had begun with the K-type engine in 1920. This was A228, which was simply a small

This photograph of one of the 75 special D2RV6G chassis built for Glasgow Corporation was taken in August 1955. At first glance, it looks much the same from this angle as any other post-war Regent with fluid transmission. The Gardner 6LW engine is hidden from view—the photographer was evidently not asked to take a view with bonnet open. However, it is just possible to discern the two control rods to the spring-operated preselective gearbox—one to the Mark III-type selector lever and the other to the gear-operating pedal. The cylinder outside the frame just behind the cab was a vacuum brake reservoir

The Glasgow Corporation D2RV6G buses had Weymann-designed bodywork basically of the style asociated with the earlier post-war period. This photograph shows A315 (FYS 621), the first of the 25 completed by Weymann, the remaining 50 were assembled by Alexander from Weymann parts. The frontal appearance of the chassis only differed from the standard Regent Mark V in regard to the somewhat uninspired grille—the 6LW engine was just shoe-horned into the standard structure (which was derived from the original Birmingham style intended for the same power unit).

One of the five buses for Aberdeen Corporation built to the same D2RV6G specification as the Glasgow vehicles is seen here shortly after entering service in 1955. No. 209 (HRG 209) was the last of the series and the last of the 80 chassis of this type, being numbered D2RV6G-080. The Crossley body originally seated 62 but this was later increased to 63. The combination of AEC chassis and Gardner engine produced an efficient and durable vehicle. When Aberdeen found that the AV470 engine fitted in 25 subsequent MD2RA buses required much more frequent major attention, a further five Gardner-engined Regents were produced by converting them, the AV470 units providing a float for over-haul of the remainder.

The final stage in the AEC-Gardner saga came in 1956, when Rochdale Corporation placed 40 Regent V buses with 6LW engines in service. These, however, had air-pressure braking systems and air-operated gearboxes and hence were type D2RA6G, the individual chassis numbers following the Aberdeen batch. Of the total, 30 had pre-selective gearboxes and No. 269 (NDK 969) of this type is seen here. Bodywork was of the four-bay Weymann curved-profile type and the distinctive Rochdale blue and cream livery helped to set off a particularly attractive appearance. Rochdale continued to buy Regent V buses with similar Weymann bodywork in 1957 and 1958-59, but reverted to standard D2RA models with AEC engines. The building in the background on the right was at this period the AEC Service Department's new premises.

size drawing sheet spelling out the specification of the Gardner 6LW engine. This included the Gardner link-type front engine mounting, which together with the standard AEC rear ring-type mounting, gave good insulation from vibration. This time the engine fitted into the standard new look bonnet length of 5ft. The overall result was an efficient and by no means unrefined bus, even though uninspiring in appearance with its plain slotted

grille—five more were also built for Aberdeen. The basic concept was also taken up by Rochdale, though that undertaking's 40 buses supplied in 1956 had air brakes and air gearbox operation, being D2RA6G models. However, the variety didn't end there for although ten had the by then standard Monocontrol gearbox, the remaining 30 had air-operated preselective gearboxes and were the only Mark V buses with this characteristically Mark III trans-

An attempt to attract business from Birmingham City Transport was made in 1956, when this MD2RA demonstrator was built and equipped with appropriate destination indicators to be sent to that city. The combination of lightweight construction and epicyclic transmission was at the time being actively examined by BCT, but 159 JHX did not succeed in drumming any business for AEC. In fact, Birmingham's big intake of buses in the 1948-54 period meant that no quantity orders for new buses would be placed until the early 'sixties, when rear-engined double-deckers were adopted and AEC had no suitable model to offer. So despite the supply of two further demonstration buses—both Bridgemasters—AEC never recovered the place it had held as Birmingham's main supplier up to 1931. However, 159 JHX did found a modest AEC empire as it was the first of several AEC double-deckers supplied to the erstwhile King Alfred fleet of R. Chisnell & Sons of Winchester.

The very last example of what was perhaps AEC's most successful bus, the Regent Mark III with 9.6-litre engine and preselective gearbox, supplied to Ipswich Corporation in 1956. Ipswich had standardised on the Mark III with Park Royal bodywork when it first ventured into motor bus operation in 1950 and it had been arranged that further vehicles of this type would be delivered over a period. Hence the final four buses to complete the order were not supplied until about two years after Mark III volume production had tailed off. Happily the very last vehicle, chassis number 9613E8260, Ipswich No. 24 (EPV 24), was purchased for preservation after withdrawal and is seen here at Southampton's Transport Centenary Rally in 1979. It is noteworthy that it has a chromium-plated radiator of the type standard up to 1950.

However, the distinction of placing the last AEC Regent Mark III in service went to Reading Corporation. Here again, an order was spread in delivery dates and of the last nine 6821A models, five, including No. 99 (LDP 946) seen here, were built in 1956 and the remainder in 1957. These also had Park Royal bodywork, but in this case of the lowbridge type. Thus the last Regent Mark III of all had an engine basically of mid 'thirties design, the 7.7-litre, and a gearbox of a type first produced in 1931, being chassis number 6812A136 (Reading No. 4, MRD 147).

mission. All 40 had standard Mark V front-ends and although I was not an enthusiast for this design, I thought these particular buses very attractive, for the then Rochdale General Manager, Ronald Cox, had persuaded Weymann to build the curved-front body style rather than the by then standard Orion version.

Just to add to the confusion, deliveries of Mark III buses, officially still available up to 1955, lingered on even later in one or two cases, where operators had arranged for supply of buses over an extended period. The last 9.6-litre Regent Mark III was completed in March 1956 for Ipswich Corporation, appropriately being a pre-selective gearbox bus with chassis number 9613E8261. This was the last Mark III of the type best remembered—happily, the vehicle is now preserved. However, strictly speaking, Reading Corporation was the last undertaking to receive Mark III buses as their last four examples did not arrive until 1957. They were, however, 7.7-litre models and indeed had the venerable crash gearbox, so were model number 6812A—perhaps one might call this series ''Mark 2½''. So farewell was said to what was AEC's most popular double-decker, in terms of popular esteem as well as numerical quantity—the Regent Mark III (either in RT or provincial form) will live on in many recollections as one of the best buses of all time.

# The Routemaster

Very shortly after the first Mark V chassis came the first of London Transport's next generation of double-decker. This, rather like a struggling unknown stage performer following the star, had at first an uphill task to build up a reputation to rival that of the RT, but like its predecessor did so by ultimately proving to be long-lasting and trouble-free. It now looks set to remain in large-scale use in the LTE fleet at least until the mid '80s. It was at first given the unofficial designation RT12 but when introduced at a press conference in August 1954 was given the name Routemaster and this was applied above the fleet number RM1 on the cab side in exactly the same way as ''London Six'' had been applied on the LS models of the late 'twenties. At first the Routemaster seemed also to be similar in the minute numbers built, but this reflected the fact that LTE at that time found itself over-stocked with buses, having put the last 100 new RT's into store. Hence the development programme was taken at a leisurely pace, it being 1959 before production quantities entered service.

A greater contrast to the ultra-conservative specification of the 6812A could hardly be imagined than the Routemaster. The prototype, RM1, looked more unorthodox than later developments in the form in which it first entered service in 1956, as seen here, as the radiator was mounted under the floor. However, it was indeed far more advanced in structural and technical specification than might have been thought from its conventional-looking layout in other respects. RM1 officially entered London Transport stock in September 1954 and was displayed both at the Commercial Motor Show that year and an Aluminium Show in 1955. However, the original destination blind equipment was considered inadequate and this and other modifications were carried out before the vehicle entered service in February 1956, though not on the route 1 for which indicator displays are shown in this offical picture.

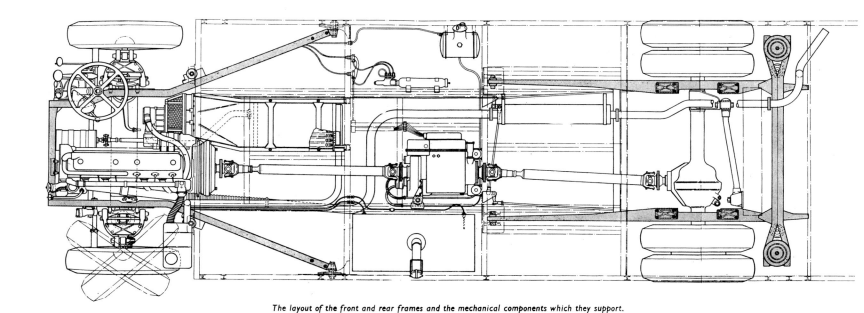

The layout of the front and rear frames and the mechanical components which they support.

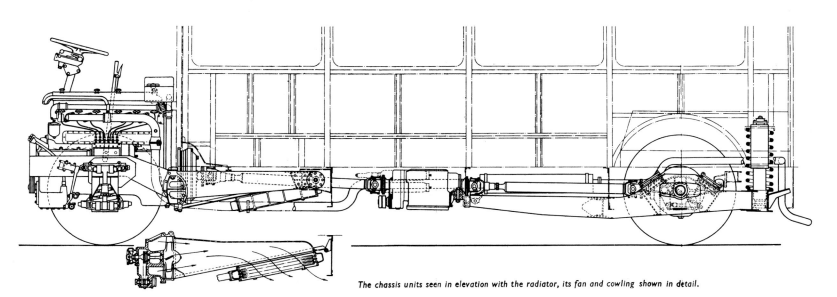

The chassis units seen in elevation with the radiator, its fan and cowling shown in detail.

(Opposite) An indication of the extent to which the Routemaster represented fresh thinking in conveyed by these plan and elevation drawings of the prototype, derived from London Transport drawings and first reproduced in "Bus & Coach" October 1954 issue. Production vehicles differed in various detail respects, most noticeably in the reversion to a conventional front-mounted radiator position. In the plan view the front and rear sub-frames are indicated by shading. The front unit performed the function of the front half of a conventional chassis, but the rear unit formed the rear suspension assembly, pivoted to the body structure just behind the amidship-mounted gearbox.

(Right) The proportions and outline of the original Routemaster provided the basis for the production vehicles, with only minor alterations. This photograph of the vehicle, taken shortly after it was first built in 1954, shows the original small side destination indicator. The low unladen weight of 6¾ tons was not quite maintained on production vehicles, but at 7¼ tons for the 64-seat version it remains as a reproach to designers of some present-day heavyweights. The wheelbase was 16ft. 10in., about 6in. more than on most 27ft. double-deckers.

This allowed plenty of time to try out alternative specifications but, even so, the production bus did reflect the ideas of 1954 in some outward aspects of its design and one wonders what might have happened if a start had been made with a clean sheet of paper in 1958. Under the skin, however, the original Routemaster prototype's most important features still seem thoroughly up to date over a quarter of a century later and many allegedly modern designs still do not match up to its bold concept.

As first designed, it conformed to the orthodox pattern of a rear-entrance half-cab double-decker of the time in layout and dimensions. It was built to the then maximum 27ft. by 8ft. length and width limits. The seating capacity was to be 64, with 36 upstairs and 28 down, and there was faint echo of the Regent IV philosophy in seeking to reduce the bonnet length by fitting the radiator and fan in an underfloor position.

Aluminium alloy integral construction was used to bring the weight down and indeed the Routemaster proved to be one of the few integral vehicles which showed a worthwhile weight reduction compared to its predecessor with conventional chassis, thanks more to the constructional material and its intelligent use than the lack of a full length frame. There was, in fact, a front sub-frame almost equivalent to the front end of a conventional chassis which carried the engine, front suspension and steering etc. At the rear, what appeared at first glance to be another "half frame" was in fact the rear suspension assembly, pivoted at its front end from near the middle of the floor assembly and supporting the rear end of the vehicle via coil springs mounted under the rear of the longitudinal seats over the rear wheel arches.

Coil springs were also used for the front suspension, but this broke new ground by being independent for each wheel, by then common on cars but not hitherto applied to a double-decker bus —

indeed, in Britain at least, only Midland Red had got as far as applying it to a single-decker intended for production.

Having revolutionised the industry's thinking on motor bus braking with the RT's air pressure system, the LTE took a similarly bold step with the power hydraulic system for the RM, though in this case Midland Red had led the way with its post-war models. Daimler had also introduced a similar system some years earlier on the CD650 model, but most operators had, so far, proved more sceptical about this than the air system of the original AEC Mark III designs. It differed from either car-type hydraulic systems or the pre-war vacuum-hydraulic bus brakes in having a hydraulic pump to give the required pressure rather than merely using hydraulic means to convey the movement.

On the first prototype the engine was a 9.6-litre unit very similar to the RT model's A204 and the epicyclic gearbox, although similar in effect to the AEC Monocontrol unit, was hydraulically operated from its own pump. Despite this quite elaborate specification, the unladen weight of RM1 was just under 6 tons 15 cwt., or ¾ ton lighter than the post-war RT. The vehicle had been built at Chiswick "with the combined help of AEC and Park Royal" to quote a contemporary account. Apart from the fairly standard engine and worm and nut steering, AEC involvement included a fair amount of the detailed mechanical design and manufacture of mechanical components.

RM1 appeared on the AEC stand at the 1954 Commercial Motor Show, but did not enter service until February 1956, and meanwhile RM2 had been built, differing mainly in at first having an AV470 engine. Two further RM prototypes were built in 1956-57, RML3 being bodied by Weymann with Leyland engine and other mechanical units and CRL4, a Green Line Coach version, by Eastern Coach Works, again with Leyland units. However, before

The production Routemaster incorporated the then recently introduced AV590 version of the 9.6-litre engine as well as being revised in frontal appearance following the decision to revert to a front-mounted radiator. Although London Transport experienced some teething troubles, particularly until the techniques of maintaining the power-hydraulic brake system had become established, it soon settled down to become an exceptionally reliable, as well as comfortable, vehicle.

they had entered service it had been decided in 1956 that the first order for 850 Routemasters should be produced by Park Royal, with AEC mechanical units, and although a minority of later examples had Leyland O.600 engines all the production vehicles were AEC-Park Royal products.

Production began in 1958 and the first complete vehicle, RM8, was at the 1958 Commercial Motor Show. By then the specification had changed somewhat. The maximum legal length for a double-decker had gone up to 30ft. in July 1956 and although no attempt was then made to take full advantage of this, LTE at the time considering 64 seats the optimum size, the radiator was moved to a more conventional position in front of the engine, the prototypes having been modified accordingly, and the length increased by about 4in. The original post-war series of 9.6-litre engines had been replaced by a new AV590 unit from 1958. This retained the cylinder dimensions of the previous unit but constructionally was a scaled-

up version of the AV470, with monobloc construction and wet cylinder liners. Production Routemasters were fitted with this engine, set to the same 115 bhp output and 1800 rpm governed speed as the post-war RT buses.

AEC was not prepared to put the hydraulically-operated gearbox into production, choosing to standardise on electro-pneumatically controlled Monocontrol design. Reluctantly, LTE agreed to this and an air compressor, reservoir, etc. had to be fitted to operate the gearbox, despite the purely hydraulic brake system, and hydraulically-assisted steering. By this date London Transport had decided to standardise on fully-automatic operation, the steering-column lever (of a design peculiar to the Routemaster) also having positions for manual selection of all but top gear. An unusual feature of the design was the handbrake, a typically AEC long lever, but to the left of the driver's seat, reminiscent of mid 'thirties Bristol practice. The result was an exceptionally easy and pleasant bus to drive, while the passenger gained from the much better ride given by the independent front suspension and the greatly reduced tendency to roll on corners compared to other double-deckers. The interior trim of the body was attractively finished and yet the production vehicles, slightly more complex than the 1954 prototype, weighed only 7 tons 5 cwt.

AEC's contribution to the finished vehicle consisted of the front and rear sub-frame assemblies, plus the gearbox, which was mounted directly to the body structure. The sets of units were given ''chassis'' numbers in a series prefixed R2RH in the usual AEC system. Production, once started, was rapid and by 1962, with well over 1,100 vehicles built, Routemasters had been used to replace virtually the whole of London's trolleybus system.

# The Bridgemaster

As if building the Routemaster alongside the very different Regent V was not complicated enough, a third type of double-decker, different again, was also in course of development in the mid 'fifties. Its design was another joint AEC-Park Royal enterprise, but, hardly surprisingly in view of the amount of work in hand at Southall and Park Royal, the detailed development was farmed out to Crossley and the first prototype vehicle was, for once, not merely an exercise in badge engineering when it appeared at the 1956 Commercial Motor Show bearing a Crossley nameplate. This was the Bridgemaster, clearly intended as AEC's answer to the Lodekka. It shared with that model the concept of a low floor, allowing centre gangway layout in both decks within a low height,

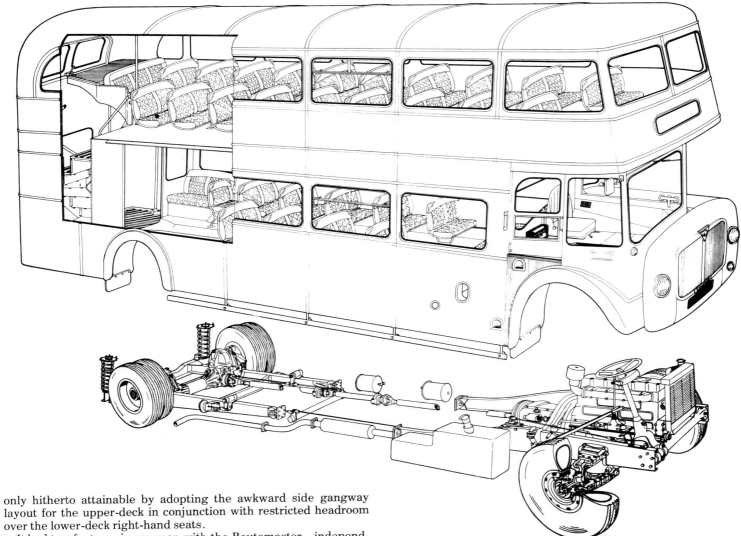

only hitherto attainable by adopting the awkward side gangway layout for the upper-deck in conjunction with restricted headroom over the lower-deck right-hand seats.

It had two features in common with the Routemaster — independent front and rear coil suspension and an integral body structure. In other respects the prototype was more akin to the standard AV470-engined version of the Regent V, with synchromesh gearbox, though it had an air-hydraulic brake system, differing from any other AEC design. By the time it appeared, a length increase to 30ft. had become possible and was incorporated in the vehicle on display. However, it was realised that a larger engine would be needed, but the new AV590, though actually in existence in

This "exploded" drawing formed part of the publicity material issued when the Bridgemaster was introduced. It shows that it shared the two-subframe concept and use of coil suspension, independent for the front wheels, with the Routemaster. But it differed both in other aspects of the specification (with drop-centre rear axle, AV470 engine and synchromesh gearbox) and even in the detailed execution of those features in which it was similar. The low-floor layout implied the use of a rearward-facing front passenger seat in the lower saloon to provide clearance for the gearbox and the oddly-shaped fuel tank was designed also to take advantage of this arrangement.

There was more than badge engineering behind the display of the first Bridgemaster on the Crossley stand at the 1956 Earls Court Show, for the detailed development had been carried out at the Crossley works, even though the basic design was a joint AEC-Park Royal venture. It was to be delivered to Walsall Corporation and hence was one of many Show vehicles built in the 'fifties which were in that undertaking's distinctive all-blue livery. It is seen on the left in this picture. Visible beyond it is one of the first 30ft. Regent V models, for F. C. Cottrell of Micheldean, Gloucestershire, the chassis of this being a purely Southall product which carried Crossley badges for display purposes — even the body was by Park Royal. The Mercury goods vehicle in the foreground was for the London Brick Co. Ltd., a long-standing AEC customer, and looked, if anything, even more out of place on the Crossley stand.

(Below) The original Bridgemaster was quite an attractive-looking vehicle, with a mildly-curved profile which matched well with the rounded bonnet contours. This was the second vehicle built, subsequently registered as 9 JML as the first of some six Bridgemaster demonstrators, and present at the demonstration park at Earls Court for the 1956 Show before going to Birmingham, firstly on trial and then being taken into stock during 1957. It remained in the fleet until 1969, but having regard to Birmingham's lack of enthusiasm for synchromesh gearboxes based on past experience, there was little chance of more being ordered, even before BCT turned to rear-engined buses.

The rear axle assembly of the Bridgemaster. The axle itself was of the drop-centre type, with gearing each side of a low-level centre portion, of much the same pattern as used on most of the low-floor double-deckers of the 'fifties onwards — the principle was, however, a modern counterpart of that used on the NS, over 30 years earlier. The suspension layout, with the axle mounted on a pivoted framework and supporting the body on the coil springs at the rear, is also clearly shown.

Lower deck interior of an early Bridgemaster. A sunken gangway helped to keep the overall height down and the rearward-facing front seat is evident. As usual with front-engined low-floor buses, forward vision from the passenger seats was poor, despite the exaggerated sweep of the bulkhead windows. Note the forward-facing seats alongside the rear wheel arches.

The first vehicle, with chassis number MB3RA001, was one of numerous Show vehicles built for the Walsall Corporation fleet during the period when Edgley Cox—no relation to Ronald—was General Manager. It was numbered 825 (YDH 825) and as it turned out the second Bridgemaster built as a demonstrator and registered 9 JML, was taken into stock by neighbouring Birmingham City Transport as No. 3228 the following year. However, the change to the larger AV590 engine delayed production and only a handful of B3RA buses with this unit had been produced before there were further upheavals. Manufacture was transferred to Park Royal and a switch to steel framing and the flat-fronted frameless dome construction by then familiar on MCW bodies helped to delay manufacture in any quantity until 1958, as well as converting possibly the neatest low-floor design into a curiously clumsy-looking vehicle.

The changes in construction had been at the request of S. C. Vince, then BET's Chief Engineer, who favoured steel construct-

By July 1958, when this photograph of what was then the latest Bridgemaster demonstrator was taken, there had been major changes to its design. In deference to BET preferences, a steel-framed structure with frameless front dome had been adopted. A much more aggressively harsh profile replaced the graceful curves of the original. This particular vehicle had been equipped and painted for a year's trial with Liverpool Corporation as that undertaking's experimental fleet number E3. It was registered 116 TMD but when it arrived in Liverpool the crews took a dislike to it, refusing to take standing passengers, so it was almost immediately returned, taking up demonstration duties in other towns.

prototype form, was not ready for public announcement. Incidentally, it is amusing to note that it was at first called the AV600 within AEC—presumably it was then decided that this was a little too close to the then rival Leyland concern's O.600 for comfort. By this date I had left AEC, though I recall Bridgemaster drawings being in evidence at least a year before the model was announced.

The low floor was achieved by adding a transfer gearbox to the back of the gearbox and using a drop-centre rear axle, similar in principle to that of the Lodekka. In other respects the general mechanical concept had a resemblance to the Routemaster, with "sawn-off" front chassis sub-frame and the use of the long trailing rear suspension framework with coil springs behind the rear wheels. Yet comparatively few parts were actually common to the two models and little, if any, attempt seemed to be made to co-ordinate their design. Similar remarks applied to the body; at first the Bridgemaster incorporated a largely aluminium alloy structure which incidentally helped to keep the weight of the prototype down to a reasonable 7 tons 17½ cwt. But little, if anything, was directly derived from the Routemaster design, though there was some family resemblance in outline to other Park Royal designs.

From bad to worse. If the post-1958 Bridgemaster was disappointing in appearance, the forward-entrance version introduced in 1960 was startlingly ungainly. This is the first of ten 72-seat examples supplied to the City of Oxford fleet in 1961, numbered 312 (312 MFC). This operator also received thirteen of a shortened version in which the short window bay behind the entrance was eliminated and corresponding reduction in upper-deck length achieved by using an ultra-short front dome. The wheelbase was reduced from the standard version's 18ft. 10in. to 16ft. 6in.

ion, and indeed the principal orders for Bridgemasters came from that Group, early operators including East Yorkshire, South Wales and Western Welsh. Municipal orders came mainly from medium-sized undertakings, though Sheffield took six. The absence of a semi-automatic option ruled the model out for bulk orders from Birmingham, for example, and there were several contradictions in the vehicle's specification which limited its appeal. Its utilitarian appearance suggested lightweight construction, yet weight was generally higher than that of more conventional buses. Ride comfort was good, particularly as air suspension had been adopted as standard for the rear axle from 1958, yet the whining gearbox gave it an old-fashioned sound.

The original design could not readily be adapted to forward-entrance layout. Major changes to its mechanical layout, notably revival of the transfer gearbox,(that had been eliminated on rear-entrance models in 1958) by mounting the engine and gearbox at an angle in the chassis, were introduced in the 2B3RA version with forward-entrance available from 1960. South Wales was the first customer, but the largest was East Yorkshire with some 50 examples. The rear-entrance B3RA continued to be available, and both 30ft. and a shorter 27ft. 8in. version of both models were built. Despite this variety, only 179 Bridgemasters had been built

when production ceased in 1962. Competition for this specialised market had been intense and the delays in production had allowed Dennis to take many orders for the Loline, which was built under Bristol licence and hence inherited much of the Lodekka's reputation, while the rear-engined Leyland Atlantean was quite popular in lowbridge form when introduced in 1959, more than equalling the Bridgemaster's entire production in this form alone within about three years, mainly for BET companies.

# Longer Regents

A much more successful, yet far simpler, development among AEC double-deckers was the introduction of 30ft. models in 1956. These were the LD2RA and LD3RA, with Monocontrol and syn-chromesh gearbox respectively, both originally having the A218 9.6-litre engine. These were very similar to the respective 27ft. 9.6-litre models apart from having an 18ft. 7in. wheelbase and such items as a slightly heavier-section frame and heavier-duty tyres. Orders soon began to come in, many operators switching over to

Just how far ideas on vehicle appearance had been allowed to slip with the later Bridgemasters can be judged by comparing the vehicle opposite with this one, delivered to the Oxford fleet three years earlier. This was H973 (973 CWL), one of the first batch of 30ft.-long Regents supplied to this concern. They were based on the LD3RA type chassis, with A218 9.6-litre engine, synchromesh gearbox and air brakes. Park Royal built the bodywork on this vehicle, one of eight similar buses—an equal number was bodied by Weymann.

Bradford Corporation's first new motorbuses since the "new look" Regent III's of 1952 were fifteen of the 30ft. long Regent V LD2RA model with Monocontrol transmission and Metro-Cammell 70-seat forward entrance bodywork delivered in 1959. Basically similar buses were to remain the Bradford standard for several years, though synchromesh transmission was adopted for the 100 examples supplied between 1962 and 1964. In this view No. 113 (PKY 113) is being followed by one of the Leyland Titan PD2 buses with Leyland-built bodywork added to the fleet in 1949. Appropriately, the car parked nearest the camera is a Jowett Javelin, built in Bradford.

(Above) The rather austere appearance given by the combination of the plain frameless-dome body style then favoured by several BET companies, particularly in conjunction with unrelieved single-colour liveries is typified by Rhondda Transport Co. Ltd. No. 426 (VTX 426), one of twenty LD3RA models supplied in 1958. Weymann built the 70-seat body.

(Right) After standardising on Guy double-deckers from 1950 to 1957, the East Kent Road Car Co. Ltd. turned to the Regent V, taking 40 of the LD3RA 30ft. synchromesh model in 1958-59. Somewhat surprisingly, this batch had fully-fronted bodywork, and as the body design was of the traditional Park Royal pattern rather than the style adopted for the Bridgemaster, they were imposing vehicles, although the frontal profile was rather upright. East Kent did not then use fleet numbers and this batch were distinguished by their PFN-prefix registration numbers.

Although the front-engined Regal single-decker was still available for export markets, it was not offered in Britain since the demand was insufficient to justify the variation of wheelbase needed to meet British turning circle requirements. So when South Wales Transport Co. Ltd. needed a couple of single-deckers to pass under some unusually low bridges in the Llanelly docks area, the choice turned to the Regent V model. The specially low-built 37-seat bodies were built by Roe. By this date, the chassis was the 2D3RA with AV590 engine.

the 30ft. version by 1958. By the end of that year the AV590 engine became available and from 1959 a new series of Regent V models using that engine, designated 2D2RA and 2D3RA available in both 27ft. and 30ft. versions replaced the previous series of models. Vehicle width, optional on most models at either 8ft. or 7ft. 6in. for the previous decade was now standardised at 8ft. and this made it possible to widen the front part of the frame without limiting steering lock. The frame was thus parallel-sided and the wider

Perhaps the most outstanding single export order obtained during the history of ACV was that to supply 250 Regent V double-deckers with Park Royal bodywork to Teheran Omnibus Board. A handing-over ceremony of the first 25 was held on 27th May 1958 and this photograph shows how they were drawn up in a circular formation at the Southall works. The photograph also shows many members of the Boards of ACV, AEC and Park Royal as well as from Teheran, in those days opening up as a market for British buses, together with journalists from the technical press. The 29ft. by 8ft. vehicles were based on D2LA chassis with the left-hand A222 version of the 11.3-litre engine, Monocontrol transmission and heavy-duty frames. The body-work seated 73 passengers. The total value of the contract was stated at the time to be worth £2½ million.

spring base improved stability without the drawbacks of the Mark III stabiliser. There was also a 2D3RV with vacuum brakes, but this was only available in the 27ft. length. By 1962, the total of 9.6-litre and AV590-engined Regent V models built exceeded 1,000, the 30ft. versions having greatly boosted demand and restored the allegiance of such fleets as Glasgow, Leeds, Bradford and South Wales to Regents of this engine size. Most of those for city fleets had Monocontrol transmission.

# Export models

Export versions of the Regent had also scored some successes in the 'fifties, Johannesburg following fourteen Regent III in 1952 with 50 Regent V in 1956, and then a further 60 in 1959. But perhaps the most outstanding was that for 250 Regent V for Teheran in 1958.

The front-engined Regal had faded from the home market in the early 'fifties, even though one or two operators had defied the trend of the time by placing 30ft. long Regal Mark III buses or coaches on the road up to 1953. But in some export markets the underfloor engine was unsuitable. The series of orders for Baghdad had been begun with a batch of left-hand drive Regal IIIs with crash gearboxes (model 9631A) in the early 'fifties and I well remember the AEC drivers struggling with the awkward linkage from what was a right-handed unit. Later deliveries of double deckers had Monocontrol transmission, so perhaps the Baghdad drivers also found them difficult.

Although unknown in Britain, a range of Regal Mark V single-deckers was offered in 1955, mainly with 11.3-litre A221 or A222 engines and Monocontrol transmission, models S2RA and S2LA, although there was also briefly an AV470 synchromesh MS3RV.

The principal market for these was Africa, but for countries with poor roads a passenger version of the contemporary Mercury was also introduced and the old Ranger model name revived for it. This was the M4RA and M4LA, and from then on until the last days of the company there was a steady flow of export Rangers of these and succeeding types to old and new markets—the Phillipines being among the latter, for example. Another Ranger success story occurred in Mosul, Iraq, where Regal III buses supplied in 'fifties were followed by Rangers in 1962 and 1967, the last being 4M4L models with Marshall bodies.

Johannesburg came back for more Regents in the late 'fifties, this time Mark V models—50 in 1956 and 60 in 1959. No. 254 is seen here, showing the characteristic appearance given by the combination of the standard Regent V front end, complete with the usual style of export-model bumper, and the Bus Bodies (SA) bodywork.

The Regal Mark VI title replaced the Regal Mark IV in 1960, largely to indicate the introduction of the AH690 wet-liner engine in place of the earlier 9.6 or 11.3-litre units. However, the design of this export model had been an evolutionary process and, from the mid 'fifties, a succession of special variations had been produced, particularly for Australian city fleets. This Regal VI, dating from 1962, was another such design, having a Spicer torque converter transmission imported from the United States, air suspension and heavy-duty axles, being designed to operate at a gross weight of up to 15.8 tons, though the chassis weight of 5½ tons was very little more than that of the original Regal IV of 1950. The frame design had by this stage become straight-topped with an outline profile very like that of the Reliance, though in this case outriggers to give direct support to the body sides were added.

The Regal Mark VI appeared at the Commercial Motor Show in 1960 as a purely export model. It was, in effect, the Regal Mark IV in updated form, with the AH690 wet-liner version of the 11.3-litre engine in place of the older A219 or A220 units. It was offered in 17ft. 6in. or 19ft. 6in. wheelbase, right or left-hand steering and Monocontrol four-speed epicyclic or ZF six-speed synchromesh transmission, designations being U2RA, U2LA, etc. Options available included air suspension and power-assisted steering. South America continued to be a big market for the firm's products, still sold under the ACLO name, and among early orders for the Regal Mark VI were two totalling 150 for operation in the Monte-

video area of Uruguay. An even bigger order came in for over 500 for operation in Buenos Aires, Argentina.

South Africa had, however, evolved its own characteristic style of bus, and in AEC terms combining some of the characteristics of Mk V and VI buses. The Kudu was, in effect, a Regal Mk VI with an AV690 vertical 11.3-litre engine mounted on the front overhang. The front-mounted engine was able to operate in relatively clean air instead of being subjected to the dust thrown up by the vehicle's front wheels as on the underfloor-engined model. Yet the layout permitted the entrance also being ahead of the front axle and hence under the direct supervision of the driver, there

By contrast, many operators in South Africa favoured a front-engined vehicle, and the Kudu was specifically designed to meet their needs. The frame was of the almost flat-topped type by then standard for AEC single-decker models, but the engine was a vertical AV690, mounted ahead of the front axle, though this was later superseded by the AV691. This picture shows an early example with Monocontrol transmission—the gearbox is barely visible, being mounted only a short distance ahead of the rear axle.

The interior layout at the front end of a Kudu allowed enough clearance for passengers to enter the bus alongside the engine, even if clearance alongside the 11.3-litre unit was hardly generous.

International co-operation was of growing importance in AEC's export trade. A joint venture between AEC and the Dutch bodybuilder Verheul to produce a vehicle to suit South American requirements led to orders for 150 Regal Mark VI vehicles to this design. Note the prominent ACLO lettering.

The style of radiator grille used on contemporary AEC goods models was generally supplied with the Kudu chassis to be incorporated into the bodywork, although some bodybuilders preferred to use their own designs. This example was one of many supplied to the Benoni municipal undertaking, operating on a dirt road surface of the type which provided the justification for the model.

being sufficient if not generous space for passengers to enter the bus alongside the engine cover. The engine was available with ratings up to 200 bhp and either Monocontrol or a six-speed constant-mesh gearbox were available—model designations being 2S2RA or 2S4RA respectively. Note that these designations used the same basic code letter as the Regal V and that '4' signified the constant mesh gearboxes. The Kudu was assembled by AEC's recently acquired Durban factory from CKD (Completely Knocked Down) kits, and proved to be a popular model, particularly for operation on dirt roads. By 1964 AEC (SA) Ltd. had followed up the first 100 with a repeat order for a further 100 to be sold to operators all over South Africa.

Orders for Kudu models soon came in from all types of South African operator and Graham B. Shields, who has surveyed the extent of their popularity, reckoned that about 1,800 were in service in 1978. The large PUTCO concern alone operated some 400, and another major user was Pietermaritzburg Municipality, with 120. Durban took 65 three-axle examples with a self-steering trailing axle behind the driver axle.

# 13  SWAN SONG

The 'sixties brought major changes to AEC. Exports had always been important, but they were to build up to nearly half the firm's output of passenger and goods vehicles. In addition to the South African venture, new assembly plants in Belgium, Holland and Portugal were set up in 1960 in association with local concerns already well-established as importers of AEC chassis — Spitals, Verheul and UTIC, respectively. Similarly, the Canadian Car Co. Ltd. of Montreal, already well-established users of AEC engines, introduced their first rear-engined buses using a special version of the AV690 engine. The following year there were links with Barreiros in Spain and Siam di Tella in Buenos Aires, the latter related to the big Regal Mark VI order for that city mentioned in the previous chapter.

At home there was a take-over, also in 1961, of the motor vehicle interests of the Thornycroft concern, and this impinged on my own life, as I had been a chassis designer there since 1957. I think I would have accepted an invitation to join the editorial staff of "Commercial Motor" in any case, but the uncertainties following the AEC take-over of Thornycroft encouraged a favourable look at other opportunities.

Thus it was that when a telephone call inviting the editor of that journal to a hastily-called press conference at Leyland's London offices came through on the afternoon of 5th June 1962, I happened to be the only technical staff member present, and was asked to accompany him. We learnt that a merger between the Leyland and ACV groups had been agreed, subject only to stockholders' acceptance, which of course was later forthcoming. The emphasis was very much on the value of co-operation in securing export orders, and it was stated that the two concerns would continue to be run as separate organisations. The Chairmen of Leyland and AEC, Sir Henry Spurrier and Sir William (later Lord) Black, were both present. Another personality on the platform, then little known outside the industry, who clearly already knew a great deal about the activities of both the two concerns was Mr. Donald (later Lord) Stokes, at that time a Leyland director, having built up a reputation as Britain's most successful bus salesman.

Thus was born what was soon to be known as the Leyland Motor Corporation. The secret had been well kept, though there had been rumours of other possible ACV mergers, mainly involving the British Motor Corporation (which in those days consisted almost entirely of the car empire based on Austin and Morris, with no commercial vehicles in as heavy a class as AEC's products) though it subsequently transpired that there had also been talks with Rolls Royce.

What would have happened had either of these other possibilities come to fruition is a matter for conjecture, though neither organisation did particularly well in the tough commercial world of subsequent years. Was it essential that ACV merge with any-one? AEC's sales of city buses on the home market had not been as strong as they were a decade earlier, but part of this decline was due to a fall in the size of that market as a whole — some 4,876 double-deckers of all makes had been registered in the peak year of 1949 whereas annual production in the early 'sixties was about half of that freak figure (which had mainly been caused by pent-up demand for vehicles frustrated due to the war). But demand was tending to rise again, if less strongly, partly because those early post-war vehicles were falling due for replacement and partly because of tram and trolleybus replacement schemes, while AEC's single-decker sales were quite healthy, both at home and abroad.

There was, however, a widespread air of uncertainty. Demand for bus travel was continuing to fall as more people bought cars and tended to spend more time at home watching television. There were still strongly divided views as to what types of bus would be in demand. The increase in the maximum size of buses to 36ft. by 8ft. 2½in., introduced the previous year had re-awakened interest in the possibility of wider use of single-deckers, but there was further diversity of opinion as to what layout they should have, with growing interest in rear-engined models, of which AEC had none. The merger made sense in the context of world markets, but the first step had been taken towards the firm's extinction.

## 36ft. Reliances

AEC had been the first manufacturer to announce chassis taking advantage of the 36ft. length legal from 1961, although volume deliveries did not begin until 1962. The new models were 18ft. 7in. wheelbase versions of the Reliance and described as the Reliance 470 or 590 according to engine size — the "30ft." Reliance with the smaller engine continued to be available, though actual coach body lengths tended to become 31ft. or so.

The principal 36ft. model was the version with the AH590 engine, set to develop up to 153 bhp at 2000 rpm and thus the most powerful home market model yet. The first British motorway had been opened three years previously and unlimited coach operating speeds became legal on such roads for a time. The standard coach transmission was the ZF six-speed synchromesh gearbox and its highest overdrive ratio gave a 70 mph capability. I vividly recall

The additional length of the 36ft. Reliance could be used to good effect in coach styling, and Harrington's Cavalier body design gave this Hove-based body-builder a style leader after a decade in the doldrums. This photograph was taken by the author when carrying out a used vehicle test for the "Bus & Coach" March 1967 issue. The subject, registered 621 TKN, had been placed in service by LeRoy Tours on Continental tours when new in May 1962 and was being offered for sale by Arlington Motor Co. Ltd., an old-established dealer in AEC coaches, from its premises in the Potters Bar London Transport garage. It must have been among the first 590-engined Reliances on the road but still seemed in very good order.

The Reliance 590 soon became a favoured type for coach rally contenders. Potteries Motor Traction Co. Ltd. entered this example with Plaxton Panorama body in the 1965 British Coach Rally and obtained the award for the highest-placed standard coach. No. C1041 (AEH 141C) is seen here during the man-oeuvering tests on Madeira Drive at Brighton.

carrying out a "Commercial Motor" road test on a laden but open chassis and driving up the M1 at this speed—an exhilarating and delightful experience on a warm day, particularly as the vehicle proved to be particularly stable in its handling character istics. I found myself having some trouble in selecting the right gear on slower routes because of the vagueness of the lever

The East Kent Road Car Co. Ltd. had been almost completely standardised on AEC vehicles, so far as new deliveries were concerned, for a decade when this photograph was taken in Folkestone in May 1967. The Reliance in the foreground was one of ten 36ft. 2U3RA models, with AH590 engine, synchromesh gearbox and Marshall 51-seat bodywork to the BET standard design of the period. They had fixed windows, relying on roof vents, but later opening windows had to be added to give adequate ventilation. The 1964 Regent on the left was also of 590-engined type, with Park Royal bodywork—East Kent had reverted to the conventional half-cab form earlier in the 'sixties. The Reliance on the right dated from 1956 and was of the MU3RV type, with Weymann dual-purpose 41-seat bodywork.

positions, but regular drivers generally developed the required sensitivity with a little practice.

The original 590-engined Reliance chassis were given 2U3RA chassis designations, and this use of the same basic series as the Regal Mark VI was apt to be confusing, the ''plain'' U3RA number signifying a Regal VI, while air-suspension versions of the Regal VI and Reliance were respectively 3U3RA and 4U3RA, though few of the Reliance version were built.

The Reliance 590 was the fastest coach chassis then generally available on the British market, a fact which undoubtedly helped sales to operators able to make use of this as the motorway network gradually spread, but the flexibility of performance given by the six-speed gearbox was perhaps more often of value. Sales steadily built up, particularly among previous Reliance users and noteworthy among regular customers were the Yelloway concern at Rochdale and Premier Travel of Cambridge, two of the best known of the few independent operators to participate in the national network of express coach services then operated mainly by BET and Tilling companies. Quite a number of BET companies placed examples in service as coaches, while others favoured the 470-engined version. For example, City of Oxford's standard single-decker in the 1962-64 period was the Reliance 470, generally with

constant mesh gearbox, and often in 36ft. 4MU4RA form. By 1965, Reliance sales were over 5,600, consolidating the position of this model as AEC's most popular single-decker.

## The low-floor Renown

The 36ft. Reliance was just coming into its own at the time of the Leyland-AEC merger, but the first model to be announced under the new regime, in July 1962, was the Renown double-decker. The third AEC model to have carried this name, the new Renown had existed in prototype form for a couple of months before the merger. It was a replacement for the Bridgemaster, and outwardly at least a standard Park Royal-bodied example looked generally very like that model.

Underneath, it differed in several respects. There was a separate chassis, it being considered that some sales were being lost because of the non-availability of alternative bodywork. A good deal of thought was given to improving the forward-entrance layout, as that offered for the Bridgemaster had been awkward

(Left) The Renown low-floor chassis was more ingenious in its design than external appearances of the complete bus suggested. This photograph shows the Monocontrol transmission prototype. To accommodate the epicyclic gearbox, the transmission line was so arranged as to bring the gearbox under the staircase of a forward-entrance body. To achieve this, the AV590 engine was inclined in all three planes. To allow a one-step entrance, the left-hand sidemember was lowered immediately behind the front axle. Also prominent in this view is the air suspension for the rear axle. The wheelbase was 18ft. 3½ in.

(Opposite) The North Western Road Car Co. Ltd. had been a frequent customer for Reliance single-deckers since 1954, but its first AEC double-deckers were eighteen Renown 3B3RA models delivered in 1963. They had the standard Park Royal bodywork for this model, seating 74.
The overall appearance was not dissimilar to that of the Bridgemaster, though considerably better proportioned than the forward-entrance version of the latter. A key identification feature was the projection of the offside front mudguard beyond the cab front panel. The flat-fronted upper-deck styling and the use of an almost unaltered version of the Regent V bonnet tended to give a somewhat dated appearance in that era of reviving interest in attractive styling.

(Opposite left and centre) City of Oxford was also still in the era of attractive liveries and No. 354 (CFC 354C) looked quite smart when photographed in 1970. It was one of twelve Renowns supplied in 1965. Like all of Oxford's Renowns, they were short-chassis vehicles, the body being one bay shorter than standard and giving a 65-seat capacity. Bodywork was by Park Royal, ten similar vehicles being supplied in 1963, nine in 1964 and eight in 1966. The 1967 batch of four had Northern Counties bodywork and were the last Renowns built. By this date No. 354 had been the subject of conversion to permit one-man operation.

(Opposite right) The use of a separate chassis for the Renown allowed a choice of bodybuilder. Leigh and Leicester Corporation both chose not only East Lancashire bodywork but also rear-entrance layout. Leicester No. 36, dating from 1965, is shown here.

the driver without intrusion into the upper-deck floor level (which was the most obvious drawback to the Leyland-Albion Lowlander of comparable design which came out a few months later).

AEC had long used inclined engine positions, but the Renown carried this much further than usual as the rear of the AV590 unit was inclined downwards and to the right, while its cylinders sloped to the left. This was done to move the transmission line far enough to the right to accommodate a Monocontrol epicyclic gearbox under the stairs, though the model was offered with synchromesh gearbox and most built were so fitted. The rear axle was similar to the Bridgemaster and, as on that model, air sprung, but the front wheels were on a conventional axle with rather stiff leaf springs.

Two demonstrators were built for the 1962 Show period, the Monocontrol example spending some time with London Transport and then being sold, while the synchromesh one visited a number of potential users. Their Park Royal bodywork was very like that on a Bridgemaster, apparently using up stocks of parts made for that model. By this date strong competition was being experienced from the rear-engined Leyland Atlantean and Daimler Fleetline, quite apart from the front-engined models mentioned above.

and wasteful of space. A twin left-hand sidemember chassis design enabled the floor height near the door to be almost as low as the 1ft. 3in. frame level at this point, giving a one-step entrance, as on contemporary Bristol Lodekka and Dennis Loline chassis. The bonnet was much the same as the contemporary Regent V but the driving position was slightly lower to give adequate headroom for

The synchromesh 3B3RA demonstrator, which I had the opportunity to drive during a press road test, had something of a dual personality. It was quite hard work to drive in town conditions, with a foolproof but heavy gear lever action, and much noisier for both driver and passengers than the Atlantean and Fleetline demonstrators against which it was compared in several fleets.

On the other hand it could be surprisingly economical on a country route—I achieved over 13 mpg on a non-stop run over quite a hilly course—and the maximum speed of 48 mph indicated how high-geared it was for a four-speed double-decker.

But it hardly looked the part of an up-to-date bus design for the swinging 'sixties, and it was not surprising that the Renown was only marginally more successful than the Bridgemaster, whose ride quality it did not equal, incidentally. A total of 251 was built, the last being delivered in 1967, although the decision to cease production of both the Renown and Lowlander had been announced in September 1965. (The decision had been made some months earlier and was not related to arrangements made the previous month to allow Bristol vehicles to be sold on the open market by the Leyland Motor Corporation taking a 25 per cent shareholding in Bristol).

The main customers for the Renown were again BET group companies, among which North Western was a newcomer to AEC double-deckers, though municipal operators included Leicester, Nottingham and Leigh. As it turned out, the 3B2RA Monocontrol version was quite rare, though it was chosen by two operators who were relatively fresh converts to AEC vehicles—Wolverhampton Corporation and R. Chisnell's Winchester-based "King Alfred" fleet. Short versions were built for the Oxford and Western Welsh fleets and it was the former who received the last examples in 1967, completing a fleet of 43, all of the 28ft. "short-tailed" type.

During the time the Renown had been in production about 700 further conventional Regent V double-deckers had been built, despite the fact that much of its design was directly inherited from the original RT of 1937-39.

# Routemaster developments

The Routemaster was also in large-scale production during the mid 'sixties and by the time construction stopped in February 1968, a total of some 2760 vehicles had been suppplied to London Transport, or roughly 275 a year for the ten year period of production. These vehicles included the 30ft. long version of which 24 had been built in 1961 and on which production was standardised with the final 500 vehicles from 1965. This had an additional bay of 2ft. 4in. in the middle of the body structure and other minor changes, giving a seating capacity of 72 in the bus version designated RML (the earlier Leyland prototype with this type classification being recoded RM). The unladen weight was increased but

These views of Routemaster front and rear "wheelbarrows" were taken in February 1961. They show the extent to which these two main AEC-manufactured contributions to the completed vehicle were built-up as self-contained assemblies, ready to be delivered to Park Royal to be attached to the body structure. The gearbox, forming part of neither, was sent separately to be mounted amidships beneath the body floor.

The extended version of the Routemaster to take full advantage of the 30ft. overall length permitted since 1966 appeared first on an experimental basis when 24 examples were built in 1961. The first is shown here with its original fleet number ER 880, at Southall before delivery to Chiswick. As can be seen, the extra length was produced by simply adding-in a short 2ft. 4in. bay to the centre of the body structure, producing a somewhat odd-looking vehicle, faintly reminiscent of LGOC buses of the S and NS era in its pillar spacing and with a 19ft. 2in. wheelbase, longer than usual for a 30ft. front-engined double-decker. In practical terms, however, it was a most efficient design, giving 72 seats with a modest unladen weight of 7 tons 15 cwt. — only 5 cwt more than an RT — with all the high standard of comfort and interior finish of the standard Routemaster. ER 880 was renumbered RML 880 before entering service and RML used as the fleet number prefix for all similar vehicles, which became standard from 1965.

only to 7 tons 15 cwt., a remarkably modest figure for so well-equipped a vehicle. There were also 68 RMC 27ft. 6in. and 43 RCL 30ft. Green Line coach versions and one forward-entrance 30ft. bus, RMF 1254, included in the above total. Additional to it were 65 forward-entrance 27ft. 6in. models, designed to tow small luggage trailers, for British European Airways services between London and Heathrow airport, owned by BEA but operated on its behalf by London Transport. These had the larger-capacity AV690 engine set to give 175 bhp to allow high-speed operation on the M4 motorway. The Green Line coaches also had the large engine; 586 standard Routemasters had Leyland O.600 engines.

Little effort seemed to be made to sell the Routemaster on the open market, although RMF 1254, exhibited at the 1962 Commercial Motor Show, was built with a view to the general sale of the model. A very limited amount of demonstration operation by various operators of this bus and standard Routemasters did

The first production Green Line coach version of the Routemaster was based on the original standard four-bay body, seating 57 with seats like those on Green Line RF coaches, parcel racks and fluorescent lighting. The first of the 68 vehicles of this type, RMC 1453, is seen here in a publicity photograph used for several years in a poster widely displayed in Underground stations. The 715 service was among those operated by this type. The equivalent 30ft. long version was designated RCL, seating 65, and 43 were built in 1965.

occur, but no attempt seems to have been made to follow this up by a genuine marketing exercise.

It was sometimes claimed at the time that the Routemaster was very expensive, though a Parliamentary investigation on expenditure appeared to suggest no more than about a 10 per cent premium above average double-deck costs. In any case, genuine "outside" orders were obtained from Northern General Transport Co. Ltd., then a member of the BET group, subject to an entirely commercial outlook and not receiving any form of subsidy. A total of 50 buses was taken, basically similar to RMF 1254, but having Leyland O.600 engines, then standard in the NGT fleet, and other minor changes from the London specification. They entered service in 1964-65 and some remain in service at the time of writing, having proved well suited to the rigours of the more severe climate of County Durham. Resistance to corrosion of the aluminium alloy structure was a particularly important benefit. This saved the company over £1,000 per bus when recertification fell due after seven years' service, by comparison with vehicles of conventional design which required extensive underframe and pillar replacement, often up to window level. NGT later bought RMF 1254 from London Transport.

In a sense, AEC's Routemaster and Regent double-deckers of the 'sixties, and indeed from the mid 'fifties, could be said to have succeeded in spite of a policy that seemed lukewarm towards

Only one operator outside London Transport (and the LTE-managed British European Airways airport service fleet) took Routemasters. This was Northern General Transport Co. Ltd., which placed in service 50 forward-entrance examples beginning in May 1964. They had Leyland O.600 engines, then standard on modern double-deckers in the NGT fleet, and other minor variations from the London Transport specification, such as semi- rather than fully-automatic transmission, worm-drive rear axle and variations in opening windows, destination blinds, etc. They proved well-suited to the inter-urban routes linking Newcastle with major towns in County Durham, standing up well to the harsher weather conditions than experienced in London.

The AEC Swift broke new ground in several directions. It was the first rear-engined AEC and the first to be introduced since the link-up with Leyland, incorporating similar side-members and steering gear as the Leyland Panther. However, the new AH505 engine and remainder of the mechanical design was by AEC. It all seemed very promising when the author carried out a road test for ''Bus & Coach'' for the December 1965 issue. This photograph was taken in Nuneaton on that occasion, the vehicle being the demonstrator FGW 498C with Willowbrook's adaptation of the standard BET-style body of the period to suit the Panther/Swift chassis, seating 53. The vehicle gave lively performance, quiet running and good fuel economy—almost the only criticism being of slightly heavy steering (a non-AEC feature!). However, it was not possible to predict the reliability problems that affected this, like many other rear-engined models. Note the low driving position derived from that of the Leyland Atlantean.

them. Had a more positive line been taken, who knows what would have happened? If a positive effort to sell the Routemaster to other operators—and to tailor its specification with options to suit varying requirements—had been made as soon as its design was finalised in 1957-58, could it have countered more of the impact of the Atlantean? A rear-engined version at that stage would have been a formidable contender for sales. Certainly more sales would have helped to reduce production costs. It also seemed a pity not to make the Bridgemaster and Routemaster more obviously related—if the former had been a low-floor version of the latter, with more common parts, further savings could have been made.

On the other hand, if integral construction was too advanced a concept for general acceptance, use of more Routemaster features in a more thoroughly redesigned Regent V would have given the latter a more modern image. The Renown low-floor concept might have been ''built-in'' as an option with fewer special parts, again cutting costs and tidying the range. As it was, it seemed as if three teams of engineers were working almost completely independently.

Of course, it is easy to be wise after the event. No doubt such factors as the drying up of quantity orders from London Transport between 1954 and 1958 and the fondness of BET for what, again

with hindsight, seem old-fashioned design features (crash gear-boxes and steel structural framing as opposed to aluminium) helped to take the momentum out of AEC's hitherto highly successful progress in this field. But it all seems a pity and undoubtedly put AEC in the position of being ripe for take-over rather than perhaps being able to make more moves in that direction itself.

# The swing to single-deckers

By the mid 'sixties, however, the wind seemed to be blowing against the double-decker. One-man operation of 36ft. single-deckers was gaining ground almost as fast as negotiations with the trade unions would allow, certainly on country routes. Early trials with amidships-underfloor-engined models such as the Reliance in urban conditions had revealed that boarding and alighting delays with the inevitable high floor level were a problem. Hence there was renewed interest in low-floor single-deckers, among which Bristol's RE model introduced in 1962 had set the pace.

The Leyland Motor Corporation's reaction was to introduce a new range of Leyland and AEC models with underfloor engines behind the rear axle. There was to be some standardisation of design, with similar frames using basically the same sidemembers and the same front-end layout including the steering, etc. However, engines and transmission were to be of each manufacturer's own standards.

The 36ft. Swift was the first AEC version to appear, being announced shortly before the 1964 Commercial Motor Show. The corresponding Leyland, the Panther, had appeared in February 1964. As with that model, there were initially both bus and coach versions, the former, type MP2R, having a low-level frame ahead of the rear axle and Monocontrol transmission as standard, and the latter, type CMP4R, a straight-framed coach chassis with the same six-speed constant mesh gearbox as had been offered in Reliance 470 models for the previous two years. The bus version was also to be made available with this box although ''not recommended'' except for services with few stops. Air brakes were standard and the previous final letter on the designation denoting the type of brake system was omitted.

The engine was a new AH505 unit, derived from the 470, but with increased bore size of 116 mm giving a swept volume of 8.2-litres, and reverting to dry cylinder liners. Operators' experience with the wet liner engines had been mixed. On the Reliance 470, the general pattern seemed to be trouble-free operation on the less arduous duties, such as most coach operation in pre-motorway days, but a tendency to gasket problems when driven hard, either in hilly terrain, or continuously at high speed. Similar remarks applied to the other versions in varying degrees, though London Transport found the AV590 generally trouble-free in the Routemaster. Although 470-engined Regents were troublesome in some fleets, others, apparently with arduous conditions, gave good reliability.

However, to return to the rear-engined single-decker story, it was also announced at that time that there was to be a new heavier-duty chassis, mainly meant for overseas, of similar design but with a larger dry-liner engine, the AH691 (of the same 11.3-litre size as the AH690, but with the different type number to indicate its altered construction) and that this was to be called the Merlin. In practice, the Swift bus-type chassis was adopted as standard, and the larger-engined version called the Swift 691, while the original version became the Swift 505. The coach version and those with constant-mesh or synchromesh gearbox, were dropped for the home market.

London Transport had announced what amounted to a revolution in its bus policy, called the Bus Reshaping Plan, with many more localised routes as well as new central routes linking main-line

Some of the first batch of fifteen AEC Swift 691 rear-engined single-deckers for London Transport in course of bodybuilding at the Hamble premises of Strachans (Coachbuilders) Ltd. towards the end of 1965. The chassis in the foreground shows the way in which the 11.3-litre engine and automatic gearbox were suspended from the rear overhang of the frame, together with the radiator and other equipment. The weight of this machinery, amounting to about a ton, overhung some distance behind the rear axle imposed considerable bending stresses in the frame and these in turn were apt to create body stress problems, often in the roof. Strachans decided to follow the convention established at the front end of conventional double-deckers and not tie the body directly to the rearmost part of the frame, and this make of bodywork is said to have given less structural trouble on rear-engined single-deckers than some others. London Transport decided to call its 36ft. rear-engined AEC single-deckers ''Merlin'' and this original experimental batch was classified XMA (six vehicles) or XMB (the remainder) according to whether they were of the 73-passenger Red Arrow standee type or of conventional seating layout.

termini with office or shopping areas. Single-deckers were to be much more widely adopted and the AH691-powered version of the new chassis was to be the basis. Chiswick had latched on to the proposed type-name Merlin and had always referred to these vehicles by that name, although they differ less than had been usual from the standard AEC model, in this case the Swift 691 (though the latter was not at first listed for general sale).

The first order, for fifteen chassis of type P2R, was placed in 1965, and six of these, fitted with Strachans bodywork with standing space for a theoretical 48 passengers and seats for only 25, all at the rear, went into service in April 1966 on the first Red Arrow route from Victoria to Marble Arch. The other nine were originally intended for London Transport's country area, with more conventional 46-seat bodywork also by Strachans and, like the Red Arrows, having a front entrance and centre exit. In fact all but one were converted to augment the central area's Red Arrow fleet.

(Right) Production of the Merlin series of buses on Swift 691 chassis was well under way before much operating experience was built up. Here MBS 42 of the first production batch and MBA 172 of the second are seen at LTE Chiswick works after delivery early in 1968, bearing SMM F-suffix registration numbers which were replaced by VLW G-suffix numbers before the buses entered service, from September that year. The photograph shows the original low and later high driving position.

(Below) Manoeuverability of 36ft. single-deckers proved to be a problem in London, with its many narrow congested streets. Here a Red Arrow MBA enters The Collonade at Waterloo station, in October 1968, a tight turn which is still carried out regularly, but some of the suburban routes proved so impracticable that only 33ft. buses were purchased subsequently.

A further 150 Merlins were ordered to form the production MB-series class, all with Metro-Cammell bodywork of various types, on a slightly modified 3P2R version of the chassis, and these were delivered early in 1968. By then a further 500, on a chassis with a higher driving position classified 4P2R, had also been ordered. Delays in placing production examples in service, due to protracted negotiations with the unions over the use of one-man operation, meant that virtually no operational experience had been gained before delivery of the final series was well under way. Delivery was completed in 1969.

Meanwhile, provincial operators had also been placing orders for Swift chassis. At first, only the Swift 505 was offered but by 1966 the provincial Swift 691 was available, designated 2P2R. All Swifts had at first been 36ft. models, but a 10 metre (33ft. 6in.) version was also introduced, based on the same frame design as the Leyland Panther Cub. This had insufficient rear overhang to accommodate the AH691 engine and hence was available only with the AH505 unit.

Orders came in from a wide variety of municipal operators, including long-standing AEC operators such as Aberdeen, Morecambe & Heysham, West Bridgford and Nottingham but less-familiar names such as Blackpool and, later, Sunderland. Sheffield

Reliability soon became a problem. By no means all was related to the buses themselves. Here MBS 56, on the right, is replaced in service by a similar bus at Turnpike Lane bus station during the first few weeks of operation on the re-organised Wood Green area suburban services. The fault was a defective coin machine, a common source of trouble. Note the driver dropping the running number into the holder on the side of the change-over vehicle.

favoured the 691 model, while Birmingham had twelve of the 33ft. 505-engined variety and six 36ft. 691 models. This was to be Birmingham's last order for AEC buses and, despite repeated attempts, and several specially-built demonstrators, was the largest order obtained since the pre-1931 era when Birmingham AEC buses were counted by the hundreds—a curious contrary strand to success elsewhere over that period.

However, operator reaction to the Swift was mixed; London Transport soon ran into difficulties with its fleet of Merlins. Some problems, however, were no fault of the chassis design. It was soon discovered that 36ft. single-deckers were not suited to operational conditions in many London suburbs with narrow streets and numerous parked cars. Not all bodybuilders had appreciated the extent to which the body structure of rear-engined single-deckers had to cope with the effect of the ton of machinery suspended from the rear overhang of the inevitably flexible chassis—a problem experienced with other similar chassis. But there were also mechanical faults and AEC ran into much the same overheating problems as on many rear-engined vehicles.

London Transport had decided to go over to the 10-metre model and so began the SM series of Swifts. Delivery of the first 150 began in November 1969, with bodywork contracts split between Marshall and Park Royal, and further orders, with further bodywork from these builders and for the last 390 by Metro-Cammell took the total to 838. Some, however, were delivered direct to London Country Bus Services Ltd. which new NBC subsidiary had by then taken over London Transport's country services. (The latter concern also took delivery of further Swifts purchased direct, including some for Green Line service with Alexander ramped-floor bodywork.) London Transport's delivery was completed by February 1972.

Investigation into overhaul requirements for the Merlin fleet led to a decision only eighteen months later, in August 1973, to replace the entire fleet. Withdrawal proceeded rapidly and the majority were out of traffic by 1975. Space was hired at the former Radlett Aerodrome and by the end of that year 350 were stored there. Many saw further service, some in Australia, and several batches were sold to Citybus, Belfast while others went to independent operators. Only the vehicles used on Red Arrow services survived and about 70 remain for these duties.

Meanwhile, the London Transport 505-engined Swifts had in turn proved unsatisfactory, being found to be susceptible to engine failures. By the end of 1976, it had been decided to replace this class, too, as soon as possible, though it was recognised that this would take time. Over half the fleet had gone by the beginning of 1979. Some of the withdrawn vehicles have been exported and

Representative of municipal orders for Swifts was that placed by Nottingham City Transport for six MP2R models with the AH505 engine and Northern Counties 43-seat bodywork, delivered in 1969. All had been withdrawn by 1975.

London Transport, as well as specifying a higher driving position for its later Swift buses, also introduced its own design of instrument panel, also used on its Daimler Fleetline double-deckers. This photograph shows one of the first examples, on a 1968 bus of the Merlin series.

London Transport's second fleet of rear-engined single-deckers was even more numerous than the first, with 838 of the 33ft.-long SM-series of Swifts delivered mainly in 1970-71. SMS 58, with Park Royal 33-seat-plus-34-standee body, demonstrates the improved manoeuverability when new in Chiswick works. Yet these vehicles were to be barely any longer lived than the Merlin 36ft. version, only a small minority remaining in LTE operational service at the time of writing.

some have, again, gone to Citybus, Belfast, to replace vehicles destroyed by terrorists.

Like other rear-engined models of that period, the Swift had, at best, a patchy reputation. The 505 engine was faster-revving than most buses in urban service, being generally governed at 2200 rpm at which speed the London examples developed 132 bhp, compared to the 165 bhp at 1800 of the Merlin version. Both types were not infrequently seen stopped with pools of water or oil beneath as a clear indication of major trouble, sometimes because a minor leak had led to serious damage before the driver became aware of anything wrong, a common problem with rear-engined vehicles. London Transport's decisions to withdraw most of its Merlins and Swifts—together some 1503 vehicles—when still quite new was certainly influenced by unreliability. But another factor was undoubtedly the surplus of single-deckers created by the abandonment of the Bus Reshaping Plan's emphasis on this type of vehicle. Certainly the Swift's reliability problems were not insuperable. I gather that those delivered to Sunderland Corporation in 1973-74, among the last built, had proved relatively trouble-free with Tyne & Wear PTE, which "inherited" the Sunderland fleet. Having recently seen a Sunderland rush-hour, I am sure they were not mollycoddled from a driving viewpoint.

Ironically, the Swift took on a new lease of life latterly as an export model, particularly after the larger AH760 engine—see page 232—was fitted. In 1974 Durban took 65 examples with semi-luxury bodies by Bus Bodies (SA). Sets of Swift units with ZF synchromesh gearboxes were still regularly being sent to UTIC in Portugal right up to 1979 for incorporation into that concern's integral rear-engined coach chassis.

# Dry-liner engines again

The AH505 and AH691 engines replaced the previous units in the Reliance and Regal Mark VI models during 1966. The Reliance 505 model replaced the 470-engined version and continued to be available in 30 or 36ft. versions (although among the first built was one short-tailed batch of seven vehicles with Pennine bodies 27ft. 6in. long by 7ft. 6in. wide for the Halifax fleet). Such models were designated 6MU3R etc. depending on transmission, which as before could be five-speed synchromesh, six-speed constant mesh or four-speed semi-automatic Monocontrol. Traditional Reliance users such as City of Oxford and South Wales tended to favour this model, in both wheelbases up to 1971. It overcame the gasket problems of the 470, but was still somewhat prone to developing water leaks and consequent engine failures were not unknown.

The 9.6-litre engine size was not produced in the new-series dry liner form because of the trend to larger engines on the corres-

The Sheffield municipal fleet was one of the largest provincial users of the Swift 691, with a total of 38 delivered between 1968 and 1971. All had Park Royal bodywork but the doorway and seating layout varied. One of the first batch of 22, No. 18, was the subject of a "Bus & Coach" road test and the author confesses to being responsible for it having a slightly bent internal handrail, caused when one of the AEC experimental department staff was thrown against it when taken off-guard during brake testing.

Standard cab interior of an AEC single-decker of the period is conveyed in this picture taken in a Reliance 690 with five-speed Monocontrol transmission and Alexander Y-type body built for Potteries Motor Traction Co. Ltd. in 1967. The steering-column mounted instrument binnacle was adopted in the mid-'50s—hitherto AEC had been rather meagre on instrumentation.

While design energies had been diverted towards rear-engined models, sales of the by-this-date "conventional" underfloor-engined Reliance went from strength to strength among coach operators. By the summer of 1969, when this photograph was taken, sales totals of this model series had reached about 7,000, making it AEC's most popular single-decker. The dry-liner AH505 and AH691 engines had been introduced in 1966. The photograph shows a 36ft. Reliance with Plaxton Panorama Elite bodywork—the design which had set the standard for British coach styling for the next decade and more—then recently delivered to the fleet of Smiths of Wigan.

ponding goods vehicles, and so models hitherto fitted with the AH590 went over to the new AH691 11.3-litre unit, although for the Reliance application it was set to develop 157 bhp at 2000 rpm which was well below the 205 bhp maximum of this unit and only slightly more than the AH590's 153 bhp. It was offered in 36ft. (11 metre) length for home market and also in 12-metre form for export, although that was not yet legal in Britain. These models had chassis designations commencing 6U, the popular ZF six-speed synchromesh version being now 6U3ZR in right-hand form. Air-suspension versions were also offered, with 8U designations and this was also used for a version with coil springs. The specification of a Reliance 691 could at this stage be very close to that of a Regal Mark VI, now designated in the 5U series, though such items as brakes remained different.

This Potteries Motor Traction Co. Ltd. Reliance 691 dating from 1967, SL 1092 (KVT 192E), had five-speed Monocontrol transmission and coil suspension, the latter employing a similar layout to that offered when air suspension was specified. The bodywork was the Alexander Y-type, then already well-established and still in production at the time of writing. The photograph was taken at the MIRA proving ground at Lindley, near Nuneaton. The Riley 2½ litre car just visible on the right of the picture is still owned by the author.

The Reliance range retained its popularity and the chassis number series had reached over 7700 by 1971. Many independent operators who had hitherto used only lightweight models found that the extra first cost of a Reliance was justified in lower maintenance costs. An interesting variation introduced in 1967 was a version with five-speed Monocontrol gearbox, five with this feature and coil spring suspension being delivered to Potteries Motor Traction that year. I road tested one for "Bus & Coach" and was impressed with its smooth performance and good fuel consumption (17.0 mpg on a cross-country route, cruising at 40 mph).

The Regent also maintained considerable popularity in the face of increasingly effective competition from the Leyland Atlantean and Daimler Fleetline rear-engined models. This Regent V 2D3RA model was one of five delivered to the Devon General company in 1966, near the end of production of the AV590 engine. Devon General had reverted to the Regent from 1962, after putting 56 Atlanteans in service in 1959-61, though there were also six Atlanteans in the 1966 order. The bodywork on the Regents was assembled from the last sets of parts for double-deck bodies to be built by Weymann's, though put together at Metro-Cammell. They had seating for 69 passengers.

The AV590-engined Regent also gave way to an AV691-engined version, but in this case the "catalogue" output of the new 11.3-litre engine, after initial exciting figures of 192 bhp had been

quoted, was cut right back to 128 bhp at 1800 rpm. This was almost identical to that of the immediate post-war Regent III, despite the inevitable increase in weight due to the 30ft. long by 8ft. 2½ in. wide bodywork found on most examples. Such conservatism was curious because the AV590 had generally been quoted with maximum ratings around 140 to 153 bhp for Regent V applications. In practice, many operators had for many years cut power below the maker's maximum mainly for economy and durability — London Transport's consistent 115 bhp for RT and Routemaster buses comes to mind — and thus engine output was apt to be variable.

The AV691-powered Regents were coded 3D2RA etc. Curiously, no corresponding change was made to the "medium weight" Regent, which remained AV470-powered to the end. Few of these were built after about 1962 because of the increased interest in the 30ft. version by then available in this form, but those built after 1959 were designated 2MD3RA etc. the prefix signifying the use of a brake system with separate air circuits for front and rear axles, also introduced on the heavier Regents at that time. The vacuum brake version was dropped. The last such vehicle was chassis number 2MD3RA645 supplied to Garelochhead Coach Services early in 1968.

Overseas sales of the larger-engined Regents had, if anything, increased under the Leyland Motor Corporation regime. Some were repeat orders reflecting satisfaction with earlier deliveries. In the Middle East, where London Transport engineers helping to set up local bus systems had understandably brought AEC influence,

the successful sale of vehicles to Baghdad from the early 'fifties had been followed by an order for 250 Regent V models for the Teheran Bus Board in Iran in 1958. A further order for 200 very similar D2LA models was fulfilled in 1966 and it is noteworthy that these retained the pre-1958 style A222 version of the 11.3-litre engine with separate cylinder block, as this was still obtainable in true left-hand form. Sir Donald Stokes, as he had then become, was by this time Chairman of AEC Ltd. as well as Leyland as a whole, and performed the handing-over ceremony himself. Another notable export order was for 210 Regent V models with AV690 engines for the Kowloon Motor Bus Co. Ltd., Hong Kong. These were of ultra-long 21ft. 6in. wheelbase type to carry bodywork over 34ft. long and accommodating 118 passengers.

Among the last major home market customers was Southampton Corporation, which had placed its first order for Regents in 1930 and had not returned for more until 1962 when a batch of 27ft. 2D3RA synchromesh models was purchased, followed by more the following two years. Over the 1965-67 period, some 30 examples of the 30ft. 3D2RA Monocontrol model with AV691 engine were purchased, all with 70-seat rear-entrance East Lancashire bodywork. These were rather old-fashioned, if attractive-looking, buses and I was slightly surprised to be offered the chance to road test one for publication in "Bus & Coach" in 1966. This proved quite pleasant to drive but acceleration and fuel economy did not quite live up to my expectations based on experience of earlier or similar models. By this date the traditional half-cab seemed to treat the driver as a second-class citizen and although good from

(Above) Among the last orders for Regents from BET companies was one for 18 of the 27ft. version of the 2D3RA model with AV590 engine and synchromesh gearbox, having Willowbrook 65-seat forward-entrance bodywork. Most entered service in 1966, one being at the Commercial Motor Show that year, but No. 641 (GWN 869E) was one of five which did not arrive until 1967.

(Below) The last Regent of all was Douglas Corporation's No. 15 (410 LMN), another Willowbrook-bodied bus, but on the 3D2RA chassis with AV691 engine and Monocontrol transmission, and first registered on 6th April 1968. Douglas had withdrawn the last of its pre-war Regents from service only a few months previously, and up to the time of writing, No. 15 remains in service with the Douglas section of Isle of Man National Transport, being relatively youthful by traditional IoM standards.

New man at the wheel. Sir Donald (later Lord) Stokes drives the prototype bus for the second big Regent V order from Teheran at the handing-over ceremony at Southall works on 13th April 1966. The order was for 200 buses with chassis generally similar to their predecessors of 1958. Park Royal supplied the bodywork, of which the design was derived from that concern's contemporary standard, but incorporating additional ventilation, etc. Only one vehicle was completed in Britain, the remainder being assembled by the Teheran Bus Board. Lord Stokes was by this date Chairman of AEC Ltd.

the vision point of view, the lack of cab interior trim and sense of being cut-off from the vehicle interior were beginning to become outdated.

The end of the road for sales of the Regent and indeed for AEC double-deckers came in 1968 when Douglas Corporation, in the Isle of Man, registered chassis number 3D2RA2024 with Willow-brook bodywork. This was appropriate, for Douglas had been a regular customer for nearly 35 years.

Well over 19,000 Regents of all types had been built since 1929— it is difficult to be precise because of left-hand export vehicles, some of which were numbered in the same series as Regal single-deckers. Not far short of half these Regents were of the Mark III family, including the almost immortal RT.

The sole rear-engined Routemaster, FRM 1, photographed at the MIRA proving ground at Lindley, near Nuneaton, during the ''Bus & Coach'' road test carried out by the author in 1967. It is seen on the horizontal straight used to carry out acceleration tests. The vehicle was then in its original form without opening windows, other than the driver's signalling window. The appearance conveys the extent to which standard Routemaster parts were used, although the windscreen assembly was similar to that of the Merlin and Swift series of single-deckers and, subsequently, the production Fleetlines.

# The might-have-been bus —
# the rear-engined Routemaster

The end of AEC double-deckers came as a blow to many people who, like the author, had been brought up in a world where the contemporary model had always been one of the leaders in its class and often the yardstick against which others could be judged.

What made it seem even more disappointing was the apparent promise of new triumphs when it became known that a rear-engined version of the Routemaster was being developed. Rumours about this came to the surface in 1966. It was said that at least one example might be exhibited at the Commercial Motor Show in September of that year. This was apparently to be in Sheffield Corporation colours. It was also said that Yorkshire Traction, as well as existing Routemaster operator Northern General, had expressed interest in the proposed model, which, as previously,

was a joint enterprise involving London Transport, Park Royal and AEC, on which work had begun in 1964. Three sets of parts were put in hand.

However, when the Show announcements were made, there was no mention of a new double-decker from AEC and indeed the 1966 Show stand (with only a left-hand Reliance chassis, admittedly with the new AH691 engine, and a Swift with Roe body for Leeds as passenger exhibits) was a distinct anti-climax. No doubt at that time, the decision not to show a new design of double-decker may have seemed understandable. London Transport was still committed to its Bus Reshaping Plan, with the emphasis on one-man-operated single-deckers, though it had already back-tracked to the extent of making it clear that double-deckers would be retained for the numerous heavily-trafficked routes. Birmingham was said to have expressed an intention of buying no more double-deckers, but Manchester had equally clearly pinned its faith in double-deckers, and large ones at that.

In fact the Government had already begun to cut the ground from under the feet of the pro-single-decker school of thought by permitting one-man-operation of double-deckers from 1st July 1966. By autumn Manchester had announced that its next 96 Atlanteans and Fleetlines would be one-man-operated and the old adage about ''what Manchester thinks today ....'' was soon proved to be true.

In the event, when the prototype rear-engined Routemaster was shown to the press in the week before Christmas 1966, it was a purely London Transport occasion. The vehicle, numbered FRM 1, signifying ''front-entrance Routemaster'', was displayed without fuss at Victoria bus garage, and it was already clear that the type would almost certainly not go into production. London Transport was not planning to buy double-deckers for a few years after the then existing Routemaster contract was completed, but it was hoped that a mechanically and structurally similar bus would be the London double-decker of the '70s.

Its design was clearly derived from the existing Routemaster — 60 per cent of standard parts were incorporated. The layout was basically the by-then conventional one with transversely-mounted rear engine and entrance ahead of the front axle. The length was 31ft. 10in., wheelbase 16ft. 10in. and seating capacity 72, no more than a standard 30ft. RML Routemaster, though this could easily have been increased. Unladen weight was 8 tons 10 cwt. and London Transport reckoned that this could have been reduced by 3 cwt. or so on a production version. Though ¾ ton more than an RML, this was among the lightest of rear-engined double-deckers, yet, as previously, the Routemaster standard of comfort and finish was much above average.

The mechanical specification retained many of the original Routemaster features—aluminium alloy integral construction,

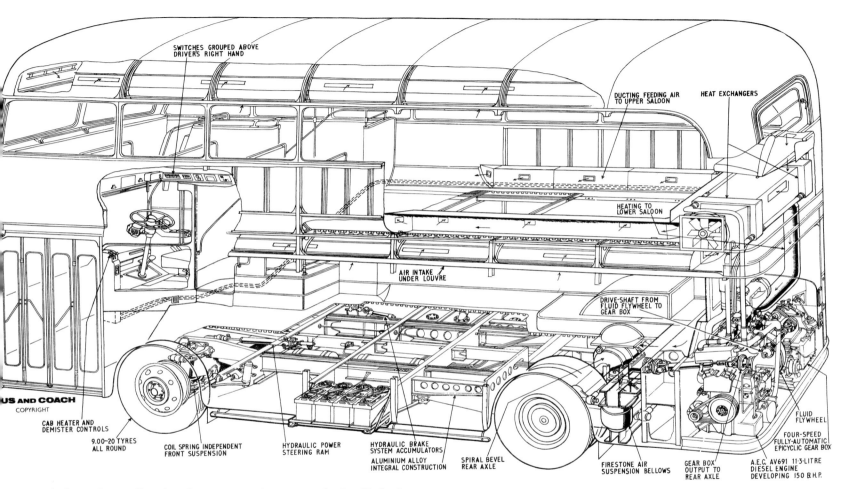

Labels on diagram:

SWITCHES GROUPED ABOVE DRIVERS RIGHT HAND

DUCTING FEEDING AIR TO UPPER SALOON

HEAT EXCHANGERS

HEATING TO LOWER SALOON

AIR INTAKE UNDER LOUVRE

DRIVE-SHAFT FROM FLUID FLYWHEEL TO GEAR BOX

US AND COACH
COPYRIGHT

CAB HEATER AND DEMISTER CONTROLS

9.00-20 TYRES ALL ROUND

COIL SPRING INDEPENDENT FRONT SUSPENSION

HYDRAULIC POWER STEERING RAM

HYDRAULIC BRAKE SYSTEM ACCUMULATORS

ALUMINIUM ALLOY INTEGRAL CONSTRUCTION

SPIRAL BEVEL REAR AXLE

FIRESTONE AIR SUSPENSION BELLOWS

GEAR BOX OUTPUT TO REAR AXLE

A.E.C. AV691 11·3-LITRE DIESEL ENGINE DEVELOPING 150 B.H.P.

FLUID FLYWHEEL

FOUR-SPEED FULLY-AUTOMATIC EPICYCLIC GEAR BOX

independent coil spring front suspension, power hydraulic brakes
and fully-automatic gearbox. The engine was the AV691, set in this
case to develop 150 bhp at the traditional 1800 rpm, and the rear
axle, carried on the usual Routemaster type of A-frame, was
equipped with air suspension. The mechanical layout at the rear
end was somewhat different from that of other rear-engined buses,
with the drive taken from the fluid flywheel by a shaft running over
the top of the gearbox casing to a train of gears in the right-hand
corner of the engine compartment. It was then taken through the

This drawing of the London Transport FRM by "Bus & Coach" artist Harry
Hodge, was reproduced in the August 1967 issue of that journal.

gearbox and forward to the axle, which was a virtually standard
Routemaster unit turned back to front.

The net result was a most impressive bus, and despite the lack of
interest from the manufacturers, I approached Kenneth Shave,
then London Transport's Chief Mechanical Engineer (Road
Services) and who was the son of George Shave, the LGOC's Chief

The rear-end design of FRM 1 had a combination of features differing from those on other rear-engined double-deckers. The recessed lower-deck rear window was reminiscent of Atlantean and Fleetline models but the use of a full-length window bay immediately ahead of the engine compartment was unusual.

FRM 1, after spending almost a year based at Chiswick, entered service from Tottenham garage on route 76 in June 1967. It suffered some of the teething troubles which seemed almost inseparable from rear-engined vehicles of that period and an engine compartment fire in August of that year caused it to be withdrawn for repair and modification for a time. When it returned to service, opening windows had been added, as shown in this picture. Subsequently, in 1969 it was converted to one-man operation and was allocated in turn to Croydon, Potters Bar and latterly Stockwell, from which it has been operated on the Round London Sightseeing Tour. It has spent a fair amount of time off the road, sometimes awaiting spare parts where these were of non-standard type. It is a matter for speculation whether a production version would have settled down to emulate the reliability of the front-engined Routemaster, but there seems no reason to doubt that with adequate development it would eventually have succeeded.

Engineer during the 'twenties, for permission to carry out a road test for ''Bus & Coach'', of which I was then editor. This was duly arranged and appeared in the August 1967 issue.

The test fully justified my interest. In the heading, I referred to ''outstanding passenger comfort'' and said that ''ease and smooth response of driving controls reach the highest degree of refinement yet experienced on a Bus & Coach test''. Flat-out acceleration, fully-laden, gave the best time for 0-30 mph of any double-decker tested by either ''Bus & Coach'' or ''Motor Transport'' at any rate in the previous seventeen years, 19.6 seconds. Fuel consumption, at 6.6 mpg with four stops per mile and using automatic gear changes, was a little below par—though many later types of vehicle have given worse results and the hydraulic drive to the two heat exchanger fans in the heating and ventilating system were blamed for possibly ½ mpg. But the overall impression was of a vehicle which made evrything previous seem out of date, in much the same way as the RT in its day.

Just when the final decision was taken not to proceed further with this design is not clear. There were reports that FRM 1 visited Leyland, but to no avail. Sir Donald Stokes was said to have been against it and it later became apparent that the Leyland group's resources were being put into a venture which was based on much larger scale use of single-deckers—the Leyland National. Yet by 1968 the revival of the double-decker was clearly well under way and there would still have been time to put a vehicle derived from FRM 1's design into production in time to catch the upsurge in double-decker demand as it gained momentum in the early '70s.

# Southall in decline

So AEC's position as one of the leading British bus and coach manufacturers was eroded away. The end of double-decker production just as city fleets were putting the emphasis back on to that type of vehicle cut off AEC from many of its biggest customers. The decision to end production of the Regent V was, like the corresponding demise of its rival, the Leyland Titan PD3, partly related to the original New Bus Grant specifications introduced in July 1968, which were intended to encourage one-man-operation, and excluded front engines for double-deckers. However, these models could hardly have survived even in its absence, such was the strength of the swing to rear-engined vehicles in the mid 'sixties.

The engineering centre of gravity of the Leyland Motor Corporation was moving from the individual member companies to the headquarters at Leyland. Bob Fryars, Chief Engineer of AEC was appointed Chief Engineer of the LMC truck division, and other once familiar faces from Southall were increasingly apt to be seen when I visited Leyland, while the design staff at AEC tended to shrink in numbers.

The formation of the British Leyland Motor Corporation as a result of the merger of LMC with British Motor Holdings (as the group linking BMC [Austin-Morris] and Jaguar-Daimler-Guy

Although the centre of gravity of design was moving away from Southall as the long-term effects of AEC's membership of the Leyland Motor Corporation and subsequently British Leyland Motor Corporation became evident, new AEC developments still came forth. Specifications for 12-metre home-market versions of the Reliance, models 9U3ZR and 9U2R, with ZF synchromesh and Monocontrol transmission respectively, were announced at the end of 1967 — AEC being the first manufacturer to offer a 12-metre model meeting British regulations. The first completed examples appeared towards the end of 1968 and among early customers was Premier Travel Ltd. of Cambridge, which favoured Reliance coaches for its express services for many years. This early example of the 12-metre version had Alexander Y-type bodywork.

organisations was called) carried the same process further. BLMC came into existence on 14th May 1968.

However, there was still some new developments from AEC. The 12-metre Reliance, by then legal in Britain, was introduced at the 1968 Commercial Motor Show where two examples with Plaxton Panorama Elite bodywork were in the demonstration park.

More dramatic was a new rear-engined coach chassis, the Sabre. This had what was called the British Leyland 800-series engine, a 12.1-litre V8 unit which had been designed at AEC, and introduced in goods models. It developed some 247 bhp at the high speed for an engine of this size of 2,600 rpm. Its bore size was 130 mm, the same as the 11.3-litre sixes, but it had a shorter stroke than any other AEC diesel of 114 mm. There was plenty of room for this compact unit and a five-speed semi-automatic gearbox behind the rear axle. The remainder of the chassis was comparatively orthodox, with a straight-topped frame ahead of the engine, coil-

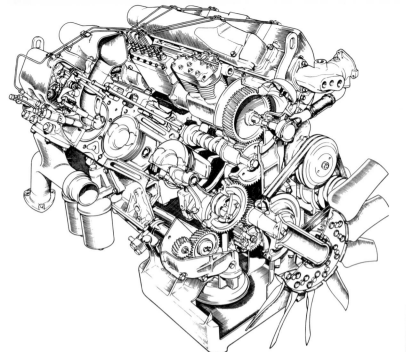

spring suspension, air-pressure brakes and power-assisted steering. It was to be offered in 11- and 12-metre lengths and both left and right-hand steering, chassis being designated VP2L and VP2R.

A left-hand chassis appeared at the 1968 Show, but little more was heard until the 1970 Show when a right-hand chassis with attractive bodywork by Eastern Coach Works was shown on the AEC stand. Sadly, this exciting design, easily the most powerful

A new V8 diesel engine of 12.1-litres capacity designed to develop some 247 bhp was designed by AEC in the mid-'sixties and introduced in May 1968 as the British Leyland 800-series engine. Intended primarily for goods vehicles, it was also offered in a new rear-engined coach chassis announced in September of that year. This was the AEC Sabre which, on paper at least, promised to be the most powerful British coach chassis ever produced. Although more power than the then usual 150 bhp or so tended to be sought for coaches in the subsequent decade to keep up with weight increases resulting from more elaborate design, the concept of a 250 bhp coach still seems very advanced over a decade later, at least for British operating conditions. The photograph below shows the 1970 Earls Court Show exhibit with Eastern Coach Works body — note the use of the ''L'' corporate symbol and the exclusion of any reference to AEC on the vehicle.

(Right) As other models faded from the scene, the Reliance emerged as the principal and, so far as the home market was concerned, ultimately the sole production passenger model offered by AEC. It tended to become increasingly regarded purely as a coach chassis, but OK Motor Services of Bishop Auckland had standardised on Reliance buses with Plaxton bodywork for several years when this photograph was taken in 1970.

(Below) Export models continued to account for a sizeable proportion of the Reliance models produced. This left-hand drive example, with both the AEC triangle and Leyland lettering, was bodied by DAB.

British coach, never got beyond the prototype stage. The 800-series engine, like many another V8, petrol or diesel, proved to be a headache to develop, and in the end the struggle was given up.

So with the double-deck range gone and the Swift about to succumb to the group's concentration on the Leyland National, AEC's only passenger model offered on the home market by the early 'seventies was the by then venerable Reliance. Both 505- and 691-engined versions continued to be available until 1972-73, the majority being 11-metre models, of which a fairly high proportion had the smaller engine. However, the shorter version of the 505 had remained in limited production with its wheelbase shortened by 2in. to 16ft. 2in. from 1969 to allow space for a slightly wider entrance door.

In 1973 further changes in engine availability meant that an engine of even larger capacity than the 691 was to be the only type available in the home market Reliance for the rest of its production life. This was the AEC 760 unit, very similar in its general design to the 691, but with cylinder bore size increased to 136 mm. The stroke remained at 142 mm and thus the engine in AEC's last passenger chassis retained this key dimension from the original A155 oil engine of 1930, the cylinder bore size having steadily risen from the original 110 mm, through the 115 mm of the 8.8-litre engine of the 'thirties, the 120 mm of the 9.6-litre and the 130 mm of the 11.3-litre units. The capacity was 12.4 litres.

However, any expectation that this engine, bigger in swept volume even than the Sabre's V8 unit, would be ultra-powerful was firmly dismissed. For this application it was set to develop a mere 165 bhp at 2000 rpm, only 11 bhp more than the 691 in Reliance form. This was enough to give good performance, even so, particularly with the ZF six-speed synchromesh gearbox. The designation, 6U3ZR, remained unaltered, as did the 6U2R of the alternative Monocontrol four- or five-speed semi-automatic version.

The remainder of the chassis was largely unaltered, though particular emphasis was laid on the adequacy of the cooling system, while provision of a 75-gallon fuel tank gave an indication of design for long-distance operation. Sales of this model continued, with several well-known coach fleets regularly returning for more examples year by year. By this time the directly comparable Leyland Leopard was no longer available with a synchromesh gearbox and this gave the Reliance a specific appeal in the group's range for operators preferring "conventional" transmission.

Production of Reliances by this time formed only a small part of the output of the Southall works, which had become very largely a goods vehicle factory. The production line had been re-organised on the assumption that the majority of vehicles produced would be short-wheelbase tractive units. There continued to be a proportion of export Ranger models, not easily distinguishable as chassis from the Mercury range of goods models, but not infrequently to be seen after bodying, parked in the service road alongside Windmill Lane, awaiting shipment. The Reliance itself continued to have an export following, examples going in sizeable numbers to Portugal as well as to New Zealand, Jamaica, Denmark and Angola.

However, home market deliveries not only continued, but even grew from admittedly modest numbers. In 1976, several of the National Bus Company's National Travel subsidiaries ordered AEC coaches. In 1977, when London Country Bus Services Ltd. decided to use coaches, in the form that word is generally understood,

(Below) National Travel chose left-hand drive Reliance chassis with Willowbrook bodywork for its contribution to the London-Athens Europabus service in 1977. The use of AEC vehicles on Europabus duties was far from new, however, as the Swedish Linjebuss concern had operated Regal Mark III vehicles on its share of this trans-continental network in the early '50s.

Export production continued to form an important part of AEC activities to the end. The Ranger left-hand drive buses with Marshall bodywork were photographed outside the factory awaiting shipment in April 1979.

One of the most faithful AEC customers among independent operators was Yelloway Motor Services Ltd. of Rochdale. Regals had been operated in the 'thirties but in the 'sixties and 'seventies 11-metre or, as in this case, 12-metre Reliances were regularly added to the fleet. This example with Plaxton bodywork was one of the 1979 deliveries.

AEC chassis remained predominant as the basis for the succeeding generations of Green Line coaches from their introduction in 1930. Over the years, there had been a tendency to use vehicles of what would nowadays be called "dual-purpose" character, with comfortable seats but basically utilitarian outline. However, in 1977 a distinct change of policy occurred, with the introduction of production Duple and subsequently Plaxton coach designs. RS 107, one of the 1979 deliveries with Plaxton Panorama Supreme IV bodywork, is seen here just after crossing the Thames.

on the Green Line services, it was appropriate that AEC Reliances chassis were used to carry the Duple Dominant bodywork chosen. Even so, total home market Reliance deliveries that year only amounted to about 160, sadly diminished from the days when this model alone was being built at about four times this rate.

The end was clearly near, and the group's decision at that time to call the vehicles Leyland Reliances gave a clear hint. However, it was noteworthy that a high proportion of vehicles carried a winged

Two of the Duple Dominant II-bodied Reliance Green Line coaches delivered in 1979, seen in Windsor. Queen Victoria's statue appears to be requiring RB 65 to draw up in front of that formidable-looking likeness. The Green Line Reliances are based on the 6U2R chassis, with Monocontrol transmission.

Another instance of international operation by a National Travel Reliance is seen in this view of BGY 584T, with Plaxton 55-seat bodywork, at Victoria Coach Station on the Frankfurt service. It is one of seven supplied to National Travel (London) in 1979.

version of the AEC triangle badge of a type more associated with the early 'fifties.

Visiting the factory at this period was a somewhat depressing experience. Many of the offices were empty even before the closure decision was announced. Yet there was a last glimmer of hope when it was revealed in 1977 that the new integral double-decker, at first code-named B15, developed by Leyland, might eventually come to the Southall works when it went into volume production. This would indeed have been fitting, for despite the rejection of the rear-engined Routemaster as a basis for development in the late 'sixties, by 1972 it was clear from preliminary announcements that the B15 was to inherit its main features from that model, even though the detail design was entirely different, for both have the following key features in common—integral construction, largely in aluminium alloy; independent front suspension, a power hydraulic brake system, and of course a transversely-mounted rear engine and fully or semi-automatic gearbox. Ironically, this is hydraulically operated—a feature London Transport wanted for the original Routemaster in the 'fifties. There was a suggestion that its model name should be "Regent", but Leyland loyalties were too strong and it was given the even more venerable, if less appropriate, name "Titan". Production began at Park Royal in

An ominous sign was the issuing of publicity material in 1977 referring to the "Leyland Reliance", an attempt to divert the goodwill associated with the model to the group, rather than the manufacturing company. The author cannot recall anyone referring to Reliance by this combination of names in conversation and it seems certain that it will be forgotten even more quickly than the references over twenty years previously to Crossley and Maudslay Reliances. Oddly enough, a seemingly higher proportion of vehicles carried the winged triangle motif, including all those shown in the leaflet, of which the cover illustration is of a Yelloway Plaxton-bodied example.

One of the last Reliance chassis, number 6U2R38500, seen outside the Southall works in April 1979. This was a Monocontrol chassis, the transmission design thus being derived from the work of Walter Gordon Wilson and completing a link with this form of epicyclic gearbox which had lasted nearly half a century.

The new-generation Leyland Titan introduced in 1977, despite the echo of a famous earlier Leyland model in its name, could be counted as a reincarnation of the rear-engined Routemaster developed jointly by London Transport, AEC and Park Royal a decade earlier. This scene in Parliament Square, with K424, built for the LGOC in 1920, preceding the first of the new Titans, could almost be regarded as a salute to half-a-century of London bus development in which AEC had played so important a role.

1978 although the idea of transfer of production to Southall once it built up was rapidly fading.

Then came the announcement towards the end of 1978 that Southall was to close and the works became even more of a ghost factory. At last, on 25th May 1979 the final closure came, and the factory which so proudly bore the slogan "Builders of London's Buses" was no more. The brief report in the following morning's "Daily Telegraph" did not even mention AEC, saying only that "British Leyland's bus and truck plant at Southall, West London, closed down yesterday, putting more than 2,000 men out of work".

The reasons for decline would form the subject of a book in themselves. The roots could certainly be partly traced back to the gradual demotion of AEC to become merely a Leyland assembly plant and in later years there was little, if any, of the old spirit still evident 25 years ago, although even then past its peak. A decline in productivity, inevitably, followed. More specifically, AEC seems to have been a victim of something almost like Dutch elm disease which attacks the motovation of management and workers alike—sadly, Park Royal has since become another victim.

# AEC Colour Cavalcade

When the first edition of this book was published, in 1980, the closure of the AEC factory had only recently occurred and examples of the marque could be seen operating throughout the country. Now, fifteen years later, AECs in front line service are not so easily found outside London, where, of course, the remaining Routemasters continue to give sterling service.

After deregulation of bus services in 1986 many operators purchased second-hand RMs; now, sadly, the ranks have thinned out. On this page we see former RM941 smartly turned out and operating with Cumberland Motor Services in Carlisle during 1988, one of many of the class to be found in locations from Blackpool to Bournemouth, Manchester or Glasgow amongst many others.

Although many Reliances continue to operate with independents they are less easily spotted, their identity being largely concealed by full-fronted coach bodywork. All is not lost, however, as the following pages will show, for thanks to the preservation movement, and in particular the AEC Society, the enthusiast can find a selection of models on display at virtually every UK bus rally and in many museums throughout the United Kingdom.

Overseas operators still have many AECs in every day service – visitors to Malta for example will find ex-London Transport single-deckers bearing very exotic liveries but still upholding the Southall tradition.

Long may it continue so !

S454, built in 1992, was one of 928 S-types produced by AEC for the London General Omnibus Co. or associated fleets. It provided seats for 54 passengers – nearly as many as were to be found on most double-deckers up to the 'fifties, yet its ultra-simple design allowed weight to be kept down to 4 tons 10 cwt. This example was found in derelict condition and purchased in 1965 by the Banfield family, of whom Charles W. Banfield had been a driver for LGOC at Nunhead Lane garage during the time when, by coincidence, S545 had been allocated there. He later founded the coach business bearing his name, and which was to have the same garage as its headquarters. His son Michael is seen at the wheel in this 1970 photograph.

The NS was indeed a milestone in bus development, setting the pattern for the modest floor levels long taken for granted on city buses in Britain but still by no means universal elsewhere. NS 1995 (YR 3844), one of the later examples, entering service with LGOC in February 1927, was preserved by London Transport after withdrawal ten years later, having been fitted with pneumatic tyres and an enclosed cab during its period of service in the capital.

T31, one of the LGOC's first 50 AEC Regals, dating from 1929, was restored to its original external condition and short-lived red and cream livery by its then owner, the late Prince Marshall. This photograph was taken in Brighton during the 1978 HCVC rally. The LGOC body had been converted to front-entrance layout, operating thus during most of its service life – see page 78.

ST 922 was one of the fleet of AEC Regents with which Thomas Tilling Ltd. modernised its London and Brighton-based fleets in the 1930-31 period. The chassis were generally similar to those of the LGOC, but the bodywork was of Tilling's own distinctive style, reminiscent of late 'twenties practice, with its open staircase layout and oddly-assorted detail features, lacking the unity of LGOC's contemporary designs. Following restoration to its condition after being taken over by London Transport in 1933, this particular bus saw regular public service in London during summer months throughout most of the 'seventies. Owned and operated by Obsolete Fleet, it was driven on the various special routes by some of the then surviving band of London Transport drivers with experience of similar buses. Its original 100 mm bore six-cylinder petrol engine was replaced by a 110-bore unit of otherwise similar design, giving slightly improved performance. Even so, its ability to cope with the traffic conditions of half-a-century after it was built, and maintain normal schedules, is remarkable. Refinement goes without saying – the engine could hardly be heard from within when idling – but reliability was also exemplary. Tim Nicholson of Obsolete Fleet kept a regular eye on ST 922's fitness for service, but remarkably little attention was needed.

Very few coaches of the early 'thirties survive and to find one in substantially original condition is rare indeed. Many Regals of this period had long lives in service, but the need to keep up-to-date in visual terms meant that many were rebodied. This 1931 example, JF 2378, is an exception, for it entered service with the Burlingham body shown here, quite a popular choice for the model, and is still substantially unaltered. The vehicle ran for Provincial (Garage) Leicester Ltd, continuing to be used for occasional duties until the 'sixties, but was preserved by Miss Muriel Morley, daughter of the proprietor. It still has the smooth-running six-cylinder petrol engine and this has been recently overhauled by Harry Pick. Marles steering is another item of the original specification still retained.

By contrast, FV 4548, though a striking vehicle recreating the style of its period, has had a complex career. It entered service with William Salisbury Ltd of Blackpool in 1934, passing to WC Standerwick Ltd, Ribble's coaching subsidiary, the following year. After the 1939-45 war it was retained as a trainer, acquiring a Leyland body originally fitted to one of Ribble's Tiger TS6 coaches of 1933, and also a 7.7-litre oil engine. It was subsequently acquired by a group of enthusiasts and, for a time, was run in the livery of Gower Vanguard, but in 1993 appeared as seen here, extensively refurbished for Clive Screaton's Grand European Touring Co, of Warrington.

Salford Corporation was one of several municipalities in the north of England which continued to favour the 8.8-litre oil engine throughout the late 'thirties, after it had been displaced as the standard power unit by the '7.7'. Number 235 (BBA 560) was among the first to have the version of the larger unit with toroidal-cavbity direct injection from new. The gearbox was of the 'crash' type. Park Royal supplied the metal-framed body, basically to its standard style of the period, though equipped to Salford's requirements. The vehicle survived by dint of having been converted to a driver trainer – with dual controls, the second driver sitting behind the first at a slightly higher level – and was purchased for preservation when finally withdrawn. It is one of the exhibits in the Greater Manchester Museum of Transport and is seen here outside the entrance to its former home, Frederick Road depot Salford.

Fortuitous, but appropriate, was the parking of former Brighton Corporation No. 63 (FUF 63) dating from the beginning of 1939, alongside RT 44 (FXT 219), which entered service with London Transport a year later, at the 1979 HCVC Rally in Brighton. The Brighton bus was one of 21 Regents with Weymann bodies. These had a mechanical specification very like that of London Transport's 1938 Green Line coaches which paved the way for the RT concept of a larger-capacity lightly-stressed engine. The author shared the driving of FUF 63 from Sussex to Halifax in 1968 as described on page 136 and still recalls this bus as one of the most enjoyable of any age he has driven – even the trip across London was a pleasure. Note the contrast of radiator heights between these two outstandingly handsome examples of a period in which elegant design was relatively commonplace. Brighton's municipal buses of that period bore the same fleet name and livery as those of the B H & D company with which they operated jointly.

Captions facing page:

Top row, left to right

The 'Blue Triangle' radiator became possibly the easiest of all those on buses to identify when introduced in 1929. This 1931 example on the Provincial Regal seen on page 240 shows the style that was standard on most models between autumn 1929 and mid-1937, with its bottom edge just below the front dumb irons.

From late 1937 the standard passenger radiator was deepened in outline, though remaining interchangeable with the earlier type. This example is one of Leicester Corporation's Renown six-wheelers of 1939, with Northern Counties bodywork.

The Mk III models a supplied to operators other than London Transport had chromium-plated radiators as standard in the 1947-49 period. This Regal with Burlingham body was supplied to Gillett Bros of Quarrington Hill, Co. Durham.

Bottom row, left to right

From about 1950, a cast aluminium radiator shell became standard in the main. Huddersfield favoured the lowbridge body by East Lancashire Coachbuilders for this Regent III.

The underfloor-engined models lost the instant identifiabilty of the traditional radiator, but were fitted with a winged version of the Blue Triangle badge. This is an example of a Reliance from the South Wales fleet, carrying Weymann Fanfare coachwork.

A mildly restyled version of the traditonal grille, broader but still with triangular badge, was used for double-deckers with the concealed radiator front cowl. This Renown with Park Royal body was in the Oxford fleet.

Leeds City Transport standardised on AEC Regent double-deckers from the mid 'thirties to the end of the 'fifties. The pre-war standard was the 7.7-litre-engined version with preselective transmission, basically similar to the contemporary standard London STL, although in post-war days at least, the Leeds examples always seemed to have that extra sparkle of performance. The final batch, delivered in the December 1939-March 1940 period, consisted of twenty buses. Like most Leeds buses, they had locally-built Roe bodywork, but their appearance, though basically of that builder's attractively curvaceous style of the period, benefited from the adoption of a windscreen with curved lower edge. The vehicle shown, No. 106 (HUM 401), had something of a charmed life, having originally been withdrawn with most of the rest of the batch as a result of Leeds' extensive fleet modernisation programme in 1952-53. However, with the others, it was reinstated until 1956 on tram replacement duties. It then became a 'learner' bus until 1962, having been renumbered 1 in 1958. Maybe this number helped its choice for use as a decorated bus for special events until 1967, when it became a mobile office. The photograph shows it at Harrogate in 1975, in early post-war livery and lacking the cream waistband relief of the original style. The radiator shown is from a pre-1937 vehicle, shorter than the original. The inclined quick-action filler cap, as widely favoured by the Tilling group, also helps to render HUM 401 non-original.

Captions: see facing page

History seems bound to give the RT premier place in the ranking of AEC's most famous models. London's streets do not seem the same without them, which is hardly surprising when it is remembered that the type formed part of London Transport's stock for 40 years.

**Facing page:**

Top left:: The London Transport STL was not only that undertaking's first major standard type of bus, but bore the brunt of the provision of public transport in London during the 1939-45 war, when normal maintenance standards had to be drastically cut back. Reliable, efficient buses were essential and the LPTB choice of chassis met this requirement, as well as giving good refinement of running if not quite the smoothness of the later RT. The body specification had not been intended for such tough conditions and the vehicle shown, STL 2093, originally of the same type as shown on page 121, received the LPTB body from an STL dating from 1939 in 1949. It was sold to an independent operator, Reliance Motor Services, of Newbury, in 1956 and purchased by D. J. Cowing for preservation in 1958. Since then, it has regularly appeared at vintage rallies, conveying the typical and attractive proportions of the majority of STL-type buses better than the earlier vehicle of the less numerous and less distinctive sloping-front variety preserved by London Transport itself.

Top right: London Transport's first post-war vehicles, delivered in the winter of 1945-46, were 20 Regents of the standard 0661/20 pattern with Weymann bodies which formed the final addition to the STL class. Because of their crash gearboxes they were allocated to the country area.

St. Helens Corporation was the only operator outside London to order complete RT-type buses to what was virtually the full London Transport specification (though Coventry eventually settled for a close approximation to it to allow completion of one chassis by Metro Cammell). The St. Helens buses, were ordered when Mr. Edgley Cox, who had begun his career at Chiswick, was General Manager and No. 67 was one of the first batch of fifteen, delivered in 1950; 25 more followed in 1952. The St. Helens livery suited the design surprisingly well, the only jarring note to an attractive effect being the curious switch round of the indicator blinds, putting the route number in the space intended for the intermediate points display. Surprisingly, No. 67 lasted only eleven years with St. Helens; in true RT fashion, however, it soon found another owner. Purchased by Hull, BDJ 67 ran for a further 11 years, definitely a better investment for its second owner than its first!

The Regal III, in its initial 0962 standard form as introduced from 1947 with 9.6-litre engine, preselective gearbox and air-pressure brakes, was seen as a very 'superior' coach chassis. Florence of Morecambe had several batches, mostly, as in this case, with Burlingham bodywork. Versions with the same appearance but alternative mechanical specifications appeared shortly afterwards, the 0682 having the 7.7-litre engine and crash gearbox, much as on the Regal I, while a crash-gearbox version with 9.6-litre engine was also offered. From 1948, these became more easily distinguished as 9621E, 6821A and 9621A respectively.

Among the last examples of the Regent III to be built was this 9613S model with Park Royal bodywork, supplied to JW Camplin of Donnington, near Spalding in Lincolnshire. It had platform doors and was used on the Spalding-Boston route and is seen here in August 1966.

The Regal Mark IV built up a reputation as a refined coach chassis. Mulley's Motorways was typical of a sizeable number of independent operators who bought examples. Number 33, now preserved, originally registered ECF 111, is a 9821E model with Burlingham 39-seat body, new in March 1952.

The British European Airways fleet of Regal Mark IV were on 8ft. wide 9822E chassis and had no fleet numbers but were in many ways part of the London Transport RF family, even to the extent of being officially classified 4RF4. Their Park Royal bodywork seated 37, with a large luggage compartment under the raised rear seats. MLL 721 is seen at Brighton.

Lisbon's fleet of AEC Mark III buses has even outlived the legendary RTs. In addition to both Regal and Regent models with original bodywork, some Regals were rebuilt as double-deckers. This photograph was taken in 1980.

The last trolleybuses of AEC design were Glasgow Corporation's fleet of 90 BUT 9613T models delivered in 1958. They were unusual among trollybuses in being 30ft-long two-axle buses and among the last British trolleybuses built.

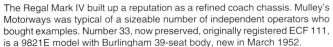

Another BET group company which purchased a high proportion of AECs over the years was the Devon General Omnibus & Touring Co. Ltd. Number 505 (505 RVO) was a Willowbrook-bodied 2D3RA-type Regent V seating 69, delivered in 1963.

The introduction of the Renown low-floor chassis allowed an improvement in appearance, though it was East Lancashire which showed what could be done in this direction while retaining the orthodox half-cab layout, by then becoming dated in itself.

The underfloor-engined Reliance broadened the market for AEC passenger chassis immensely, particularly among independent operators. Chiltern Queens Ltd., of Woodcote, near Reading, took delivery of three examples with Duple 44-seat bus bodywork, including the vehicle shown.

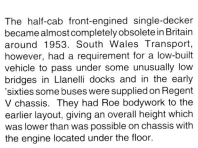

The half-cab front-engined single-decker became almost completely obsolete in Britain around 1953. South Wales Transport, however, had a requirement for a low-built vehicle to pass under some unusually low bridges in Llanelli docks and in the early 'sixties some buses were supplied on Regent V chassis. They had Roe bodywork to the earlier layout, giving an overall height which was lower than was possible on chassis with the engine located under the floor.

(Above) British European Airways chose 65 examples of a 27ft. 6in. forward-entrance version of the Routemaster to replace its Regal IV fleet in 1966-67. The 56-seat capacity came nearer to meeting the growing passenger capacity of contemporary airliners, but meant that luggage had to be conveyed in trailers, not hitherto legal for British PSVs, except insofar as the wartime producer gas trailers had been permitted. One of the later vehicles is seen at Heathrow, to which the extension of the Piccadilly underground railway line has now made the provision of a special-purpose fleet to link the airport to central London unnecessary.

(Above) RML 2672, one of the last Routemasters to be built, in 1967-68, seen passing under the famous Iron Bridge at Southall, on which large AEC publicity signs had been used for over half-a-century to indicate the turn into Windmill Lane, on the right just beyond the bridge in this view, which led to the factory.

(Right) Possibly the most promising design of double-decker of its time, but one that was never allowed to develop beyond the completion of one prototype was the rear-engined Routemaster. Number FRM 1, built in 1966, was destined to be the only vehicle of its kind, and although it spent periods in normal service tended to be used for special duties, as was the case here.

London Country's Swifts included a batch of 21 for Green Line duties, originally intended for South Wales Transport Co. Ltd., on which the combination of low frame height at the front and the higher floor level necessary to clear the engine at the rear was used to permit a ramped seating layout, giving improved forward vision for passengers sitting towards the rear. Alexander built the 45-seat bodywork. SMA 7 is seen when new, early in 1972 at Windsor.

SMS 168 was one of a second batch of 75 AEC Swift chassis sent by London Transport to Marshall for bodybuilding in 1970-71 – the first 50 examples of the 10-metre SM class had also been bodied by this concern. It is seen at Hornchurch. London Transport's decision that vehicles of this type did not meet its requirements led to many withdrawals at an age that would have been considered premature for earlier generations of London AECs. However, many found homes elsewhere.

Contemporary with the Green Line Swifts was a batch of 90 vehicles also for this part of the London Country fleet, based on Reliance 11-metre chassis and having Park Royal bodywork reminiscent of BET practice. RP 37 is also seen at Windsor in 1972.

Portugal, an old-established market for AEC buses and coaches, seems likely to be the location of the last new examples to enter service in quantity. Sizeable orders for sets of Swift units and for Reliance chassis were supplied to UTIC during the years right up to the very end of production.

Over the years, many AEC buses were rebuilt to make them suitable for changing conditions or tastes. Northern General Transport obtained excellent reliability and durability from its Routemaster buses, the only examples supplied new to an operator outside London. In the early 'seventies, it was experimenting with the possibilities of converting them to permit one-man operation, and 2085 (RCN 685) was rebuilt so as to have a semi-forward-control layout to this end, being given the name Wearsider.

# AEC IN RETROSPECT

The reasons for the decline and ultimate closure of AEC would provide subject matter for a book in themselves. However, it is important to set down the main factors.

Three other famous vehicle manufacturers had, after all, been brought into the AEC empire and, on the face of it, shut down with considerably more haste than the seventeen years it took from the merger of AEC and Leyland to the final close-down of Southall. However, Maudslay was already building AEC engines and gearboxes into almost all its output of passenger and goods vehicles even before it was taken over. Crossley chassis, though built in sizeable numbers in the days of vehicle shortage just after the war, were not sufficiently competitive in the harsher climate that became evident in the early 'fifties, though the body-building side continued for several years. Thornycroft's special-purpose vehicles for airfield or cross-country operation remained in production at Basingstoke until the factory was sold by British Leyland in the early 'seventies, though it is true that the home market goods range ended soon after the merger with AEC.

Overall, AEC, or the ACV group, took a harsher line over the continuation of duplication by existing vehicle designs originating from concerns that had been taken over than did Leyland. However, the latter concern's attitude to Albion and Scammell, taken over by Leyland in the same period, was no doubt tempered by the niche that those concerns had carved for themselves in the medium-to-light goods vehicle market and in specialised types of heavy haulage respectively. The larger Albion passenger models went as soon after take-over as those from Crossley and Maudslay.

Leyland had become involved with AEC in an entirely different level of ball-game. The 1962 merger that formed the Leyland Motor Corporation was triggered off by the conviction that for AEC and Leyland to be under-cutting each other when tendering for potentially valuable orders from all over the world was mutually harmful. Indeed, export successes during the middle 'sixties for both Leyland and AEC tended to confirm the logic of this view.

But I still recall having the feeling right from the first day of the merger that the end of AEC had been brought nearer. Inevitably, it was soon seen to be illogical and prohibitively expensive for both concerns to design and develop new types of vehicle for the same market. The first step was that taken with the closely related Panther and Swift rear-engined bus chassis—common frame assemblies but Leyland and AEC engine and transmission units for the respective ranges.

Then what can be called primary design was centralised at Leyland, with the AEC drawing office at Southall left with work of a more immediate kind, tailoring vehicles or units to meet specific requirements. AEC had thus become a satellite of Leyland for design and a similar approach applied to the factory.

The formation of the British Leyland Motor Corporation, bringing in the Austin-Morris car empire, as well as the Jaguar-Daimler-Guy combine, did not, on the surface, directly affect AEC's position, nor did the subsequent nationalisation of the group. However, the decision not to proceed with the rear-engined Routemaster effectively cut AEC off from the city bus market, by then rapidly climbing back on to the double-decker bandwagon after the flirtation with single-deckers that led to the heavy investment in what became the Leyland National.

Apart from the sucking away of finance into the car business that severely handicapped all the group commercial-vehicle activities, there were major new problems to face. Tougher legislation was being introduced in many parts of the world as part of the increased consciousness of the need to protect the environment, and that concerning vehicle noise and exhaust emissions (either smoke or invisible but noxious gases) was a particular headache for vehicle builders. Ironically, the AEC-designed 800-series V8 diesel engine, the biggest design plum handled by AEC since the merger, was to be a casualty of this.

Yet this was only one aspect of international legislation that had sprung up. In Europe, with the formation of the Common Market (EEC), a stream of Directives affecting vehicle design began to emerge from Brussels, the aim being to harmonise requirements so as to allow freer trade. The effect was to give the designer much less freedom of action. By the 'seventies, a complex inter-relation of EEC and Economic Commission for Europe (ECE) requirements had been built up, the latter being a United Nations offshoot. Almost all aspects of vehicle design were affected.

At home, the protection of the working environment for employees was raised to new levels with the Health and Safety at Work legislation, often calling for expensive reconstruction. So far as AEC was concerned, development of the factory was also hamstrung by green belt requirements for open space around London. When the original Southall works was opened in 1926-27, it was able to draw skilled labour from new housing estates in the surrounding areas, built to house people moved from the overcrowded inner areas of London. A sports field was provided on the site and although this was gradually almost surrounded by successive extensions to the factory and the associated service department workshops, it remained sacrosant, even though latterly almost invisible to the passer-by.

Older parts of the factory had become outdated by the 'seventies and yet green belt prohibition of building on any part of the designated open space meant that modernisation would have implied a lengthy shut-down of at least part of the works. Moreover, it was becoming increasingly difficult to hold the top-quality skilled labour force on which the firm had built its name. Other newer industries calling for similar skills had grown up in the area and, in particular, Heathrow Airport, with its giant facilities for overhauling airliners was only 15 minutes away by car. Furthermore, the Southall area now had a large immigrant population lacking the previous tradition of engineering skills.

The successive upheavals as British Leyland was repeatedly reorganised to cope with the harshly competitive world in which it lived, did at least give reasonable autonomy for the commercial vehicle business, which was given the title "Leyland Vehicles" in 1977. There were at one stage plans for development of Southall works as a passenger vehicle centre. Indeed the offices of the Passenger Vehicle Division were moved to the relatively modern premises which had been built in the early 'sixties for the AEC

Service Department, operating from there from 1978 until the beginning of 1980. The intention to move production of the new Titan double-decker to Southall was leaked, (incidentally disastrously affecting morale at Park Royal where it was just beginning production), but this was not to be, and the decision was eventually taken to concentrate Leyland Vehicles' future development largely in Lancashire and Scotland.

So AEC is already a memory, though it will probably be some months after this book is published before the last AEC passenger vehicles go into service. Large orders for both 505 and 760-engined versions of the Reliance chassis were supplied to UTIC up to 1979 and 100 of the former are destined to receive a variety of UTIC bodywork. The 10-metre 505-powered Reliance (long obsolete in Britain) is well suited to the twisting roads found on the Portuguese islands and is also popular with schools, colleges and the armed forces. The 760-powered Reliance has latterly found favour as a suburban bus, with two-door bodywork for up to 100 passengers. Customers have included Rodoviaria Nacional (the state-owned equivalent of our NBC), some of the smaller municipalities and the

The factory view, above left, shows the open space in the centre of the site. Below is the impressive frontage, and, right, the auction notices after the final closure.

independent operators who retain shareholdings in UTIC. However, some have received more luxurious bodywork, including one superbly equipped as an executive coach for the President of Portugal. Some home market Reliances have still to enter service with British operators.

Even the Swift is not quite dead, as the last of a long line of UTIC integral coaches incorporating Swift units including the 760 engine and ZF six-speed gearbox are due to enter service in 1980, including some for Rodoviaria Nacional. The Ranger had all but disappeared, but quite a number, frustrated from an Iraqi order, were only finding homes early in 1980.

But if nothing is left of AEC in terms of factory ownership and vehicles bearing the familiar name, echoes of AEC will still survive for some time to come. The Reliance has gone, but the forthcoming new underfloor-engined Leyland passenger chassis, at present still code-named B43, will include a ZF gearbox option to cater for Reliance customers. Meanwhile, a ZF option has been added to the Leopard range. Even on engines, there is a fascinating carry-over. The Leyland L12 and the turbocharged TL12 are derived from the 760 and, fascinatingly, retain the 142 mm stroke dimension that has been found on a continuous sequence of units since the first production AEC oil engine, the A155, half-a-century ago.

All one can do now is salute the old firm and what it achieved. The general public was probably unaware of AEC, yet the average cartoonist's idea of a bus generally had—and still has—a recognisable AEC radiator. More specifically, the men and women who together comprised AEC may not have always got things right. But they produced many fine vehicles and many which made big advances in design. They will long be remembered.

This magnificent coach, built on a Reliance chassis by UTIC, is used by the President of Portugal.

# ERRATA

Since the original book was published in 1980 the following information has come to light:

## Pages 33 and 35
There is evidence to suggest that the numbers built of early trolleybus types 602, 604 and 607 may have been slightly greater than those given, though there is some conflict of evidence as to the exact figures. It seems possible that this may have been because some were supplied as sets of chassis parts.

## Page 92
In the second paragraph, the fourth line should read 'drawing office when the author worked there in the 'fifties, visiting the'

## Page 94
In the second column, second full paragraph, the fourth last line should read:
'at this stage that 62 (LT1355-1416) of the next orders for the 260'

## Page 96
Caption to lower picture. A contemporary account (AEC Gazette, April 1932) quotes the fuel consumption for the northbound journey of 12.05 mpg, which compares well with much later vehicles, though it seems that the contemporary speed limit of 30 mph was rigorously observed.

## Page 101
An account of Capt. Eyston's record-breaking runs in the 'thirties in his car fitted with an AEC diesel engine which appeared in 'Motor Sport' of January 1981 quotes the engine type as A1650 (which may be a misunderstanding as suffix letter O was avoided in AEC engine types. The information quoted appeared to imply that the only 'tuning' to what was basically a standard A165 engine as then in use in buses was to allow the governed speed to reach 2,400 rpm, at which the power output was 141 bhp.

## Page 105 and 106
It is now known that the body on the double-deck Q-type prototype registered AHX 63 was built by Metropolitan Cammell to AEC's specification – subsequent bodies on this chassis by that concern incorporated a little more of Metro-Cammell's standard practice, though still to the AEC outline, which was a registered design.

## Page 107
The caption to the top picture should have mentioned that the registration number had been incorrectly signwritten as AXH 801 instead of AHX 801, London United Tramways vehicles being registered in Middlesex.

## Page 139
In the ninth line of text, the reference to completed production RT chassis not reaching LPTB until January 1940 should have referred to entry into service of bodied vehicles.

# INDEX